X Manual Set

Volume 1:
X User Commands

ASP, Inc.

San Jose CA

X Manual Set

First Edition

ASP, Inc.
San Jose CA

629-7993

Printed in the United States of America

The ASP X Manual Set is a compilation and reprint of the standard MIT X11.3 Window System documentation and is provided "as-is" without express or implied warranty.

X Window System is a trademark of MIT
UNIX is a registered trademark of AT&T
ULTRIX is a trademark of Digital Equipment Corporation

NOTICE

Table of Contents

NAME

X - a portable, network transparent window system

SYNOPSIS

X is a network transparent window system developed at MIT which runs on a wide range of computing and graphics machines. The core distribution from MIT has both client and server support for the following operating systems:

> 4.3+tahoe
> Ultrix 3.0 FT2 (also compiles under Ultrix 2.0)
> SunOS 3.4
> HP-UX 6.01
> Apollo Domain/IX 9.7 (and 9.6 according to its developers)
> IBM AOS 4.3 (according to its developers)
> A/UX 1.0

Commercial implementations are also available for a much wider range of platforms.

The X Consortium requests that the following names be used when refering to this software:

> X
> X Window System
> X Version 11
> X Window System, Version 11
> X11

X Window System is a trademark of the Massachusetts Institute of Technology.

DESCRIPTION

X window system servers run on computers with bitmap displays. The server distributes user input to and accepts output requests from various client programs through a variety of different interprocess communication channels. Although the most common case is for the client programs to be running on the same machine as the server, clients can be run transparently from other machines (including machines with different architectures and operating systems) as well.

X supports overlapping hierarchical subwindows and text and graphics operations, on both monochrome and color displays. For a full explanation of the functions that are available, see the *Xlib - C Language X Interface* manual, the *X Window System Protocol* specification, and various toolkit documents.

The number of programs that use *X* is growing rapidly. Of particular interest are: a terminal emulator (*xterm*), a window manager (*uwm*), a display manager (*xdm*), mail managing utilities (*xmh* and *xbiff*), a manual page browser (*xman*), a bitmap editor (*bitmap*), an access control program (*xhost*), user preference setting programs (*xrdb*, *xset*, *xsetroot*, and *xmodmap*), a load monitor (*xload*), clock (*xclock*), a font displayer (*xfd*), utilities for listing information about fonts, windows, and displays (*xlsfonts*, *xlswins*, *xwininfo*, *xdpyinfo*, and *xprop*), a protocol translator for running X10 programs (*x10tox11*), a diagnostic for seeing what events are generated and when (*xev*), screen image manipulation utilities (*xwd*, *xwud*, *xpr*, and *xmag*), and various demos (*xeyes*, *ico*, *muncher*, *puzzle*, etc.).

Many other utilities, window managers, games, toolkits, etc. are available from the user-contributed distribution. See your site administrator for details.

STARTING UP

There are currently 3 ways of getting the X server and an initial set of client applications started. The particular method used depends on what operating system you are running and on whether or not you use other window systems in addition to X.

xdm (the X Display Manager)

If you want to always have X running on your display, your site administrator can set your machine up to use the X Display Manager *xdm*. This program is typically started by the system at boot time and takes care of keeping the server running and getting users logged in. If you are running *xdm*, you will see a window on the screen welcoming you to the system and asking for your username and password. Simply type them in as you would at a normal terminal, pressing the Return key after each. If you make a mistake, *xdm* will display an error message and ask you to try again. After you have successfully logged in, *xdm* will start up your X environment. By default, if you have an executable file named *.xsession* in your home directory, *xdm* will treat it as a program (or shell script) to run to start up your initial clients (such as terminal emulators, clocks, a window manager, user settings for things like the background, the speed of the pointer, etc.). Your site administrator can provide details.

xterm −L (started from /etc/init)

Some versions of UNIX that are derived from 4.3bsd support starting the window system and an initial *xterm* window from the system terminal line configuration file */etc/ttys*. As with *xdm*, there will be a window requesting your username and password. However, this window will become your primary window and is not configurable on a per-user basis. Sites using this method should switch to *xdm* as *xterm -L* may not be supported in future releases.

xinit (run manually from the shell)

Sites that support more than one window system might choose to use the *xinit* program for starting X manually. If this is true for your machine, your site administrator will probably have provided a program named "x11", "startx", or "xstart" that will do site-specific initialization (such as loading convenient default resources, running a window manager, displaying a clock, and starting several terminal emulators) in a nice way. If not, you can build such a script using the *xinit* program. This utility simply runs one user-specified program to start the server, runs another to start up any desired clients, and then waits for either to finish. Since either or both of the user-specified programs may be a shell script, this gives substantial flexibility at the expense of a nice interface. For this reason, *xinit* is not intended for end users.

DISPLAY NAMES

From the user's prospective, every X server has a *display name* of the form:

hostname:displaynumber.screennumber

This information is used by the application to determine how it should connect to the server and which screen it should use by default (on displays with multiple monitors):

hostname

The *hostname* specifies the name of the machine to which the display is physically connected. If the hostname is not given, the most efficient way of communicating to a server on the same machine will be used.

displaynumber

The phrase "display" is usually used to refer to collection of monitors that share a common keyboard and pointer (mouse, tablet, etc.). Most workstations tend to only have one keyboard, and therefore, only one display. Larger, multi-user systems, however, will frequently have several displays so that more than one person can be doing graphics work at once. To avoid confusion, each display on a machine is assigned a *display number* (beginning at 0) when the X server for that display is started. The display number must always be given in a display name.

screennumber

Some displays share a single keyboard and pointer among two or more monitors. Since each monitor has its own set of windows, each screen is assigned a *screen number* (beginning at 0) when the X server for that display is started. If the screen number is not given, then screen 0 will be used.

On UNIX systems, the default display name is stored in your DISPLAY environment variable. This variable is set automatically by the *xterm* terminal emulator. However, when you log into another machine on a network, you'll need to set DISPLAY by hand to point to your display. For example,

% setenv DISPLAY myws:0
$ DISPLAY=myws:0; export DISPLAY

Finally, most X programs accept a command line option of **-display** *displayname* to temporarily override the contents of DISPLAY. This is most commonly used to pop windows on another person's screen or as part of a "remote shell" command to start an xterm pointing back to your display. For example,

% xeyes -display joesws:0 -geometry 1000x1000+0+0
% rsh big xterm -display myws:0 -ls </dev/null &

X servers listen for connections on a variety of different communications channels (network byte streams, shared memory, etc.). Since there can be more than one way of contacting a given server, The *hostname* part of the display name is used to determine the type of channel (also called a transport layer) to be used. The sample servers from MIT support the following types of connections:

TCP/IP

The hostname part of the display name should be the server machine's IP address name. Full Internet names, abbreviated names, and IP addresses are all allowed. For example: *expo.lcs.mit.edu:0*, *expo:0*, *18.30.0.212:0*, *bigmachine:1*, and *hydra:0.1*.

UNIX domain sockets
>The hostname part of the display name should be the string "unix" (in lower case letters). For example: *unix:0*, *unix:1*, and *unix:0.1*.

DECnet
>The hostname part of the display name should be the server machine's nodename followed by two colons instead of one. For example: *myws::0*, *big::1*, and *hydra::0.1*.

GEOMETRY SPECIFICATIONS

One of the advantages of using window systems instead of hardwired terminals is that applications don't have to be restricted to a particular size or location on the screen. Although the layout of windows on a display is controlled by the window manager that the user is running (described below), most X programs accept a command line argument of the form **-geometry** *WIDTHxHEIGHT+XOFF+YOFF* (where *WIDTH*, *HEIGHT*, *XOFF*, and *YOFF* are numbers) for specifying a prefered size and location for this application's main window.

The *WIDTH* and *HEIGHT* parts of the geometry specification are usually measured in either pixels or characters, depending on the application. The *XOFF* and *YOFF* parts are measured in pixels and are used to specify the distance of the window from the left or right and top and bottom edges of the screen, respectively. Both types of offsets are measured from the indicated edge of the screen to the corresponding edge of the window. The X offset may be specified in the following ways:

+XOFF The left edge of the window is to be placed *XOFF* pixels in from the left edge of the screen (i.e. the X coordinate of the window's origin will be *XOFF*). *XOFF* may be negative, in which case the window's left edge will be off the screen.

-XOFF The right edge of the window is to be placed *XOFF* pixels in from the right edge of the screen. *XOFF* may be negative, in which case the window's right edge will be off the screen.

The Y offset has similar meanings:

+YOFF The top edge of the window is to be *YOFF* pixels below the top edge of the screen (i.e. the Y coordinate of the window's origin will be *YOFF*). *YOFF* may be negative, in which case the window's top edge will be off the screen.

-YOFF The bottom edge of the window is to be *YOFF* pixels above the bottom edge of the screen. *YOFF* may be negative, in which case the window's bottom edge will be off the screen.

Offsets must be given as pairs; in other words, in order to specify either *XOFF* or *YOFF* both must be present. Windows can be placed in the four corners of the screen using the following specifications:

+0+0   upper left hand corner.

-0+0   upper right hand corner.

-0-0   lower right hand corner.

+0-0   lower left hand corner.

In the following examples, a terminal emulator will be placed in roughly the center of the screen and a load average monitor, mailbox, and clock will be placed in the upper right hand corner:

>xterm -fn 6x10 -geometry 80x24+30+200 &

```
xclock -geometry 48x48-0+0 &
xload -geometry 48x48-96+0 &
xbiff -geometry 48x48-48+0 &
```

WINDOW MANAGERS

The layout of windows on the screen is controlled by special programs called *window managers*. Although many window managers will honor geometry specifications as given, others may choose to ignore them (requiring the user to explicitly draw the window's region on the screen with the pointer, for example).

Since window managers are regular (albeit complex) client programs, a variety of different user interfaces can be built. The core distribution comes with a window manager named *uwm* which supports overlapping windows, popup menus, point-and-click or click-to-type input models, and minimal use of screen real estate (i.e. it doesn't provide title bars around windows). It tries to stay out of the way as much as possible, but can be somewhat difficult to master.

Several other window managers are available in the user-contributed distribution:

awm   This window manager is descended from *uwm* but provides optional title bars whose layout can be tailored by the user.

twm   This window manager provides title bars, resize and reposition boxes, and specially-designed icons. It is known for its small size and simplicity.

rtl   This is a *tiling* window manager that rearranges and resizes windows on the screen to prevent them from ever overlapping.

People who find that none of these window managers are acceptable are encouraged to write their own.

FONT NAMES

Collections of characters for displaying text and symbols in X are known as *fonts*. A font typically contains images that share a common appearance and look nice together (for example, a single size, boldness, slant, and character set). Similarly, collections of fonts that are based on a common type face (the variations are usually called roman, bold, italic, bold italic, oblique, and bold oblique) are called *families*.

Sets of font families of the same resolution (usually measured in dots per inch) are further grouped into *directories* (so named because they were initially stored in file system directories). Each directory contains a database which lists the name of the font and information on how to find the font. The server uses these databases to translate *font names* (which have nothing to do with file names) into font data.

The list of font directories in which the server looks when trying to find a font is controlled by the *font path*. Although most installations will choose to have the server start up with all of the commonly used font directories, the font path can be changed at any time with the *xset* program. However, it is important to remember that the directory names are on the **server**'s machine, not on the application's.

The default font path for the sample server contains three directories:

/usr/lib/X11/fonts/misc

This directory contains several miscellaneous fonts that are useful on all systems. It contains a very small family of fixed-width fonts (**6x10, 6x12, 6x13, 8x13, 8x13bold,** and **9x15**) and the cursor font. It also has font name aliases for the commonly used fonts **fixed** and **variable**.

/usr/lib/X11/fonts/75dpi
>   This directory contains fonts contributed by Adobe Systems, Inc. and Digital Equipment Corporation and by Bitstream, Inc. for 75 dots per inch displays. An integrated selection of sizes, styles, and weights are provided for each family.

/usr/lib/X11/fonts/100dpi
>   This directory contains 100 dots per inch versions of some of the fonts in the *75dpi* directory.

Font databases are created by running the *mkfontdir* program in the directory containing the source or compiled versions of the fonts (in both compressed and uncompressed formats). Whenever fonts are added to a directory, *mkfontdir* should be rerun so that the server can find the new fonts. To make the server reread the font database, reset the font path with the *xset* program. For example, to add a font to a private directory, the following commands could be used:

```
%  cp newfont.snf ~/myfonts
%  mkfontdir ~/myfonts
%  xset fp rehash
```

The *xlsfonts* program can be used to list all of the fonts that are found in font databases in the current font path. Font names tend to be fairly long as they contain all of the information needed to uniquely identify individual fonts. However, the sample server supports wildcarding of font names, so the full specification

-adobe-courier-medium-r-normal--10-100-75-75-m-60-iso8859-1

could be abbreviated as:

-courier-medium-r-normal---100-*

Because the shell also has special meanings for * and *?*, wildcarded font names should be quoted:

```
%  xlsfonts -fn '*-courier-medium-r-normal--*-100-*'
```

If more than one font in a given directory in the font path matches a wildcarded font name, the choice of which particular font to return is left to the server. However, if fonts from more than one directory match a name, the returned font will always be from the first such directory in the font path. The example given above will match fonts in both the *75dpi* and *100dpi* directories; if the *75dpi* directory is ahead of the *100dpi* directory in the font path, the smaller version of the font will be used.

COLOR NAMES

Most applications provide ways of tailoring (usually through resources or command line arguments) the colors of various elements in the text and graphics they display. Although black and white displays don't provide much of a choice, color displays frequently allow anywhere between 16 and 16 million different colors.

Colors are usually specified by their commonly-used names (for example, *red*, *white*, or *medium slate blue*). The server translates these names into appropriate screen colors using a color database that can usually be found in */usr/lib/X11/rgb.txt*. Color names are case-insensative, meaning that *red*, *Red*, and *RED* all refer to the same color.

Many applications also accept color specifications of the following form:

#rgb
#rrggbb
#rrrgggbbb
#rrrrggggbbbb

where *r*, *g*, and *b* are hexidecimal numbers indicating how much *red*, *green*, and *blue* should be displayed (zero being none and ffff being on full). Each field in the specification must have the same number of digits (e.g., #rrgb or #gbb are not allowed). Fields that have fewer than four digits (e.g. #rgb) are padded out with zero's following each digit (e.g. #r000g000b000). The eight primary colors can be represented as:

black	#000000000000 (no color at all)
red	#ffff00000000
green	#0000ffff0000
blue	#00000000ffff
yellow	#ffffffff0000 (full red and green, no blue)
magenta	#ffff0000ffff
cyan	#0000ffffffff
white	#ffffffffffff (full red, green, and blue)

Unfortunately, RGB color specifications are highly unportable since different monitors produce different shades when given the same inputs. Similarly, color names aren't portable because there is no standard naming scheme and because the color database needs to be tuned for each monitor.

Application developers should take care to make their colors tailorable.

KEYS

The X keyboard model is broken into two layers: server-specific codes (called *keycodes*) which represent the physical keys, and server-independent symbols (called *keysyms*) which represent the letters or words that appear on the keys. Two tables are kept in the server for converting keycodes to keysyms:

modifier list

Some keys (such as Shift, Control, and Caps Lock) are known as *modifier* and are used to select different symbols that are attached to a single key (such as Shift-a generates a capital A, and Control-l generates a formfeed character ^L). The server keeps a list of keycodes corresponding to the various modifier keys. Whenever a key is pressed or released, the server generates an *event* that contains the keycode of the indicated key as well as a mask that specifies which of the modifer keys are currently pressed. Most servers set up this list to initially contain the various shift, control, and shift lock keys on the keyboard.

keymap table

Applications translate event keycodes and modifier masks into keysyms using a *keysym table* which contains one row for each keycode and one column for each of the modifiers. This table is initialized by the server to correspond to normal typewriter conventions, but is only used by client programs.

Although most programs deal with keysyms directly (such as those written with the X Toolkit), most programming libraries provide routines for converting keysyms into the appropriate type of string (such as ISO Latin-1). However, programs that use such routines are usually less portable and not as flexible.

OPTIONS

Most X programs attempt to use the same names for command line options and arguments. All applications written with the X Toolkit automatically accept the following options:

–display *display*
> This option specifies the name of the X server to use.

–geometry *geometry*
> This option specifies the initial size and location of the window.

–bg *color*, **–background** *color*
> Either option specifies the color to use for the window background.

–bd *color*, **–bordercolor** *color*
> Either option specifies the color to use for the window border.

–bw *number*, **–borderwidth** *number*
> Either option specifies the width in pixels of the window border.

–fg *color*, **–foreground** *color*
> Either option specifies the color to use for text or graphics.

–fn *font*, **-font** *font*
> Either option specifies the font to use for displaying text.

–iconic
> This option indicates that the user would prefer that the application's windows initially not be visible as if the windows had be immediately iconified by the user. Window managers may choose not to honor the application's request.

–name
> This option specifies the name under which resources for the application should be found. This option is useful in shell aliases to distinguish between invocations of an application, without resorting to creating links to alter the executable file name.

–rv, **–reverse**
> Either option indicates that the program should simulate reverse video if possible, often by swapping the foreground and background colors. Not all programs honor this or implement it correctly. It is usually only used on monochrome displays.

+rv
> This option indicates that the program should not simulate reverse video. This is used to override any defaults since reverse video doesn't always work properly.

–synchronous
> This option indicates that requests to the X server should be sent synchronously, instead of asynchronously. Since *Xlib* normally buffers requests to the server, errors do not necessarily get reported immediately after they occur. This option turns off the buffering so that the application can be debugged. It should never be used with a working program.

–title *string*

> This option specifies the title to be used for this window. This information is sometimes used by a window manager to provide some sort of header identifying the window.

–xrm *resourcestring*

> This option specifies a resource name and value to override any defaults. It is also very useful for setting resources that don't have explicit command line arguments.

RESOURCES

> To make the tailoring of applications to personal preferences easier, X supports several mechanisms for storing default values for program resources (e.g. background color, window title, etc.) Resources are specified as strings of the form

$$name*subname*subsubname...: value$$

> that are read in from various places when an application is run. The *Xlib* routine *XGetDefault(3X)* and the resource utilities within the X Toolkit obtain resources from the following sources:

RESOURCE_MANAGER root window property

> Any global resources that should be available to clients on all machines should be stored in the RESOURCE_MANAGER property on the root window using the *xrdb* program. This is frequently taken care of when the user starts up X through the display manager or *xinit*.

application-specific files

> Any application- or machine-specific resources can be stored in the class resource files located in the XAPPLOADDIR directory (this is a configuration parameter that is /usr/lib/X11/app-defaults in the standard distribution). Programs that use the X Toolkit will also look in the directory named by the environment variable XAPPLRESDIR (default value is user's home directory) for files named *Class* where *Class* is the class name of the particular application. XAPPLOADDIR and XAPPLRESDIR configuration files are actually loaded *before* the RESOURCE_MANAGER property, so that the property can override the values.

XENVIRONMENT

> Any user- and machine-specific resources may be specified by setting the XENVIRONMENT environment variable to the name of a resource file to be loaded by all applications. If this variable is not defined, the X Toolkit looks for a file named .Xdefaults-*hostname*, where *hostname* is the name of the host where the application is executing.

–xrm *resourcestring*

> Applications that use the X Toolkit can have resources specified from the command line. The *resourcestring* is a single resource name and value as shown above. Note that if the string contains characters interpreted by the shell (e.g., asterisk), they must be quoted. Any number of **–xrm** arguments may be given on the command line.

> Program resources are organized into groups called *classes*, so that collections of individual resources (each of which are called *instances*) can be

set all at once. By convention, the instance name of a resource begins with a lowercase letter and class name with an upper case letter. Multiple word resources are concatentated with the first letter of the succeeding words capitalized. Applications written with the X Toolkit will have at least the following resources:

background (class **Background**)
> This resource specifies the color to use for the window background.

borderWidth (class **BorderWidth**)
> This resource specifies the width in pixels of the window border.

borderColor (class **BorderColor**)
> This resource specifies the color to use for the window border.

Most X Toolkit applications also have the resource **foreground** (class **Foreground**), specifying the color to use for text and graphics within the window.

By combining class and instance specifications, application preferences can be set quickly and easily. Users of color displays will frequently want to set Background and Foreground classes to particular defaults. Specific color instances such as text cursors can then be overridden without having to define all of the related resources. For example,

```
bitmap*Dashed: off
XTerm*cursorColor: gold
XTerm*multiScroll: on
XTerm*jumpScroll: on
XTerm*reverseWrap: on
XTerm*curses: on
XTerm*Font: 6x10
XTerm*scrollBar: on
XTerm*scrollbar*thickness: 5
XTerm*multiClickTime: 500
XTerm*charClass: 33:48,37:48,45-47:48,64:48
XTerm*cutNewline: off
XTerm*cutToBeginningOfLine: off
XTerm*titeInhibit: on
XTerm*ttyModes: intr ^c erase ^? kill ^u
XLoad*Background: gold
XLoad*Foreground: red
XLoad*highlight: black
XLoad*borderWidth: 0
emacs*Geometry: 80x65-0-0
emacs*Background: #5b7686
emacs*Foreground: white
emacs*Cursor: white
emacs*BorderColor: white
emacs*Font: 6x10
xmag*geometry: -0-0
xmag*borderColor: white
uwm*bordercolor: black
uwm*Foreground: #f00
uwm*Background: #ede7e2
uwm*borderwidth: 0
uwm*iborderwidth: 0
uwm*mborderwidth: 1
```

If these resources were stored in a file called *Xresources* in your home directory, they could be added to any existing resources in the server with the following command:

> % xrdb -merge $HOME/.Xresources

This is frequently how user-friendly startup scripts merge user-specific defaults into any site-wide defaults. All sites are encouraged to set up convenient ways of automatically loading resources. See the *Xlib* manual section *Using the Resource Manager* for more information.

EXAMPLES

The following is a collection of sample command lines for some of the more frequently used commands. For more information on a particular command, please refer to that command's manual page.

> % xrdb -load $HOME/.Xresources
> % xmodmap -e "keysym BackSpace = Delete"
> % mkfontdir /usr/local/lib/X11/otherfonts
> % xset fp+ /usr/local/lib/X11/otherfonts
> % xmodmap $HOME/.keymap.km
> % xsetroot -solid '#888'
> % xset b 100 400 c 50 s 1800 r on
> % xset q
> % uwm
> % xmag
> % xclock -geometry 48x48-0+0 -bg blue -fg white
> % xeyes -geometry 48x48-48+0
> % xbiff -update 20
> % xlsfonts '*helvetica*'
> % xlswins -l
> % xwininfo -root
> % xdpyinfo -display joesworkstation:0
> % xhost -joesworkstation
> % xrefresh
> % xwd | xwud
> % bitmap companylogo.bm 32x32
> % xcalc -bg blue -fg magenta
> % xterm -geometry 80x66-0-0 -name myxterm $*

DIAGNOSTICS

A wide variety of error messages are generated from various programs. Various toolkits are encouraged to provide a common mechanism for locating error text so that applications can be tailored easily. Programs written to interface directly to the *Xlib* C language library are expected to do their own error checking.

The default error handler in *Xlib* (also used by many toolkits) uses standard resources to construct diagnostic messages when errors occur. The defaults for these messages are usually stored in */usr/lib/X11/XErrorDB*. If this file is not present, error messages will be rather terse and cryptic.

When the X Toolkit encounters errors converting resource strings to the appropriate internal format, no error messages are usually printed. This is convenient when it is desirable to have one set of resources across a variety of displays (e.g. color vs. monochrome, lots of fonts vs. very few, etc.), although it can pose problems for trying to determine why an application might be failing. This behavior can be overridden by the setting the *StringConversionsWarning* resource.

To force the Toolkit to always print string conversion error messages, the following resource should be placed at the top of the file that gets loaded onto the RESOURCE_MANAGER property using the *xrdb* program (frequently called *.Xresources* or *.Xres* in the user's home directory):

    *StringConversionWarnings: on

To have conversion messages printed for just a particular application, the appropriate instance name can be placed before the asterisk:

    xterm*StringConversionWarnings: on

BUGS

If you encounter a **repeatable** bug, please contact your site administrator for instructions on how to submit an X Bug Report.

SEE ALSO

Xserver(1), mkfontdir(1), bitmap(1), uwm(1), x10tox11(1), xbiff(1), xcalc(1), xclock(1), xdpyinfo(1), xedit(1), xev(1), xfd(1), xhost(1), xinit(1), xkill(1), xload(1), xlogo(1), xlsfonts(1), xlswins(1), xmag(1), xman(1), xmh(1), xmodmap(1), xpr(1), xprop(1), xrdb(1), xrefresh(1), xset(1), xsetroot(1), resize(1), xterm(1), xwd(1), xwininfo(1), xwud(1), Xapollo(1), Xqdss(1), Xqvss(1), Xsun(1), XmacII(1), Xplx(1), bdftosnf(1), kbd_mode(1), todm(1), tox(1), biff(1), init(8), ttys(5), *Xlib – C Language X Interface, X Toolkit Intrinsics - C Language X Interface*, and *Using and Specifying X Resources*

COPYRIGHT

The following copyright and permission notice outlines the rights and restrictions covering most parts of the standard distribution of the X Window System from MIT. Other parts have additional or different copyrights and permissions; see the individual source files.

Copyright 1984, 1985, 1986, 1987, 1988, Massachusetts Institute of Technology.

Permission to use, copy, modify, and distribute this software and its documentation for any purpose and without fee is hereby granted, provided that the above copyright notice appear in all copies and that both that copyright notice and this permission notice appear in supporting documentation, and that the name of M.I.T. not be used in advertising or publicity pertaining to distribution of the software without specific, written prior permission. M.I.T. makes no representations about the suitability of this software for any purpose. It is provided "as is" without express or implied warranty.

This software is not subject to any license of the American Telephone and Telegraph Company or of the Regents of the University of California.

AUTHORS

A cast of thousands. See the file *doc/contributors* in the standard sources for some of the names.

NAME
> X - X Window System server

SYNOPSIS
> **X** [:displaynumber] [-option ...] [ttyname]

DESCRIPTION
> *X* is the generic name for the X Window System server. It is frequently a
> link or a copy of the appropriate server binary for driving the most fre-
> quently used server on a given machine. The sample server from MIT
> supports the following platforms:

Xqvss	Digital monochrome vaxstationII or II
Xqdss	Digital color vaxstationII or II
Xsun	Sun monochrome or color Sun 2, 3, or 4
Xhp	HP Topcat 9000s300
Xapollo	Apollo monochrome (Domain/IX 9.6)
Xibm	IBM APA and megapel PC/RT
XmacII	Apple monochrome Macintosh II
Xplx	Parallax color and video graphics controller

STARTING THE SERVER
> The server is usually started from the X Display Manager program *xdm*.
> This utility is run from the system boot files and takes care of keeping the
> server running, prompting for usernames and passwords, and starting up
> the user sessions. It is easily configured for sites that wish to provide
> nice, consistent interfaces for novice users (loading convenient sets of
> resources, starting up a window manager, clock, and nice selection of ter-
> minal emulator windows).
>
> Since *xdm* now handles automatic starting of the server in a portable way,
> the *-L* option to *xterm* is now considered obsolete. Support for starting a
> login window from 4.3bsd-derived */etc/ttys* files may not be included in
> future releases.
>
> Installations that run more than one window system will still need to use
> the *xinit* utility. However, *xinit* is to be considered a tool for building
> startup scripts and is not intended for use by end users. Site adminstrators
> are **strongly** urged to build nicer interfaces for novice users.
>
> When the sample server starts up, it takes over the display. If you are
> running on a workstation whose console is the display, you cannot log
> into the console while the server is running.

NETWORK CONNECTIONS
> The sample server supports connections made using the following reliable
> byte-streams:
>
> *TCP/IP*
>> The server listens on port htons(6000+*n*), where *n* is the display
>> number.
>
> *Unix Domain*
>> The sample server uses */tmp/.X11-unix/X***n** as the filename for the
>> socket, where *n* is the display number.
>
> *DECnet*
>> The server responds to connections to object X$X**n**, where *n* is the
>> display number.

OPTIONS
> All of the sample servers accept the following command line options:

–a *number*
> sets pointer acceleration (i.e. the ratio of how much is reported to how much the user actually moved the pointer).

–bs   disables backing store support on all screens.

–c   turns off key-click.

c *volume* sets key-click volume (allowable range: 0-8).

–f *volume*
> sets feep (bell) volume (allowable range: 0-7).

–logo   turns on the X Window System logo display in the screen-saver. There is currently no way to change this from a client.

nologo turns off the X Window System logo display in the screen-saver. There is currently no way to change this from a client.

–p *minutes*
> sets screen-saver pattern cycle time in minutes.

–r   turns off auto-repeat.

r   turns on auto-repeat.

–s *minutes*
> sets screen-saver timeout time in minutes.

–su   disables save under support on all screens.

–t *numbers*
> sets pointer acceleration threshold in pixels (i.e. after how many pixels pointer acceleration should take effect).

–to *seconds*
> sets default screensaver timeout in seconds.

v   sets video-on screen-saver preference.

–v   sets video-off screen-saver preference

–co *filename*
> sets name of RGB color database

–help   prints a usage message

–fp *fontPath*
> sets the search path for fonts

–fc *cursorFont*
> sets default cursor font

–fn *font* sets the default font

–wm   forces the default backing-store of all windows to be When-Mapped; a cheap trick way of getting backing-store to apply to all windows.

Many servers also have device-specific command line options. See the manual pages for the individual servers for more details.

SECURITY

The sample server uses an access control list for deciding whether or not to accept connections from clients on a particular machine. This list initially consists of the host on which the server is running as well as any machines listed in the file */etc/Xn.hosts*, where **n** is the display number of the server. Each line of the file should contain either an Internet hostname (e.g. expo.lcs.mit.edu) or a DECnet hostname in double colon format (e.g. hydra::). There should be no leading or trailing spaces on any lines. For example:

> joesworkstation
> corporate.company.com
> star::
> bigcpu::

Users can add or remove hosts from this list and enable or disable access control using the *xhost* command from the same machine as the server. For example:

> % xhost +janesworkstation
> janesworkstation being added to access control list
> % xhost -star::
> public:: being removed from access control list
> % xhost +
> all hosts being allowed (access control disabled)
> % xhost -
> all hosts being restricted (access control enabled)
> % xhost
> access control enabled (only the following hosts are allowed)
> joesworkstation
> janesworkstation
> corporate.company.com
> bigcpu::

Unlike some window systems, X does not have any notion of window operation permissions or place any restrictions on what a client can do; if a program can connect to a display, it has full run of the screen. The core protocol does have support for providing authentication information when establishing connections, but is not used in the sample implementation. Sites that have authentication and authorization systems (such as Kerberos) might wish to make use of the hooks in the libraries and the server to provide additional security.

SIGNALS

The sample server attaches special meaning to the following signals:

SIGHUP This signal causes the server to close all existing connections, free all resources, and restore all defaults. It is sent by the display manager whenever the main user's main application (usually an *xterm* or window manager) exits to force the server to clean up and prepare for the next user.

SIGTERM
This signal causes the server to exit cleanly.

FONTS

Fonts are usually stored as individual files in directories. The list of directories in which the server looks when trying to open a font is controlled by the *font path*. Although most sites will choose to have the server start up with the appropriate font path (using the *-fp* option mentioned above), it can be overridden using the *xset* program.

The default font path for the sample server contains three directories:

/usr/lib/X11/fonts/misc
This directory contains several miscellaneous fonts that are useful on all systems. It contains a very small family of fixed-width fonts (**6x10, 6x12, 6x13, 8x13, 8x13bold,** and **9x15**) and the cursor font. It also has font name aliases for the commonly

used fonts **fixed** and **variable**.

/usr/lib/X11/fonts/75dpi
>This directory contains fonts contributed by Adobe Systems, Inc. and Digital Equipment Corporation and by Bitstream, Inc. for 75 dots per inch displays. An integrated selection of sizes, styles, and weights are provided for each family.

/usr/lib/X11/fonts/100dpi
>This directory contains versions of some of the fonts in the *75dpi* directory for 100 dots per inch displays.

Font databases are created by running the *mkfontdir* program in the directory containing the compiled versions of the fonts (the *.snf* files). Whenever fonts are added to a directory, *mkfontdir* should be rerun so that the server can find the new fonts. **If *mkfontdir* is not run, the server will not be able to find any fonts in the directory.**

DIAGNOSTICS
Too numerous to list them all. If run from *init(8)*, errors are logged in the file */usr/adm/X*msgs*,

FILES
/etc/X*.hosts   Initial access control list

/usr/lib/X11/fonts/misc, /usr/lib/X11/fonts/75dpi, /usr/lib/X11/fonts/100dpi
>Font directories

/usr/lib/X11/rgb.txt   Color database

/tmp/.X11-unix/X*   Unix domain socket

/usr/adm/X*msgs   Error log file

SEE ALSO
X(1), xdm(1), mkfontdir(1), xinit(1), xterm(1), uwm(1), xhost(1), xset(1), xsetroot(1), ttys(5), init(8), Xqdss(1), Xqvss(1), Xsun(1), Xapollo(1), XmacII(1) *X Window System Protocol, Definition of the Porting Layer for the X v11 Sample Server, Strategies for Porting the X v11 Sample Server, Godzilla's Guide to Porting the X V11 Sample Server*

BUGS
The option syntax is inconsistent with itself and *xset(1)*.

The acceleration option should take a numerator and a denominator like the protocol.

If *X* dies before its clients, new clients won't be able to connect until all existing connections have their TCP TIME_WAIT timers expire.

The color database is missing a large number of colors. However, there doesn't seem to be a better one available that can generate RGB values tailorable to particular displays.

The *xterm -L* method for starting an initial window from */etc/ttys* is completely inadequate and should be removed. People should use *xdm* instead.

COPYRIGHT
Copyright 1984, 1985, 1986, 1987, 1988, Massachusetts Institute of Technology.
See *X(1)* for a full statement of rights and permissions.

AUTHORS
The sample server was originally written by Susan Angebranndt, Raymond Drewry, Philip Karlton, and Todd Newman, with support from a cast of thounds. See also the file *doc/contributors* in the sample distribution for a more complete list.

NAME
>   Xapollo – Apollo server for X Version 11

SYNOPSIS
>   **Xapollo** [option] ...

DESCRIPTION
>   *Xapollo* is the server for Version 11 of the *X* window system on Apollo
>   systems. It will normally be started by *xinit (1)*, or by a shell script run
>   from an interactive shell. Note that you will probably need to give com-
>   mand line options to *xinit (1)* in order to get it to run the server with the
>   desired command line options, and to run *xterm (1)* with the desired
>   options, display, etc. See the man page for *xinit (1)*.

CONFIGURATIONS
>   *Xapollo* operates under DOMAIN/IX, with at least Apollo software release
>   SR9.6. It operates on any Apollo display hardware. It requires a key-
>   board with a mouse. TCP/IP software must also be installed and running.

OPTIONS
>   The Xapollo server program takes device dependent options as follows.
>   In addition, the "standard" X11 server command line options can be used.
>   These options are described under *Xserver(1)*.

>   **-D**<unit>
>>   This option gives the display unit number to which the following
>>   string giving per-display options should apply. Presently, only
>>   **-D1**, meaning display unit 1, is meaningful. The string following
>>   has, for the present, the following simple syntax: **d**<depth>,
>>   which means use the given number as the depth of the screen.
>>   The actual depth will be the minimum of the available number of
>>   planes, and the depth given. If the resulting number is not 1, 4 or
>>   8, the next smallest number in that list will be used. In the
>>   absence of any option, the server will use the full depth available.
>>   For example, *-D1 d1* means treat display unit 1 as a monochrome
>>   display, regardless of how many planes it has. *-D1 d4* means use
>>   only 4 planes of display unit 1, assuming that it has at least 4
>>   planes.

KEYBOARD
>   We assume Apollo keyboard number 2 (with mouse, without numeric
>   keypad or lighted CapsLock key). (Keyboard number 1 is unsupported,
>   since it can't have a mouse. Keyboard number 3, with the numeric
>   keypad and lighted CapsLock key, is a superset of keyboard number 2. It
>   has the ability to generate raw key up/down transitions; this should be
>   supported but isn't. Keyboard number 2 cannot generate raw key
>   up/downs.)

>   Only the white keys, the four basic arrow keys and F1-F8 are imple-
>   mented now. Up transitions for the white keys are faked. Positions of the
>   real control and shift keys are inferred from the raw input character; their
>   transitions are faked if necessary.

>   "Mouse" Control, Shift and Meta keys are as follows:

>   Control:
>>   KBD_$LD, Boxed up-arrow, Lower left corner of left-hand
>>   keypad

>   Shift:
>>   KBD_$LF, Boxed down-arrow, Lower right corner of left-hand
>>   keypad

Meta:
KBD_$R1, "POP", Lower right corner of main keyboard

You can bail out of the server by hitting the ABORT/EXIT key (KBD_$R5 and KBD_$R5S, upper right corner of keyboard). Unshifted, it will exit the server in an orderly fashion. If this doesn't work (i.e. server is wedged), the shifted version is the system quit character.

SWITCHER

The server has a feature called the switcher, which allows you to alternate between the X server and the Apollo DM environment. (This feature is included by defining the symbol SWITCHER when the Apollo driver is compiled; this happens by default.) Once the X server is running, you can switch from it to the DM by running the program *todm,* found in the *server/ddx/apollo* directory. You may wish to bind this program to a *uwm (1)* menu entry, if you use that window manager.

While in the DM, you can switch back to an already-running X server by running the program *tox,* also in the *server/ddx/apollo* directory. You may wish to bind this program to a DM programmable key.

While you are "switched away" from the X server to the DM, the X server is blocked.

SEE ALSO

Xserver(1),   xinit   (1),   todm   (1),   tox   (1),   and   the *server/ddx/apollo/README* file on the X distribution tape.

LIMITATIONS

When running in monochrome, the server uses the portable but slow MFB driver. When in color, it uses Apollo native graphics interfaces, but more optimizations are still called for.

Due to differing implementation techniques for the color switcher and the monochrome switcher, you will find that running the X server in monochrome leaves the DM free to continue execution (for example, processing typed-ahead input), while running the server in color blocks the DM, so that typed-ahead input will not be processed until you switch back to the DM.

The pointer motion buffer, threshhold and acceleration factors are not implemented.

The keyboard hardware does not allow for keyclick, bell pitch or volume control, or autorepeat control. The keyboard support for keyboard 3 could allow more natural use of control and shift, and it could add more Apollo keys to the keymap.

BUGS

If the server exits abnormally on a color display, it will not restore the hardware color map to its former state, making the DM screen hard to read. You can fix this by running the program */systest/ssr_util/lcm,* which will reload the DM's default color map.

There is a known race condition in the pre-SR9.7 versions of TCP/IP which may make local clients hang just after establishing connections to the server. This problem does not exist with remote clients. At SR9.7, this problem has been fixed.

COPYRIGHT

Copyright 1987, 1988, Apollo Computer Inc.

AUTHORS

Dave Gorgen, Jim Hamilton, Steve Reber, Bob Terek
Apollo Computer Inc.

NAME

Xplx – Parallax Graphics 1280 server for X Version 11

SYNOPSIS

Xplx [option] ...

DESCRIPTION

Xplx is the server for Version 11 of the X window system on the Parallax 1280 video graphics processor. This server includes extensions for providing live and still video images within a window. It will normally be started by *xinit(1)*.

CONFIGURATIONS

Xplx operates under SunOS versions 3.5 on Sun/3 workstations and under Ultrix 2.0 on Microvax-II's.

The server is configured to run on an 8-bit 1280 video graphics processor plugged into either of those machines. It supports a Logitech mouse and a DEC LK201 keyboard connected to the 1280 graphics processor via the serial port.

VIDEO EXTENSIONS

This server uses a set of sample video extensions to provide the ability of showing a video image in an X Window. The extensions can be found in the *extensions* directory. A sample video program can be found in the *contrib* directory.

SOFTWARE REQUIRMENTS.

The *Xplx* server requires the standard Parallax Graphics base software. This package contains the device driver for 1280 processor, 'C' Language interface code and diagnostic programs.

The server uses the **EIS** (Extended Instruction Set) microcode package to handle clipping windows, cursor tracking and image loading. This microcode can be resident in EPROM of the Parallax 1280 processor or downloaded to the board by the server.

Please contact the factory for these items.

OPTIONS

-microcode ucodefile

This specifies the **EIS** microcode file (ucodefile) and if the currently running microcode is a different revision, the server will reload upon startup.

-device takes the following argument as the name of the special file for a display device. If no device is specified, the enviroment variable **PLX** is used, if PLX environment variable is not present then **/dev/plx0** is used.

Other options are described under *Xserver(1)*.

ENVIRONMENT VARIABLES

PLX   If present, and if no explicit **-device** options are given, specifies the display device to use.

PLXMICROCODE If present, and if no explicit

-microcode option is given, specifies the microcode file to use.

FILES

/dev/plx0

default Parallax display device name.

SEE ALSO

Xserver(1), xinit(1), X(1),

BUGS & RESTRICTIONS

1   The server does not use the *CFB* or *MFB* directories for drawing. All drawables are kept either on the screen or as off-screen pixmaps. All drawing operations, such as lines, copies, stipple's and text are done by the 1280 graphics processor. With this scheme comes the restriction that pixmaps are limited in size.

2   The server code does not implement thick lines.

AUTHORS

Parallax Graphics Inc.

Greg Cockroft (Parallax Graphics & Univ Michigan CITI),
Bob Goodwin,
Martin Levy,
Murali Srinivasan.

MIT Project Athena.

Mark Levine.

NAME

Xqdss - VAXStation II/GPX server for the X Window System

DESCRIPTION

The QDSS hardware in the VAXStation II/GPX supports 8 plane or 4 plane displays.

OPTIONS

-bp *pixel-value*   set default black-pixel color
-wp *pixel-value*   set default white-pixel color

The server also takes all of the standard server options (See *Xserver(1)* for a complete list.)

NOTE

You need to make sure your kernel is configured with DMA_BUFSIZ set to 10 in sys/data/qd_data.c, or things won't work right.

BUGS

Currently only numeric arguments from #000000 to #ffffff are accepted for default BlackPixel and WhitePixel, and no screen number is accepted.

The GPX hardware contains a polygon edge address generation engine which does not conform to the polygon edge model specified in the X11 protocol document. The effect is that GPX polygon edges extend on average one-half pixel farther out than they ought.

Masks do not work correctly in most cases. The fact that scrollbars look fine is a fluke. This bug affects stipple operations, copyPlane operations, and XYbitmap putImage as well.

ImageText does not paint enough background color -- the last character will have too few bits filled in on the right side (all bits from the edge of the character bitmap to the 'width' field of the character). (The "ultimate sleazoid hack" in tlpolytext.c doesn't work right.)

Any tile or stipple which is too large to fit off-screen will not work at all. There should be provisions for punting to MI code in these cases.

The console driver for the QDSS mashes the state of the drawing engine -- this causes massive lossage when doing GetImage or PutImage (which shut the engine down), and causes other strange effects. Use xcons to avoid the problem.

This driver uses MI code for all off-screen pixmap drawing operations, including scrolling and text painting. This is incredibly slow. This could be replaced with cfb, but would require reengineering much of the pixmap management code as it doesn't conform to the cfb model at all. Besides, cfb isn't known for it's speed anyway...

GetImage is also amazingly slow, it fetches one pixel at a time from the screen through a long sequence of instructions. This can be fixed, but requires rethought in how the template rams are managed.

Because BackingStore uses the GetImage code to fetch stuff from the screen, it is useless on all but the fastest VaxStations (works reasonably well on my 3200, don't bother on a 2000 or VaxStar). For this reason, the -bs and -su options were added to the server (see the *Xserver* manual). Also, because the on-screen lines are drawn with the hardware, they don't match off screen lines exactly, the differences are quite noticeable in some contexts.

Be patient with this server, some operations are amazingly slow (such as scrolling a partially-occluded window with backing store), but others are

quite fast (like text painting). Make very sparing use of backing store and
save unders.

SEE ALSO

Xserver(1), xdm(1), X(1)

COPYRIGHT

Copyright 1987, 1988, Digital Equipment Corporation.
Copyright 1987, 1988, Massachusetts Institute of Technology.
See *X(1)* for a full statement of rights and permissions.

AUTHORS

Donald Mullis and Matt Pappas, Digital Equipment Corporation.

Thanks to Ram Rao, Vasudev Bhandarkar and Mary Larsen of UEG for
their 4-plane code and numerous bug fixes.

NAME
         Xqvss - QVSS server for the X Window System
DESCRIPTION
         This driver supports the QVSS and SM displays.

         The QVSS hardware in the DEC VS2 is monochrome. The usable size is
         864 lines by 1024 pixels/line. (Under some versions of Ultrix, the driver
         thinks the screen is 960 pixels wide; to fix this for a VR260 monitor,
         patch the kernel variable qv_def_scrn to 2 and rebuild the kernel.).

         The SM hardware in the DEC VaxStation is functionally identical with the
         QVSS hardware, except for new cursor support and slightly different
         cabling.

         Probably the most irritating problem with the QVSS hardware is the cur-
         sor support, which is limited to 16x16. As only "and" and "or" opera-
         tions are available in the hardware, the driver inverts the cursor depending
         upon the pixels below the cursor. The server displays a reasonable cursor
         in most (but not all) circumstances. The SM hardware has better support
         — two planes instead of one; exactly what X needs.

         Under Ultrix-32 release 1.1 and 4.2BSD, the window system will be
         slightly unreliable due to a kernel problem. Fixed in Ultrix32 release 1.2.
         Under Ultrix-32 1.1, your best bet is to use unix domain connections
         (unix:0 as host spec's) for local connections.
OPTIONS
         -bp *pixel-value*   set default black-pixel color
         -wp *pixel-value*   set default white-pixel color

         The server also takes all of the standard server options (See *Xserver(1)* for
         a complete list.)

         Performance needs to be better, but the server is usable; it uses the X11
         portable   monchrome   framebuffer   code.   Look   in
         contrib/server/speedups/donohue.shar for some ideas which could speed
         up this server.
SEE ALSO
         Xserver(1), xinit(1), X(1)
COPYRIGHT
         Copyright 1988, Massachusetts Institute of Technology.
         See *X(1)* for a full statement of rights and permissions.
AUTHORS
         Phil Karlton wrote the QVSS-specific pieces of X11; thanks to David
         Carver of the DEC Workstations group for work on X10.

NAME
XmacII – Macintosh II server for X Version 11

SYNOPSIS
XmacII [option] ...

DESCRIPTION
XmacII is the server for Version 11 of the X window system on Macintosh II hardware running A/UX. It will normally be started by the shell script *X11*.

CONFIGURATIONS
XmacII operates under A/UX Release 1.0 and later. Under A/UX Release 1.0, the server supports a single monochrome display. Color and multiple screens are supported under A/UX Release 1.1 and later.

OPTIONS
The following options can be given on the command line to the X server.

–screen *number* **–depth** *number*
> arranges that the given screen will operate at the given depth. Screens are numbered from 0 and correspond to the relative position of video cards in the Macintosh II slots. Supported depths are 1 (monochrome at 1 bit per pixel, the default value), and 8 (color at 8 bits per pixel, indexing a colormap with 256 entries). Multiple screens and color support require A/UX Release 1.1 or later.

–a *number*
> sets pointer acceleration (i.e. the ratio of how much is reported to how much the user actually moved the pointer).

–logo turns on the X Window System logo display in the screen-saver. There is currently no way to change this from a client.

nologo turns off the X Window System logo display in the screen-saver. There is currently no way to change this from a client.

–p *minutes*
> sets screen-saver pattern cycle time in minutes.

–r   turns off auto-repeat.

r   turns on auto-repeat.

–s *minutes*
> sets screen-saver timeout time in minutes.

–t *numbers*
> sets pointer acceleration threshold in pixels (i.e. after how many pixels pointer acceleration should take effect).

–to *seconds*
> sets default screensaver timeout in seconds.

–co *filename*
> sets name of RGB color database

–help prints a usage message

–fp *fontPath*
> sets the search path for fonts

–fc *cursorFont*
> sets default cursor font

–fn *font* sets the default font

2

BUTTON MAPPINGS

Many X clients assume the mouse has three buttons. The A/UX X server simulates the middle and right mouse buttons with keystrokes -- the left-arrow key generates middle button events, and the right-arrow key generates right button events -- the real mouse button generates left button events. The open-apple or cloverleaf key is the "Meta" modifier, Meta can also be obtained by pressing the up-arrow key. The down-arrow key duplicates the Control key. Meta, Control, and Shift are often used in combination with other keystrokes or mouse clicks. For example, the terminal emulator xterm pops up menus in response to control-left and control-middle. The original function of the arrow keys may be obtained by holding down the Option key while pressing one of the arrow keys.

SECURITY

X uses an access control list for deciding whether or not to accept a connection from a given client. This list initially consists of the machine on which the server is running, and any hosts listed in the file */etc/X0.hosts* This file should contain one line per host name, with no white space.

The user can manipulate a dynamic form of this list in the server using the *xhost(1)* program from the same machine as the server.

Unlike some window systems, *X* does not have any notion of window operation permissions or place any restrictions on what a client can do; if a program can connect to a display, it has full run of the screen. There is support for using authentication services on connection startup beyond the simple host name check, but it is not used in the standard distribution.

FONTS

Fonts are stored in individual files in the directory(ies) named by the font search path. These files may be created by the *fc* utility. The name of the file must correspond to the name of the font in lowercase with the suffix ".snf" appended. Font files may be stored in *compress*(1) format, in which case an additional suffix (usually ".Z", defined when the server is built) must be appended to the usual filename.

FILES

/usr/bin/X11/X11	Bourne shell script which starts the server and initial *xterm* client
$HOME/.x11start	Bourne shell script executed by initial *xterm* client which starts a slew of other clients. Reference copy in /usr/lib/X11/.x11start
/usr/bin/X11/XmacII	the server binary
/usr/bin/X11/Xrepair	ensures console viability after server exits
/usr/bin/X11/*	client binaries
/usr/lib/X11/fonts/*	
/usr/lib/X11/rgb.{dir,pag,txt}	color names to RGB mapping
/etc/X0.hosts	Initial access control list
/tmp/.X11-unix/X0	Unix domain socket
/usr/adm/X0msgs	Error log file
$HOME/.twmrc	customization for the *twm* window manager. Reference copy in /usr/lib/X11/Sample.twmrc

$HOME/.uwmrc	customization for the *uwm* window manager. Reference copy in /usr/lib/X11/default.uwmrc
/usr/lib/X11/XErrorDB	client error message database
/usr/lib/X11/app-defaults	client specific resource specifications
/usr/lib/X11/examples/Xaw/*	source code examples of applications built on the *X* Toolkit
/usr/lib/terminfo/x/xterm*	*terminfo* database entries descibing the terminal emulation capabilities of the *xterm* client. Reference copies in /usr/lib/X11/xterm*.tic
/usr/include/X11/bitmaps/*icon	bitmap representations of icons used by the *twm* window manager

SEE ALSO

xinit(1), X(1)

BUGS

In the unlikely event the server crashes, it may leave the keyboard in a non-useful state. The X11 script executes the *Xrepair* command in an attempt to repair the damage.

COPYRIGHT

Copyright 1988, Massachusetts Institute of Technology.
See *X(1)* for a full statement of rights and permissions.

2

NAME

Xsun – Sun server for X Version 11

SYNOPSIS

Xsun [option] ...

DESCRIPTION

Xsun is the server for Version 11 of the X window system on Sun hardware. It will normally be started by *xinit*(1), or *xdm*(1), or perhaps by some script such as:

```
#!/bin/sh
home=/disk1d/x11

case "$1" in
"")     X=$home/Bin/X;;
/*)     X=$1;;
*)      X='pwd'/$1;;
esac

clear
xinit -- $X -fp $home/Lib/fonts -co $home/Lib/rgb
kbd_mode -a
```

CONFIGURATIONS

Xsun operates under SunOS versions 3.2, 3.4, and 4.0, on Sun/2, Sun/3 and Sun/4 architectures. It normally auto-configures to use all available displays; it supports the following display types:

bwtwo in both 1152*900 and 1600*1280 versions.

cgtwo used both as a color and a monochrome display (for 3/160C, 3/260C. 4/260C).

cgfour used both as a color and a monochrome display (for 3/110, 4/110, 3/60).

It does not support the GP, GP+, or GP2. If you have one of these installed, use the **-dev** argument to select */dev/cgtwo0*.

On a **cgfour**, *Xsun* will use both the monochrome and color screens as if they were two separate screens side-by-side. Sliding the mouse off the left and right edges will swap screens.

USE WITH SUNWINDOWS OR NeWS

The server can be run from outside **suntools**, in which case it configures for all available displays (unless overridden by **-dev** options). Otherwise, it can be run "on top of" either **suntools** or **NeWS**. In this case, it takes over the entire screen it was invoked from.

If you have multiple displays, you can run **suntools** on both, use **adjacentscreens** to move the mouse between them, and then run *Xsun* on top of one of the desktops. **Adjacentscreens** will still be in effect, so you can move between window systems by sliding the mouse from one screen to another.

OPTIONS

-mono means use a **cgtwo**, if present, as a monochrome device. Default is use it as a color device. Using it as a monochrome device is, for the present, mush faster.

-debug means that the server is being run from a debugger, such as *dbx*(1), and that it should *not* set its standard input, output and error files into non-blocking mode.

-dev   takes the following arument as the name of the special file for a display device. If any **-dev** arguments are supplied, they are used. The server does not auto-configure in this case.

Other options are described under *Xserver(1)*.

ENVIRONMENT
XDEVICE
If present, and if no explicit **-dev** options are given, specifies the (colon separated) list of display devices to use.

WINDOW_PARENT
If present, specifies the */dev/win* file of the **suntools** desktop.

SEE ALSO
Xserver(1), xinit(1), X(1), *Godzilla's Guide to Porting the X V11 Sample Server.*

BUGS

1   If the server crashes, it may leave the keyboard in a non-useful state. The script above uses the *kbd_mode* command (found in the *server/ddx/sun* directory) to repair the damage.

2   The server code is completely untuned, and has inferior performance. In particular, the color code is very slow (but it is very portable).

3   The auto-configuration depends on there being appropriate special files in the */dev* directory for the framebuffers which are to be used. Spurious entries can disturb the process. For example, the X/160C in fact has the hardware for a monochrome **bwtwo0** on the CPU board. So if your */dev* has a special file for */dev/bwtwo0*, the server will use it, even though there is no monitor attached to the monochrome framebuffer. The server will appear to start, but not to paint a cursor, because the cursor is on the monochrome frame buffer. The solution is to remove the */dev* entries for any device you don't have a monitor for.

4   There is a bug in pre-FCS operating systems for the Sun/4 which causes the server to crash driving a **cgtwo**.

5   There is a race condition that sometimes happens when running "on top of" NeWS. The symptom is that parts of NeWS show through, and that the keyboard is in a non-useful state. There is no simple work-around.

6   Autorepeat for the keyboard cannot be turned off.

7   Use of the pattern (as opposed to the blanking) screensaver may cause the server to loop forever.

8   The cursor colors are correct. If you are skeptical, try running *hacks/cursorcolor/cursorcolor*.

AUTHORS
U. C. Berkeley
Adam de Boor.

Sun Microsystems
David Rosenthal, Stuart Marks, Robin Schaufler, Mike Schwartz, Frances Ho, Geoff Lee, and Mark Opperman.

NAME
    alert – display a warning message in a window

SYNOPSIS
    alert [**–z**] [**–standard X Toolkit options ...**] "TITLE" text to be
    displayed

DESCRIPTION
    Alert is a utility to issue a warning message to the user. It displays a
    warning symbol, some justified text and a button in a window. The button
    should be clicked with the mouse to acknowledge the alert and close the
    window.

    If the connection to the X server cannot be established, the title and text is
    printed on *alert*'s standard output and the user is requested to press
    RETURN to acknowledge the message.

    Alert can take the following option:

    -z   No Zoom. The window will attempt to by pass the window
              manager and appear immediately, rather than going through the
              window manager's placement and sizing scheme.

    Alert additionally recognizes the following standard X Toolkit command
    line arguments:

    –bg *colour* or **–background** *colour*
              This option specifies the colour to use for the background of the
              window and widgets. The default is 'white.'

    –bd *colour* or **–bordercolor** *colour*
              This option specifies the colour to use for the border of the main
              window. The default is 'black.'

    –bw *number* or **–borderwidth** *number*
              This option specifies the width in pixels of the border surround-
              ing the main window.

    –fg *colour* or **–foreground** *colour*
              This option specifies the colour to use for all text and symbols.
              The default is 'black'.

    –fn *font*   This option specifies the font to be used for displaying the text
              warning message. The default is 'serif10'.

    –name *name*
              This option specifies the application name under which resources
              are to be obtained, rather than the default executable file name,
              'alert'.

    –geometry *geometry*
              This option specifies the preferred size and position of the alert
              window; see *X(1)*;

    –display *display*
              This option specifies the X server to contact; see *X(1)*.

    –xrm *resourcestring*
              This option specifies a resource string to be used. This is espe-
              cially useful for setting resources that do not have separate com-
              mand line options.

X DEFAULTS
    Alert is implemented using the Athena widgets. Each widget can indivi-
    dually or in groups have various visual and operational aspects changed
    via   a   '.Xdefaults'   file   on   the   client   machine   or   the

'RESOURCE_MANAGER' property on the server. All widgets have a common set of resources (background, backgroundPixmap, etc.) and resources unique to each type of widget; a 'command button' widget, for example, also has a cursor resource. For a full list see the document *X Toolkit Widgets - C Language X Interface*.

The path names and types of all widgets used by *alert* are as follows:

XXX.alert/yorn
> The widget that is a child of root. All the other widgets used by the alert box are children or grand children of this widget.

XXX.alert/yorn.contents
> A form widget that manages the layout of the alert box. Normally completely covers the alert/yorn widget.

XXX.alert/yorn.contents.symbol
> A widget to display the alert symbol.

XXX.alert/yorn.contents.ok/yes button
> A command button widget to obtain an acknowledgement from the user, normally displaying an 'equals' symbol.

XXX.alert/yorn.contents.message
> A widget to display and format the text message.

The '*XXX*' may be replaced by either *alert*'s classname, 'Xopentop', or its application name, 'alert'.

Additionally, the following items are also fetched from the resource database:

alertsym The pathname of a bitmap file to use as an alternative to the 'exclamation-mark-in-a-triangle' symbol displayed in the 'symbol' widget.

oksym The pathname of a bitmap file to use as an alternative to the 'equals' symbol displayed in the 'ok/yes button' widget.

backgroundPixmap.foreground
> One of two colours (the other is the widget's background colour) required when converting a bitmap file into a pixmap for use as the widget's background pixmap.

RETURN CODES
> 0 – Termination via the acknowledge box.
>
> 2 – Termination due to some internal error.

ENVIRONMENT
> DISPLAY - the default host name and display number of the X server.
>
> XENVIRONMENT - the name of the Xdefaults file to use, normally $HOME/.Xdefaults.

EXAMPLES
> alert "Low disk space" Warning: There are less than 200 free disk blocks
>
> Will open an alert box with the title *Low disk space* and containing the text *Warning: There are less than 200*

FILES
> $HOME/.Xdefaults /usr/lib/X11/app-defaults/Xopentop

SEE ALSO
> gs(1), yorn(1)

BUGS

If the font is too large or the message too long, the text will be clipped.

The title may not be displayed if the window manager does not provide title bars around windows or the −z option is used.

AUTHOR

Gary Henderson & Mark E. Howells, Torch Computers Ltd.

3

NAME
      awm - Window Manager X Client Application
SYNOPSIS
      awm [**–f** filename] [**–e** execfile] [**–b**] [**–i**]
DESCRIPTION
      The *awm* command is a window manager client application of the window
      server. It is heavily based on an earlier work by M. Gancarz of Digital
      Equipment Corporation (see the end of this document for appropriate ack-
      nowledgments).

      When the command is invoked, it traces a predefined search path to locate
      any *awm* startup files. If no startup files exist, *awm* initializes its built-in
      default file.

      If startup files exist in any of the following locations, it adds the variables
      to the default variables. In the case of contention, the variables in the last
      file found override previous specifications. Files in the *awm* search path
      are:

              $LIBDIR/*awm*/*system.awmrc*
              $HOME/*.awmrc*

      To use only the settings defined in a single startup file, include the vari-
      ables, **resetbindings**, **resetmenus** and **resetgagdets** at the top of that
      specific startup file.

OPTIONS
      –f filename
              Names an alternate file as an *awm* startup file.

      –e execfile
              Names a file to exec (typically a shell script invoking other
              clients) after all startup files have been loaded. This is useful for
              minimizing the number of map/unmaps that occur when titlebars
              are added.

      –b   Causes *awm* to ignore the system startup file.

      –i   Causes *awm* to ignore $HOME/*.awmrc*.

STARTUP FILE VARIABLES
      Variables are typically entered first, at the top of the startup file. Because
      of a merge with the resource manager, very few variables are set here
      now. The directives **resetbindings**, **resetmenus** and **resetgadgets** are still
      allowed, as are gadget declarations of the form:

              gadgetˈ]=*expr*

      Where *n* is a positive integer indicating the gadget to initialize and *expr* is
      one of the following:

      string or "*string*" [ˆ *attributes*]
              Set the name of the gadget to *string*. The name will be painted in
              the gadget box with the **gadget.font** resource or an overriding
              font attribute (see below). *string* may contain embedded non-
              alphanumeric characters in the form of \# where # is one or more
              decimal digits (i.e. \54) or \c where *c* is a character in the stan-
              dard C string literal set (i.e. n, r, t, f). This is useful if you've
              specified a gadget font with glyphs in it (such as cursor) and you
              want to paint a specific glyph from it in a gadget box. Many such
              glyphs are not represented by ascii characters.

(*string*) [^ *attributes*]
> Load a pixmap from the file named by *string* and tile the gadget with it (see also: **path**).

Additional *attributes* may be specified after a '^' (caret) character in the form:

offset\gravity\foreground\background\font
> Any omitted parameters will be set to default values.

> *offset* is an integer specifying how far to place this gadget from its nearest neighbor (or an edge). Default offset is **gadget.pad**, or 2 if **gadget.pad** is not defined.

> *gravity* is one of **NoGravity, LeftGravity, RightGravity** or **CenterGravity. NoGravity** specifies that the gadget is to be placed opposite of wherever the last gadget was placed. **LeftGravity** specifies that the gadget should stick to the left of the title bar, **RightGravity** to the right and **CenterGravity** to the center.

> *foreground* and *background* specify the colors used to tile the gadget or draw the text.

> *font* is the name of the font you want the gadget's name drawn in. This overrides the **gadget.font** setting for this gadget.

> The default values for *attributes* are 0, **NoGravity**, black (**reverse**: white) and white (**reverse**: black), the setting of **gadget.font**.

It is important to note that in the absence of a *gravity* specification (i.e. we've defaulted to **NoGravity**), the window manager will automatically place a gadget on the side opposite of the last gadget placed. If it's the first gadget placed, it will go to the right. Thus in the absence of any *gravity* (or *offset*) specifications, the window manager will place gadgets in a right-left-right fashion until all gadgets have been placed.

For example:

```
gadget[0] = "die"
gadget[1] = (resize.b) ^ 2 | red | orange
gadget[2] = (iconbox.b) ^ | LeftGravity
gadget[3] = "\56" ^ | LeftGravity | green | black | cursor
```

These declarations will create 4 gadget boxes, situated in the following manner:

The first gadget box will be created wide enough to print the word "die" in it (in whatever gadget font has been defined) and will be placed on the right side (since it hasn't chosen a gravity) against the edge (since it hasn't chosen an offset). Background and foreground colors will be black and white (assignment depending on whether **reverse** is set).

The second gadget box will be tiled with the contents of the file "resize.b" (assuming that it's a valid bitmap file) and will go on the left side (since it also has no gravity and the last one went on the right). It will be offset from the edge by 2 pixels since there was an offset for it. Foreground will be red, background will be orange.

The third gadget will be tiled with the contents of "iconbox.b" and will be placed against the second gadget on the left hand side since we specified a gravity. Colors will be black and white (depending on **reverse**).

The fourth gadget will display glyph #56 from the cursor font in green and black (it's gumby of course).

IMPORTANT: Gadgets may be declared in any order, but you are not allowed to leave gaps, i.e..it's perfectly acceptable to declare gadgets in the order 0, 2, 3, 1, but **not** legal to declare gadgets in the order 0, 3, 2, 4 as gadget #1 has been omitted. This restriction may be removed in the future, but for now you'll get a diagnostic and *awm* will exit.

All other variables controlling window manager behavior are described in the **X DEFAULTS** section of this man page.

BINDING SYNTAX

Mouse buttons may be bound to particular window manager functions with:

"function=[modifier key(s)]:[context]:mouse events:" menu name "

or

"function=[modifier key(s)]:[context]:mouse events:" text action "

Function and mouse events are the only required fields. The menu name is required with the *f.menu* function definition only. Similarly, text action is required only with the *f.action* function definition.

Function

f.action Invokes a text action. 'text' should be in quotes with a preceding "action" character (one of '^', '!' or 'l'). The syntax is identical to menu text actions which are discussed in greater detail under the **Menus** section of this document.

f.action=*[modifier key(s)]:[context]:mouse events:action"* text "

f.beep	emits a beep from the keyboard. Loudness is determined by the volume variable.
f.circledown	causes the top window that is obscuring another window to drop to the bottom of the stack of windows.
f.circleup	exposes the lowest window that is obscured by other windows.
f.continue	releases the window server display action after you stop action with the **f.pause** function.
f.destroy	calls XKillClient on the selected window. Use with caution!! Binding it to naked mouse buttons is probably not a good idea!
f.exit	exits the window manager. If you've started *awm* from *xinit* (actually sort of useful now that the −e flag has been added), this will also exit the window system.
f.focus	directs all keyboard input to the selected window. To reset the focus to all windows, invoke *f.focus* from the root window.
f.iconify	When implemented from a window, this function converts the window to its respective icon. When implemented from an icon, f.iconify converts the icon to its respective window.
f.lower	lowers a window that is obstructing a window below it.
f.menu	invokes a menu. Enclose 'menu name' in quotes if it contains blank characters or parentheses.

f.menu=[*modifier key(s)*]:[*context*]:*mouse events*:" *menu name* "

f.move	moves a window or icon to a new location, which becomes the default location.
f.moveopaque	moves a window or icon to a new screen location. When using this function, the entire window or icon is moved to the new screen location. The grid effect is not used with this function.
f.neaten	neatens the desktop using the RTL neaten package. See the **X DEFAULTS** for the resources necessary to customize this somewhat complex feature. This function only works if *awm* has been compiled with the -DNEATEN flag (which compiles in the neaten package). Invoking this function without this is a noop (though a warning diagnostic is printed to stderr). See the INSTALLATION section of the README document for more details.
f.newiconify	allows you to create a window or icon and then position the window or icon in a new default location on the screen.
f.pause	temporarily stops all display action. To release the screen and immediately update all windows, use the **f.continue** function.
f.pushdown	moves a window down. The distance of the push is determined by the push variables.
f.pushleft	moves a window to the left. The distance of the push is determined by the push variables.
f.pushright	moves a window to the right. The distance of the push is determined by the push variables.
f.pushup	moves a window up. The distance of the push is determined by the push variables.
f.raise	raises a window that is being obstructed by a window above it.
f.refresh	results in exposure events being sent to the window server clients for all exposed or partially exposed windows. The windows will not refresh correctly if the exposure events are not handled properly.
f.resize	resizes an existing window. Note that some clients, notably editors, react unpredictably if you resize the window while the client is running.
f.restart	causes the window manager application to restart, retracing the *awm* search path and initializing the variables it finds.
f.[no]decorate	adds or removes "decorations" on the selected window. What decorations are added (or deleted) depends on the settings of various booleans and client-specific resources (see: **SPECIAL RESOURCES**).

The booleans **titles**, **gadgets** and **borderContext.width** currently influence **awm**'s choice of default decorations.

Modifier Keys

It is preferable to use meta as a modifier key for **awm** (or any other window manager, for that matter), but one may also use ctrl, shift, lock, or null (no modifier key). Modifier keys must be entered in lower case, and can be abbreviated as: c, l, m, s for ctrl, lock, meta, and shift, respectively. It's also permissible to refer to the the modifier keys directly as "mod1, mod2, mod3, mod4 or mod5". A mouse button with no modifier key(s) is often referred to as a "naked" mouse button.

You may bind any number of modifier keys to a function, use the bar (|) character to combine them.

Context

The context refers to the screen location of the cursor when a command is initiated. When you include a context entry in a binding, the cursor must be in that context or the function will not be activated. The window manager recognizes the following seven contexts: icon, window, root, title, gadget[*n*] (where *n* is the gadget number), border and (null).

The icon context refers to any icon and may be safely bound without interfering with window events.

The window context refers to application windows and should be used carefully to avoid usurping button events that applications may want for their own purposes.

The root context refers to the root, or background window.

The title context refers to the titlebar area of a window, if one exists.

The gadget context (with mandatory index) specifies a given gadget box. Binding to a gadget that's undefined (not initialized to anything) is an error.

The border context refers to the artificial border area created when the resource **borderContext.width** is defined (see **borderContext.width** under **X DEFAULTS**). Using this context when no border area exists (i.e. **borderContext.width** is not defined) is a noop.

A (null) context is indicated when the context field is left blank, and allows a function to be invoked from any screen location. This is basically equivalent to specifying all the possible contexts.

Combine contexts using the bar (|) character.

Mouse Buttons

Any of the following mouse buttons are accepted (in lower case) and may be abbreviated as l, m, or r, respectively: left, middle, right.

With the specific button, you must identify the action of that button. Mouse actions can be:

down   function occurs when the specified button is pressed down.

up   function occurs when the specified button is released.

delta   indicates that the mouse must be moved the number of pixels specified with the delta variable before the specified function is invoked. The mouse can be moved in any direction to satisfy the delta requirement.

MENU DEFINITION

After binding a set of function keys and a menu name to **f.menu**, you must define the menu to be invoked, using the following syntax:

menu = (*string*) " *menu name* " {
"*item name*" : "*action*"

      .
      .
      .

}

The *string* in parenthesis is an optional argument which names a pixmap file (see also: **path**) to use as the menu title rather than just using the name of the menu. This is generally only useful if you're using pixmaps for the menu panes as well (see below). Though the *menu name* isn't displayed when you specify *string*, you still need to specify one for *awm* to use when looking up the binding to it.

Enter the *menu name* exactly the way it is entered with the **f.menu** function or the window manager will not recognize the link. If the *menu name* contains blank strings, tabs or parentheses, it must be quoted here and in the **f.menu** function entry. If you haven't chosen to display a pixmap title in *string*, the menu name will be displayed at the top of the menu in whatever font has been chosen for **menu.boldFont** (or its default).

You can enter as many menu items as your screen is long. You cannot scroll within menus.

Any menu entry that contains quotes, special characters, parentheses, tabs, or strings of blanks must be enclosed in double quotes. Follow the item name by a colon (:).

A special case is an item surrounded by parenthesis, which designates the *item name* as the name of a pixmap file to tile the menu pane with. Given a pixmap for the menu title as well (see above), it's possible to create menus that are totally pictorial in nature. There are, however, two caveats. Due to the fact that it's easier to do, the pixmaps are used as backgrounds for the menu panes rather than painting them on whenever a given pane in exposed. This has rather ugly consequences if one of the pixmaps (or a line of text if a pane is textual) is larger than the others. Since the server replicates pixmaps over the entire window, it results in a "wallpaper" effect on the smaller pixmaps. The solution is to make all the pixmaps the same size and/or not mix in any text items that will need a wider pane.

The second problem is that the check marks and pull-right indicators are always displayed in fixed positions on the right and left edges of menu panes. If your pixmaps try to use this real-estate, they may be partially covered by a check mark or pull-right pixmap. Design your menus with this in mind.

Menu Action
    Window manager functions

        Any function previously described, e.g., **f.move** or **f.iconify**. Using **f.menu** results in a pull-right pane which you can use to "walk" between menus (see below). A "walk" can be done by moving the cursor onto the pull-right arrow displayed at the right edge of the pane, or by clicking another button in the pane while holding the original one down.

    Walking menus

        Select the function **f.menu** and separate it from the *menu name* with a colon (:) i.e.

```
menu = "foo" {
Walking Menu:        f.menu:  "NextMenu"
}
```

Text actions
> There are two kinds of special "actions" involving arbitrary strings of text. These are:

Shell commands
> Begin with an exclamation point (!) and set to run in background. You cannot include a new line character within a shell command.

Text strings
> Text strings are placed in the window server's cut buffer.

> Strings with a new line character must begin with an up arrow (^), which is stripped during the copy operation.

> Strings without a new line must begin with the bar character (|), which is stripped during the copy operation.

Booleans
> Any boolean variable previously described, e.g., **reverse** or **autoraise**. The current state of a boolean variable in a menu will be indicated with a check mark (a check mark means the boolean is set to true).

SPECIAL NOTE:

Menus bound to title bars, gadget boxes or borders cause (where logical) the selected menu action to occur automatically on the titled window as opposed to having to select a window for the action. However, actions requiring mouse tracking (i.e. move, resize) will usually **not** work well in this context. While this limitation will be eliminated in the near future, it is suggested that you use this feature to do things that do not require mouse tracking, such as raise, lower, iconify, etc.

Color Defaults
> Colors default to the colors of the root window under any of the following conditions:

> 1)   If you run out of color map entries, either before or during an invocation of *awm*.

> 2)   If you specify a foreground or background color that does not exist in the RGB color database ($LIBDIR/*rgb.txt*).

> 3)   If you omit a foreground or background color.

> 4)   If you specify no colors in the resource database.

X DEFAULTS

A number of variables that were previously specified in the *.uwmrc* file have been moved out of the *.awmrc* file and are now retrieved from the resource database. When a value cannot be found, a default (compiled into *awm*) is substituted. The resource database is also now queried to determine whether or not to title a given window. See the end of this section for details.

In the descriptions below, variable names are listed in boldface, their type in parenthesis, and their default value in double quotes.

autoraise (boolean) "off"
> Automatically raise a window to the top when it gains the input focus. See also: **raiseDelay**

autoselect (boolean) "off"
> Specifies that the pointer be placed over the first item in a menu, rather than the title, when the menu is popped up.

background (string)
> The default background color for all other color choices in *awm*. If **reverse** is not set, this defaults to white, otherwise it defaults to black. References to **background** in this document refer to this resource.

border.foreground (boolean) "foreground"
> Specifies the border color to use for all windows (this color may be drawn solid or stippled, depending on the window focus and the setting of **border.hilite**).

border.hilite (boolean) "on"
> Specifies whether or not window border colors are to be changed on focus changes. On focus in, the window border is changed to solid **border.foreground**. On focus out, it is changed to a "gray" stipple.

borderContext.background (string) "background"
> Background color to use for border context pixmap. Value is meaningless if **borderContext.width** and **borderContext.pixmap** are undefined.

borderContext.boldPixmap (string) "none"
> The name of a pixmap file to load and tile the border context area with when the focus is in. If this is defined, and **hilite** is set, focus changes will cause the border context background to alternate between **borderContext.pixmap** and **borderContext.boldPixmap**. If **borderContext.boldPixmap** is defined, but **borderContext.pixmap** is not, a blank pixmap will be used in place of **borderContext.pixmap**.

borderContext.cursor (int) "XC_cross"
> Glyph (in decimal) to retrieve from cursor font for use in border context.

borderContext.foreground (string) "foreground"
> Foreground color to use for border color pixmap. Value is meaningless if **borderContext.width** and **borderContext.pixmap** are undefined.

borderContext.pixmap (string) "background
> Pixmap to display as border context area background. Value is meaningless is **borderContext.width** is undefined (or set to zero).

Used exclusively as the background unless
borderContext.boldPixmap and **hilite** are defined.

borderContext.width (int) "0"

Number of pixels wide to make the border context. Though functions may be bound to the border context (see: **Context**) without
setting this, they will be impossible to invoke due to the fact that
there will be nothing to click on. The border context should not
be confused with the actual window border. It is an artificial area
around each window that resembles a border.

delta (int) "1"

Number of pixels that must be moved over before a "delta" action
is taken (see: **BINDING SYNTAX**).

foreground (string)

The default foreground color for all other color choices in *awm*.
If **reverse** is not set, this defaults to black, otherwise it defaults to
white. References to **foreground** in this document refer to this
resource.

frameFocus (boolean) "off"

[De]highlight when the pointer [leaves] enters the "frame" of the
window (the frame includes the client window, title bar and
border context areas, if present). Setting this option also causes
the focus to follow the pointer so that keyboard input will go the
the client regardless of where the pointer is in the "frame".

freeze (boolean) "off"

Lock out all other clients during certain window manager tasks,
such as move and resize.

gadget.border (int) "1"

The width of all gadget borders in pixels.

gadget.font (string) "fixed"

Which font to use for (textual) gadget labels.

gadget.pad (int) "3"

The number of pixels to pad a gadget from its neighbor if it has
no offset defined.

gadgets (boolean) "off"

Display gadgets in title bars, if any are declared.

grid (boolean) "off"

Display a finely ruled grid when positioning or resizing
windows/icons.

hilite (boolean) "off"

Causes the following actions to occur when a window gains the
input focus:

1. If **showName** is on:

1a.   If **title.boldFont** is defined, the window name is
redrawn in this font.

1b.   If it's not, then the window name is redrawn in
reverse video.

2. If **title.boldPixmap** is defined, the background of the
title bar is set to it.

3. If **borderContext.boldPixmap** is defined, the
background of the border context area is set to it.

On focus out, the window name is redrawn in **title.font** the title
background to **title.pixmap** and the border context to
borderContext.pixmap, respectively.

If **border.hilite** is undefined, this variable will set it automatically.

Note that most icon variables only affect icons owned by *awm*. Except
for foreground and background colors, client created icons are left
alone.

icon.background (string) "**background**"
Icon (pixmap) background color.

icon.border (string) "**icon.foreground**"
Color to use for icon borders.

icon.borderWidth (int) "**2**"
Width of icon border in pixels.

icon.font (string) "**8x13**"
Which font to use for icon text.

icon.foreground (string) "**foreground**"
Icon (pixmap) foreground color.

icon.hPad (int) "**2**"
Number of pixels to pad icon text horizontally.

icon.vPad (int) "**2**"
Number of pixels to pad icon text vertically.

icon.text.background (string) "**icon.background**"
Background color to use for icon text.

icon.text.foreground (string) "**icon.foreground**"
Foreground color to use for icon text.

icon.pixmap (string) "**grey**"
Pixmap to display as icon background. Since this pixmap will be
used to tile all icons owned by *awm*, it's probably not a good
idea to put application specific pictures in it. More typically, this
will be a cross hatch pattern or some similar background weave.
See also: **path, icon.foreground, icon.background**.

installColormap (boolean) "**false**"
Install a given window's colormap when the pointer enters it.
When the pointer leaves, the default colormap is installed.

menu.background (string) "**background**"
Menu background color.

menu.boldFont (string) "**8x13bold**"
Which font to use for (textual) menu panes. Currently, the only
pane using this font is the title pane (unless, of course, it's a pixmap).

menu.border (string) "**foreground**"
Menu border color.

menu.borderWidth (int) "**2**"
Width of menu border in pixels.

menu.delta (int) "20"
> Number of pixels to move on a "pull-right" pane before the sub-menu attached to it is popped up.

menu.font (string) "8x13"
> Which font to use in (textual) menu panes.

menu.foreground (string) "**foreground**"
> Menu foreground color.

menu.itemBorder (int) "1"
> Width of individual (menu) item borders.

menu.pad (int) "2"
> Number of pixels to pad menu text/pixmaps vertically.

The following resources pertain only to the RTL Neaten package and are ignored if *awm* has not been compiled with that option (see the INSTALLATION file).

neaten.absMinWidth (int) "64"
> Indicates the amount of space in pixels, that is used as the absolute minimum width of a window during the neaten operation.

neaten.absMinHeight (int) "64"
> Indicates the amount of space in pixels, that is used as the absolute minimum height of a window during the neaten operation.

neaten.retainSize (boolean) "true"
> Forces to windows to be at least their current size. Windows may overlap as a side effect.

neaten.fill (boolean) "true"
> Allows windows to grow to their maximum size during the neaten operation. Normally a window will grow only to the maximum of its desired (based on the WM_NORMAL_HINTS property) and current size.

neaten.fixTopOfStack (boolean) "true"
> Fixes the size and location of the window at the top of the window hierarchy. If necessary, this window will overlap even other windows which can not be tiled.

neaten.keepOpen (boolean) "true"
> Constrains all windows to remain open during the neaten operation. No windows will be iconized. This operation may cause windows to overlap.

neaten.usePriorities (boolean) "true"
> Assigns the windows priorities based on their stacking order (windows closer to the top in the stacking order are given higher priorities). Priorities are used when determining size and location of windows on the screen.

neaten.primaryIconPlacement (string) "**Top**"
> Selects the side of the screen where icons are first placed. Legal values are: **Top, Left, Bottom, Right** and **Closest** (to its current position).

neaten.secondaryIconPlacement (string) "**Left**"
> Determines where along the specified primary side the icon should be placed. Legal values are those for **neaten.primaryIconPlacement** plus **Center**. Not used if **neaten.primaryIconPlacement** is **Closest**

normali (boolean) ''on''
> Make sure that icons created with **f.newiconify** stay wholly within the root window (on screen), regardless of attempted placement. If off, put icons wherever the cursor is placed.

normalw (boolean) ''on''
> Make sure that windows mapped with **f.newiconify** are placed on-screen, regardless of cursor position. If off, put windows wherever the cursor is placed.

path (string) ''null''
> A number of items (titles, menus, etc) now allow you to specify a pixmap file, rather than just a text string to display. Since it would be tedious to type in full pathnames for these files if they all lived in the same places, the directory(s) named by **path** are searched if the pixmap file's pathname does not begin with a slash (/) or tilde (~) and is not found in the current directory.

> **path** is a white-space separated list of one or more directories to search, much like that used by the Unix C-shell. The ~ notation used to designate your (or someone else's) home directory is supported, but wildcards are not.

popup.background (string) ''background''
> Background color to use for pop-up text.

popup.borderWidth (int) ''2''
> Width of pop-up window border in pixels.

popup.font (string) ''9x15''
> Which font to use for popup window text.

popup.foreground (string) ''
> Foreground color to use for pop-up text.

popup.pad (int) ''4''
> Number of pixels to pad pop-up text horizontally.

pushRelative (boolean) ''on''
> When a window is pushed, push 1/**push** of the window. If off, move window **push** pixels.

pushDown (boolean) ''false''
> When adding a title bar or border context to a window, put the border or title bar area at the current x, y position and "push" the window down to make room. For windows with an upper edge at or near the top of the screen, this gives the most asthetically pleasing results. For windows near the bottom, it does not. If set to false, the title bar/border will be added "on top" and the window will not be moved down. Note that the setting of this resource also affects how the window is maniplated during resizes, title removals, etc.

raiseDelay (int) ''100''
> Amount of time in milliseconds to wait (while window has focus) before raising. If pointer leaves window before time elapses, raise is not performed.

reverse (boolean) ''on''
> Reverse background/foreground colors for titles, menus, gadget windows, popup windows, etc. In the absence of any color specifications, this results in black-on-white.

rootResizeBox (boolean) "on"
> Put the resize (popup) window in the upper left corner of the root window, rather than on the window being resized. This saves a potentially expensive refresh that would occur when the popup was unmapped. If your server supports save-unders, it's generally (but not always) better to turn **saveUnder** on instead.

saveUnder (boolean) "off"
> Use save-unders for menus and pop-up windows. If the server does not support save-unders, this action does nothing.

showName (boolean) "on"
> Display the window name in a title (assuming that the window is titled in the first place).

title.background (string) "background"
> Background color to use for title pixmap.

title.boldFont (string) "none"
> Which font to use for titlebar labels if focus is and **hilite** is enabled. If this isn't set, and **hilite** is, the title text will be displayed with **title.font** in reverse video.

title.boldPixmap (string) "none"
> The name of a pixmap file to load and tile titlebars with when the focus is in. If this is defined, and **hilite** is set, focus changes will cause title backgrounds to alternate between **title.pixmap** and **title.boldPixmap**. If **title.boldPixmap** is defined, but **title.pixmap** is not, a blank pixmap will be used in place of **title.pixmap**.

title.cursor (int) "XC_left_ptr"
> Glyph (in decimal) to retrieve from cursor font for use in title bar.

title.font (string) "vtsingle"
> Which font to use for titlebar labels. Used exclusively unless **title.boldFont** and **hilite** are set.

title.foreground (string) "foreground"
> Foreground color to use when drawing background (both normal and bold) pixmaps.

title.pad (int) "2"
> Number of pixels to pad title bar text vertically.

title.pixmap (string) "none"
> The name of a pixmap file to load and tile titlebars with. This background is use exclusively unless the **title.boldPixmap** is defined and **hilite** is set.

title.text.background (string) "title.background"
> Background color to use when drawing title bar text.

title.text.foreground (string) "title.foreground"
> Foreground color to use when drawing title bar.

titles (boolean) "off"
> Put title bars on all windows (both existing windows and new ones as they're created. See also: **f.title**

volume (int) "2"
> Specifies the bell volume (delta on volume set with *xset*).

wall (boolean) "off"
> Restrict window movement to edges of screen (rootwindow). This feature is fairly handy and should probably be bound to a menu so that it can readily be turned on and off.

warpOnDeIconify (boolean) "off"
> Warp pointer to upper right corner of window on de-iconify.

warpOnIconify (boolean) "off"
> Warp pointer to center of icon on iconify.

warpOnRaise (boolean) "off"
> Warp pointer to upper left corner of window on raise.

windowName.offset (int) "0"
> Number of pixels from the right or left edge of a titlebar to print the window name (assuming that **showName** is set). If this value is negative, the name will be offset **nameOffset** (plus the name length) pixels from the right edge. If the value is positive, then the name will be offset **nameOffset** pixels from the left edge. If the value is zero, the name will be centered. Since the length of a window name can vary dynamically, this value will be adjusted, when necessary, to ensure that the name is visible in the title bar.

zap (boolean) "off"
> Causes ghost lines to follow the window or icon from its previous location to its new location during a move, resize or iconify operation.

SPECIAL RESOURCES

name.**wm_option.autoRaise** (boolean)

name.**wm_option.borderContext** (boolean)

name.**wm_option.gadgets** (boolean)

name.**wm_option.title** (boolean)

> These resources determine whether or not a given application really wants a title, gadgets, border context area or to be auto-raised. The application's CLASS and NAME (in the WM_CLASS property) are checked against the string supplied for *name* (for example: Xclock*wm_option.title: off).

> Specifying one of these resources overrides any other boolean settings (I.E. **awm.titles** or **awm.gadgets**) and may be used to turn things on and off at the application and/or class level for applications, regardless of **awm**'s settings.

> Note: Both class and name resources are checked, and in that order. Thus specific applications may override settings for their class, if desired.

> These resources are "special" as they are checked for under the application's name, not *awm*'s; I.E. **xclock.wm_option.autoRaise** is not **awm.xclock.wm_option.autoRaise** as one might think.

EXAMPLES
>The following sample startup file shows the default window manager options:

```
# Global variables
#
resetbindings
resetmenus
#
# Mouse button/key maps
#
# FUNCTION   KEYS CONTEXT  BUTTON    MENU(if any)
# ========   ==== =======  ======    ===========
f.menu =      meta :     :left down   :"WINDOW OPS"
f.menu =      meta :     :middle down :"EXTENDED WINDOW OPS"
f.move =      meta :wli :right down
f.circleup =  meta :root :right down
#
# Menu specifications
#
menu = "WINDOW OPS" {
"(De)Iconify":  f.iconify
Move:           f.move
Resize:         f.resize
Lower:          f.lower
Raise:          f.raise
}


menu = "EXTENDED WINDOW OPS" {
Create Window:               !"xterm &"
Iconify at New Position:     f.lowericonify
Focus Keyboard on Window:      f.focus
Freeze All Windows:          f.pause
Unfreeze All Windows:         f.continue
Circulate Windows Up:         f.circleup
Circulate Windows Down:        f.circledown
}
```

RESTRICTIONS
>The color specifications have no effect on a monochrome system. There's currently no way to specify a keysym in place of a button (up/down/delta) specification. This restriction will be removed in the near future.

FILES
>$LIBDIR/rgb.txt
>$LIBDIR/font
>/usr/skel/.awmrc
>$LIBDIR/awm/system.awmrc
>$HOME/.awmrc

SEE ALSO
>X(1), X(8C)

AUTHOR

Copyright 1988
Ardent Computer Corporation
Sunnyvale, Ca
COPYRIGHT 1985, 1986
DIGITAL EQUIPMENT CORPORATION
MAYNARD, MASSACHUSETTS

NAME

bdf2vf – convert BDF format to vfont format

SYNOPSIS

bdf2vf vffile < bdffile

DESCRIPTION

Bdf2vf converts the BDF file on stdin to vfont format.

DIAGNOSTICS

No error recovery in parser, just quits.

BUGS

Vfont format can only handle glyphs smaller than 127 per side. Sun vfont glyphs is 16-bit word aligned. I haven't provided for this. Hack it yourself.

AUTHOR

Ken Yap

3

NAME

bdf2gf – convert BDF format to GF (TeX generic font) format

SYNOPSIS

bdf2gf gffile [plfile] < bdffile

DESCRIPTION

Bdf2gf converts the BDF file on stdin to a TeX GF (generic font) file and optionally a PL (property list) file.

DIAGNOSTICS

No error recovery in parser, just quits.

AUTHOR

Ken Yap

NAME
>   bdfresize – Resize BDF Format Font

SYNOPSIS
>   bdfresize [-w *factor*] [-h *factor*] [-f *factor*] [*bdf-file*]

DESCRIPTION
>   *Bdfresize* is a command to magnify or reduce font which is described with
>   the standard BDF format. If *bdf-file* is not specified, it reads from stdin.
>   *Bdfresize* outputs the result to stdout in BDF format. A few COMMENT
>   lines are inserted to the result font. FONT, ATTRIBUTES, STARTCHAR
>   and ENCODING lines are copied from source font. If a syntax error
>   occurs in source font, *bdfresize* stop its process.

OPTIONS
>   **–w** *factor*
>   >   Specifies resize factor for the font width.
>
>   **–h** *factor*
>   >   Specifies resize factor for the font height.
>
>   **–f** *factor* Same as specifying both **-w** and **-h** with same *factor*.
>
>   *factor* is described either of following forms.
>   >   <digits>
>   >   <digits>/<digits>

SEE ALSO
>   Character Bitmap Distribution Format 2.1 (Adobe Systems, Inc.)

AUTHOR
>   Copyright (C) 1988 by Hiroto Kagotani.
>   kagotani@cs.titech.junet
>
>   Everyone is permitted to do anything on this program including copying,
>   transplanting, debugging, and modifying.

NAME

bdftosnf - BDF to SNF font compiler for X11

SYNOPSIS

bdftosnf [-p#] [-s#] [-m] [-l] [-M] [-L] [-w] [-W] [-t] [-i] [bdf-file]

DESCRIPTION

bdftosnf reads a Bitmap Distribution Format (BDF) font from the specified file (or from standard input if no file is specified) and writes an X11 server normal font (SNF) to standard output.

OPTIONS

–p#   Force the glyph padding to a specific number. The legal values are 1, 2, 4, and 8. **–s#** Force the scanline unit padding to a specific number. The legal values are 1, 2, and 4.

–m   Force the bit order to most significant bit first.

–l   Force the bit order to least significant bit first.

–M   Force the byte order to most significant bit first.

–L   Force the byte order to least significant bit first.

–w   Print warnings if the character bitmaps have bits set to one outside of their defined widths.

–W   Print warnings for characters with an encoding of -1; the default is to silently ignore such characters.

–t   Expand glyphs in "terminal-emulator" fonts to fill the bounding box.

–i   Don't compute correct ink metrics for "terminal-emulator" fonts.

SEE ALSO

X(1), Xserver(1)

"Bitmap Distribution Format 2.1"

NAME
> bitimp – generic bitmap to imPress program

SYNOPSIS
> **bitimp** [options] [Ifile]

DESCRIPTION
> *bitimp* converts a bitmap *file* to imPress format for printing on an IMAGEN printer.
>
> The options are:
>
> **–a** *mode*
>> Sets *bitimp's* mode of operation to *mode*, which may be one of *genimp*, *isimp*, *macimp*, *sunimp* or *xwdimp*, (default taken from the invocation line if possible, otherwise the default is *xwdimp*.)
>
> **–b** *string*
>> Sets the banner string for the job.
>
> **–c** *n*   Prints *n* copies. Since this is done via the Imagen DCL, this switch is meaningful even if the output is not to be immediately printed.
>
> **–d**   Turns on debugging.
>
> **–f** *string*
>> Identifies *string* as the value of the variable **file** in the DCL.
>
> **–gs** *num*
>> For *genimp* mode, indicates that *num* bitmaps are in the input stream. (default 8)
>
> **–gh** *num*
>> For *genimp* mode, indicates that each bitmap is *num* bits wide. (default 512)
>
> **–gv** *num*
>> For *genimp* mode, indicates that each bitmap is *num* bits tall. (default 512)
>
> **–g** *num* For *genimp* mode, indicates that each bitmap is *num* bits wide and tall. (default 512)
>
> **–h**   Prevents a banner page for being printed for this job.
>
> **–i** *file*   Directs *bitimp* to send its output to the named file. This disables the *–p* and *–s* switches.
>
> **–l**   Print in landscape mode.
>
> **–p**   Directs *bitimp* to spool its output for printing. This disables the *–s* switch. (default OFF unless stdout is a tty)
>
> **–r**   Directs *bitimp* to remove its input file if everything goes well.
>
> **–s**   Directs *bitimp* to send its output to the standard output. This diables the *–i* and *–p* switches. (default ON unless stdout is a tty)
>
> **–t**   Toggles page reversal for the job. If the job is to be sent to an Imagen 12/300, pagereversal actually does the wrong thing.
>
> **–v**   Turns on verbose output to the diagnostic output.
>
> **–D** *string*
>> Identifies *string* to be appended to the DCL for the job.
>
> **–H** *host*
>> Identifies the *host* of the user spooling the job.

−J *string*
>   Identifies *string* as the name of this job.

−M *num*
>   Sets the bitmap magnification to two raised to the *num*. *num* may
>   be 0, 1, or 2. (default 1)

−P *printer*
>   Sets the printer for this job.

−R *resolution*
>   Sets the resolution of the printer for this job. (default 300)

−U *user*
>   Identifies the *user* spooling the job.

SEE ALSO
>   iprint(1), catimp(1), dviimp(1)

DIAGNOSTICS
>   Obvious.

BUGS

>   For *xwdimp*, only XY pixmaps of a single plane are handled.

NAME
        bitmap, bmtoa, atobm – bitmap editor and converter utilities for X

SYNOPSIS
        bitmap [-options ...] *filename WIDTHxHEIGHT*

        bmtoa [-chars ...] [*filename*]

        atobm [-chars *cc*] [-name *variable*] [-xhot *number*] [-yhot *number*]
        [*filename*]

DESCRIPTION
        The *bitmap* program is a rudimentary tool for creating or editing rectangu-
        lar images made up of 1's and 0's. Bitmaps are used in X for defining
        clipping regions, cursor shapes, icon shapes, and tile and stipple patterns.

        The *bmtoa* and *atobm* filters convert *bitmap* files (FILE FORMAT) to and
        from ASCII strings. They are most commonly used to quickly print out
        bitmaps and to generate versions for including in text.

USAGE
        Bitmap displays grid in which each square represents a single bit in the
        picture being edited. Squares can be set, cleared, or inverted directly with
        the buttons on the pointer and a menu of higher level operations such as
        draw line and fill circle is provided to the side of the grid. Actual size
        versions of the bitmap as it would appear normally and inverted appear
        below the menu.

        If the bitmap is to be used for defining a cursor, one of the squares in the
        images may be designated as the *hotspot*. This determines where the cur-
        sor is actually pointing. For cursors with sharp tips (such as arrows or
        fingers), this is usually at the end of the tip; for symmetric cursors (such
        as crosses or bullseyes), this is usually at the center.

        Bitmaps are stored as small C code fragments suitable for including in
        applications. They provide an array of bits as well as symbolic constants
        giving the width, height, and hotspot (if specified) that may be used in
        creating cursors, icons, and tiles.

        The *WIDTHxHEIGHT* argument gives the size to use when creating a new
        bitmap (the default is 16x16). Existing bitmaps are always edited at their
        current size.

        If the *bitmap* window is resized by the window manager, the size of the
        squares in the grid will shrink or enlarge to fit.

OPTIONS
        Bitmap accepts the following options:

        –help
                This option will cause a brief description of the allowable options and
                parameters to be printed.

        –display *display*
                This option specifies the name of the X server to used.

        –geometry *geometry*
                This option specifies the placement and size of the bitmap window on
                the screen. See *X* for details.

        –nodashed
                This option indicates that the grid lines in the work area should not
                be drawn using dashed lines. Although dashed lines are prettier than

solid lines, on some servers they are significantly slower.

–name *variablename*
This option specifies the variable name to be used when writing out the bitmap file. The default is to use the basename of the *filename* command line argument.

–bw *number*
This option specifies the border width in pixels of the main window.

–fn *font*
This option specifies the font to be used in the buttons.

–fg *color*
This option specifies the color to be used for the foreground.

–bg *color*
This option specifies the color to be used for the background.

–hl *color*
This option specifies the color to be used for highlighting.

–bd *color*
This option specifies the color to be used for the window border.

–ms *color*
This option specifies the color to be used for the pointer (mouse).

Bmtoa accepts the following option:

–chars *cc*
This option specifies the pair of characters to use in the string version of the bitmap. The first character is used for 0 bits and the second character is used for 1 bits. The default is to use dashes (-) for 0's and sharp signs (#) for 1's.

Atobm accepts the following options:

–chars *cc*
This option specifies the pair of characters to use when converting string bitmaps into arrays of numbers. The first character represents a 0 bit and the second character represents a 1 bit. The default is to use dashes (-) for 0's and sharp signs (#) for 1's.

–name *variable*
This option specifies the variable name to be used when writing out the bitmap file. The default is to use the basename of the *filename* command line argument or leave it blank if the standard input is read.

–xhot *number*
This option specifies the X coordinate of the hotspot. Only postive values are allowed. By default, no hotspot information is included.

–yhot *number*
This option specifies the Y coordinate of the hotspot. Only postive values are allowed. By default, no hotspot information is included.

CHANGING GRID SQUARES
Grid squares may be set, cleared, or inverted by pointing to them and clicking one of the buttons indicated below. Multiple squares can be changed at once by holding the button down and dragging the cursor across them. Set squares are filled and represent 1's in the bitmap; clear squares are empty and represent 0's.

Button 1
This button (usually leftmost on the pointer) is used to set one or more squares. The corresponding bit or bits in the bitmap

are turned on (set to 1) and the square or squares are filled.

Button 2

This button (usually in the middle) is used to invert one or more squares. The corresponding bit or bits in the bitmap are flipped (1's become 0's and 0's become 1's).

Button 3

This button (usually on the right) is used to clear one or more squares. The corresponding bit or bits in the bitmap are turned off (set to 0) and the square or squares are emptied.

MENU COMMANDS

To make defining shapes easier, *bitmap* provides 13 commands for drawing whole sections of the grid at once, 2 commands for manipulating the hotspot, and 2 commands for updating the bitmap file and exiting. A command buttons for each of these operations is located to the right of the grid.

Several of the commands operate on rectangular portions of the grid. These areas are selected after the command button is pressed by moving the cursor to the upper left square of the desired area, pressing a pointer button, dragging the cursor to the lower right hand corner (with the button still pressed) , and then releasing the button. The command may be aborted by pressing any other button while dragging or by releasing outside the grid.

To invoke a command, move the pointer over that command and click any button.

Clear All

This command is used to clear all of the bits in the bitmap as if Button 3 had been dragged through every square in the grid. It cannot be undone.

Set All

This command is used to set all of the bits in the bitmap as if Button 1 had been dragged through every square in the grid. It cannot be undone.

Invert All

This command is used to invert all of the bits in the bitmap as if Button 2 had been dragged through every square in the grid.

Clear Area

This command is used to clear a region of the grid as if Button 3 had been dragged through each of the squares in the region. When this command is invoked, the cursor will change shape to indicate that the area to be cleared should be selected as outlined above.

Set Area

This command is used to set a region of the grid as if Button 1 had been dragged through each of the squares in the region. When this command is invoked, the cursor will change shape to indicate that the area to be set should be selected as outlined above.

Invert Area

This command is used to inverted a region of the grid as if Button 2 had been dragged through each of the squares in the region. When this command is invoked, the cursor will change shape to indicate that the area to be inverted should be selected as outlined above.

Copy Area

This command is used to copy a region of the grid from one location to another. When this command is invoked, the cursor will change shape to indicate that the area to be copied should be selected as outlined above. The cursor should then be clicked on the square to which the upper left hand corner of the region should be copied.

Move Area

This command is used to move a region of the grid from one location to another. When this command is invoked, the cursor will change shape to indicate that the area to be moved should be selected as outlined above. The cursor should then be clicked on the square to which the upper left hand corner of the region should be moved. Any squares in the region's old position that aren't also in the new position are cleared.

Overlay Area

This command is used to copy all of the set squares in a region of the grid from one location to another. When this command is invoked, the cursor will change shape to indicate that the area to be copied should be selected as outlined above. The cursor should then be clicked on the square to which the upper left hand corner of the region should be overlaid. Only the squares that are set in the region will be touched in the new location.

Line

This command will set the squares in a line between two points. When this command is invoked, the cursor will change shape to indicate that the pointer should be clicked on the two end points of the line.

Circle

This command will set the squares on a circle specified by a center and a point on the curve. When this command is invoked, the cursor will change shape to indicate that the pointer should be clicked on the center of the circle and then over a point on the curve. Small circles may not look very round because of the size of the grid and the limits of having to work with discrete pixels.

Filled Circle

This command will set all of the squares in a circle specified by a center and a point on the curve. When this command is invoked, the cursor will change shape to indicate that the pointer should be clicked on the center of the circle and then over a point on the curve. All squares side and including the circle are set.

Flood Fill

This command will set all clear squares in an enclosed shape. When this command is invoked, the cursor will change shape to indicate that the pointer should be clicked on any empty square inside the shape to be filled. All empty squares that border horizontally or vertically with the indicated square are set out to the enclosing shape. If the shape is not closed, the entire grid will be filled.

Set Hot Spot
> This command designates one square in the grid as the hot spot if this bitmap to be used for defining a cursor. When the command is invoked, the cursor will change indicating that the pointer should be clicked on the square to contain the hot spot.

Clear Hot Spot
> This command removes any designated hot spot from the bitmap.

Write Output
> This command writes a small fragment of C code representing the bitmap to the filename specified on the command line. If the file already exists, the original file will be renamed to *filename˜* before the new file is created. If an error occurs in either the renaming or the writing of the bitmap file, a dialog box will appear asking whether or not *bitmap* should use */tmp/filename* instead.

Quit
> This command causes *bitmap* to display a dialog box asking whether or not it should save the bitmap (if it has changed) and then exit. Answering *yes* is the same as invoking *Write Output*; *no* causes *bitmap* to simply exit; and *cancel* will abort the *Quit* command so that more changes may be made.

FILE FORMAT

The *Write Output* command stores bitmaps as simple C program fragments that can be compiled into programs, referred to by X Toolkit pixmap resources, manipulated by other programs (see *xsetroot*), or read in using utility routines in the various programming libraries. The width and height of the bitmap as well as the hotspot, if specified, are written as preprocessor symbols at the start of the file. The bitmap image is then written out as an array of characters:

```
#define name_width 11
#define name_height 5
#define name_x_hot 5
#define name_y_hot 2

static char name_bits[] = {
    0x91, 0x04, 0xca, 0x06, 0x84,
    0x04, 0x8a, 0x04, 0x91, 0x04
};
```

The **name** prefix to the preprocessor symbols and to the bits array is constructed from the *filename* argument given on the command line. Any directories are stripped off the front of the name and any suffix beginning with a period is stripped off the end. Any remaining non-alphabetic characters are replaced with underscores. The *name_x_hot* and *name_y_hot* symbols will only be present if a hotspot has been designated using the *Set Hot Spot* command.

Each character in the the array contains 8 bits from one row of the image (rows are padded out at the end to a multiple of 8 to make this is possible). Rows are written out from left to right and top to bottom. The first character of the array holds the leftmost 8 bits of top line, and the last characters holds the right most 8 bits (including padding) of the bottom line. Within each character, the leftmost bit in the bitmap is the least signficant bit in the character.

This process can be demonstrated visually by splitting a row into words containing 8 bits each, reversing the bits each word (since Arabic numbers have the significant digit on the right and images have the least significant bit on the left), and translating each word from binary to hexidecimal.

In the following example, the array of 1's and 0's on the left represents a bitmap containing 5 rows and 11 columns that spells *X11*. To its right is is the same array split into 8 bit words with each row padded with 0's so that it is a multiple of 8 in length (16):

```
10001001001        10001001 00100000
01010011011        01010011 01100000
00100001001        00100001 00100000
01010001001        01010001 00100000
10001001001        10001001 00100000
```

Reversing the bits in each word of the padded, split version of the bitmap yields the left hand figure below. Interpretting each word as hexidecimal number yields the array of numbers on the right:

```
10010001 00000100        0x91 0x04
11001010 00000110        0xca 0x06
10000100 00000100        0x84 0x04
10001010 00000100        0x8a 0x04
10010001 00000100        0x91 0x04
```

The character array can then be generated by reading each row from left to right, top to bottom:

```
static char name_bits[] = {
    0x91, 0x04, 0xca, 0x06, 0x84,
    0x04, 0x8a, 0x04, 0x91, 0x04
};
```

The *bmtoa* program may be used to convert *bitmap* files into arrays of characters for printing or including in text files. The *atobm* program can be used to convert strings back to *bitmap* format.

USING BITMAPS IN PROGRAMS

The format of *bitmap* files is designed to make bitmaps and cursors easy to use within X programs. The following code could be used to create a cursor from bitmaps defined in *this.cursor* and *this_mask.cursor*:

```
#include "this.cursor"
#include "this_mask.cursor"

XColor foreground, background;
/* fill in foreground and background color structures */
Pixmap source = XCreateBitmapFromData (display, drawable,
        this_bits, this_width, this_height);
Pixmap mask = XCreateBitmapFromData (display, drawable,
        this_mask_bits, this_mask_width, this_mask_height);
Cursor cursor = XCreatePixmapCursor (display, source, mask,
        foreground, background, this_x_hot, this_y_hot);
```

Additional routines are available for reading in *bitmap* files and returning the data in the file, in Bitmap (single-plane Pixmap for use with routines that require stipples), or full depth Pixmaps (often used for window backgrounds and borders). Applications writers should be careful to understand the difference between Bitmaps and Pixmaps so that their programs function correctly on color and monochrome displays.

For backward compatibility, *bitmap* will also accept X10 format *bitmap* files. However, when the file is written out again it will be in X11 format

X DEFAULTS

Bitmap uses the following resources:

Background
> The window's background color. Bits which are 0 in the bitmap are displayed in this color. This option is useful only on color displays. The default value is *white*.

BorderColor
> The border color. This option is useful only on color displays. The default value is *black*.

BorderWidth
> The border width. The default value is 2.

BodyFont
> The text font. The default value is *variable*.

Foreground
> The foreground color. Bits which are 1 in the bitmap are displayed in this color. This option is useful only on color displays. The default value is *black*.

Highlight
> The highlight color. *bitmap* uses this color to show the hot spot and to indicate rectangular areas that will be affected by the *Move Area*, *Copy Area*, *Set Area*, and *Invert Area* commands. If a highlight color is not given, then *bitmap* will highlight by inverting. This option is useful only on color displays.

Mouse
> The pointer (mouse) cursor's color. This option is useful only on color displays. The default value is *black*.

Geometry
> The size and location of the bitmap window.

Dimensions
> The *WIDTHxHEIGHT* to use when creating a new bitmap.

SEE ALSO

X(1), *Xlib - C Language X Interface* (particularly the section on *Manipulating Bitmaps*), *XmuReadBitmapDataFromFile*

BUGS

The old command line arguments aren't consistent with other X programs.

If you move the pointer too fast while holding a pointer button down, some squares may be missed. This is caused by limitations in how frequently the X server can sample the pointer location.

There is no way to write to a file other than the one specified on the command line.

There is no way to change the size of the bitmap once the program has started.

There is no *undo* command.

COPYRIGHT

Copyright 1988, Massachusetts Institute of Technology.
See *X(1)* for a full statement of rights and permissions.

AUTHOR

bitmap by Ron Newman, MIT Project Athena; documentation, *bmtoa*, and *atobm* by Jim Fulton, MIT X Consortium.

3

NAME
> brushtopbm - convert doodle brush files into portable bitmaps

SYNOPSIS
> brushtopbm [brushfile]

DESCRIPTION
> Reads a Xerox doodle brush file as input. Produces a portable bitmap as output.
>
> Note that there is currently no pbmtobrush tool.

SEE ALSO
> pbm(5)

AUTHOR
> Copyright (C) 1988 by Jef Poskanzer.
>
> Permission to use, copy, modify, and distribute this software and its documentation for any purpose and without fee is hereby granted, provided that the above copyright notice appear in all copies and that both that copyright notice and this permission notice appear in supporting documentation. This software is provided "as is" without express or implied warranty.

NAME

cbmtopbm - convert compact bitmaps into portable bitmaps

SYNOPSIS

cbmtopbm [cbmfile]

DESCRIPTION

Reads a compact bitmap as input. Produces a portable bitmap as output.

SEE ALSO

pbmtocbm(1), pbm(5)

AUTHOR

Copyright (C) 1988 by Jef Poskanzer.

3

NAME
>   checkw – check and patch up PXL files whose TFM widths are wrong

SYNOPSIS
>   **checkw** [**-f**] [**-q**] [**-s**] *tfmfile pxlfile*

DESCRIPTION
>   *Checkw* is a program that ought to be unnecessary, but there is a bug in
>   Metafont that produces incorrect TFM widths in PXL files for characters
>   that are zero pixels wide. *Checkw* reads the named TFM and PXL files,
>   which should be for the same font, and compares the width tables of each.
>   A message is printed indicating whether the tables match. If the **-f**
>   ("fix") option is given, *checkw* writes the correct widths back to the PXL
>   file.
>
>   The **-s** ("silent") option makes *checkw* operate silently (only exit status is
>   returned). The **-q** ("quiet") option makes checkw complain if the TFM
>   and PXL files do not match, but otherwise run silently.

DIAGNOSTICS
>   Exit value is 0 if the fonts match or were corrected, 1 if they do not, and
>   2 for any other error. Various messages may be printed to the standard
>   error output if things go wrong; they are intended to be self explanatory,
>   unless they should "never happen". If the message does not mention a
>   damaged PXL file, the file has not been touched.

AUTHOR
>   Chris Torek, University of Maryland

BUGS
>   The bugs are in Metafont.

NAME

   constype - print type of Sun console

SYNOPSIS

   constype

DESCRIPTION

   Consoletype prints on the standard output the Sun code for the type of
   display that the console is. It is one of:

   bw?   Black and White, where ? is 1-4. (eg) 3-50s are bw2
   cg?   Colour Graphics display, where ? is 1-4
   gp?   Optional Graphics Processor board, where ? is 1-2
   ns?   Not Sun display - where ? is A-J

   This is useful in determining startup values and defaults for window systems.

BUGS

   Not tested on all monitor types

COPYRIGHT

   Copyright 1988, SRI

AUTHOR

   Doug Moran <moran@ai.sri.com>

NAME
       cpicker – colormap editor for X11

SYNTAX
       /usr/bin/X11/cpicker [-id *id*] [-root] [-wname *name*] [-display *display*]

OPTIONS
       -id *id*   This option allows the user to specify a target window *id* on
                    the command line rather than using the mouse to select the tar-
                    get window.

       -wname *name*
                    This option allows the user to specify that the window named
                    name is the target window on the command line rather than
                    using the mouse to select the target window.

       -root   This option specifies that X's root window is the target win-
                    dow.

       -display *display*
                    This option allows you to specify the server to connect to; see
                    X(1).

DESCRIPTION
       Cpicker makes temporary changes to the installed colormap, allowing the
       user to observe the effects. It's useful for trying to pick that perfect color
       or find the appropriate color combination for an application.

       When cpicker first starts, it either uses the colormap of the window
       specified, or asks you to click on the window whose colormap you wish to
       edit. Then, it displays a grid of the color cells in the installed colormap.
       Click on the cell you wish to edit. Then, in the upper right there will be a
       box containing the current color along with a label showing the current
       RGB values in X11 hex format.

       To adjust the current color you can use one of the nine sliders, each con-
       trolling one of the RGB, HSV, or CMY values for the current color. Or
       you can click on a cell displayed in the palette to use its color. The but-
       ton underneath the hex label switches between the three palettes: range,
       narrow, and wide.

       The "select" button allows you to choose another cell to edit, the "cancel"
       button restores the current color to its original value, the "restore" button
       restores all the cells of the colormap to their original value, and the "quit"
       button exits out of cpicker.

SEE ALSO
       pixedit(1)

AUTHOR
       Mike Yang

BUGS
       When clicking in a window to select its colormap, be sure to click in the
       window contents. Clicking in window manager real estate may or may
       not result in the correct colormap.

NAME

dclock - digital clock for X

SYNOPSIS

dclock [*-toolkitoption* ...] [-option ...]

DESCRIPTION

The *dclock* program displays the time in digital format only. The time is updated on a per second basis or on a per minute basis. This program is nothing more than a wrapper around the dclock widget not associated with the Athena Widget Set.

When the clock is running, the user may change attributes by typing:

r Toggles **Reverse Video**.
s Toggles the **seconds** display.
b Toggles the **bell** attribute (see below).
j Toggles the **jump/scroll** attribute (see below).

OPTIONS

Dclock accepts all of the standard X Toolkit command line options along with the additional options listed below:

–help   This option indicates that a brief summary of the allowed options should be printed on the standard error.

–bell   This option indicates that the beel will beep once on the half hour and twice on the hour.

–scroll

–noscroll When the time changes, the digits scroll from the previous digit to the next digit. Since this is on by default, the -noscroll option can turn it off.

–date format

The date is printed under the time in the specified font. The string displayed is in the "format" argument. If the string contains a formatting character (%), then the next character is examined and a value is inserted into the string. Example:

dclock -date "Today is %W"

The date string will print "Today is Friday" if the weekday name happens to be friday. The formatting characters that are understood are:

%W   Full weekday name
%w   Three-char weekday name (Sun, Mon, Tue...)
%M   Full month name
%m   Three-char abbreviation for that month (Jan, Feb...)
%d   The date (numerical day number of the month)
%Y   Full year (4 digits)
%y   2-digit year number

–seconds

This option will update the clock every second and display the time including the seconds.

–bg *color*

This option specifies the color to use for the background of the window. The default is ''white.''

–bd *color*

This option specifies the color to use for the border of the window. The default is "black."

–bw *number*

This option specifies the width in pixels of the border surround-ing the window.

–fg *color*

This option specifies the color to use for displaying text. The default is "black".

–fn *font*   This option specifies the font to be used for displaying normal text. The default is "Fixed."

–rv   This option indicates that reverse video should be simulated by swapping the foreground and background colors.

–geometry *geometry*

This option specifies the prefered size and position of the clock window.

–display *host:display*

This option specifies the X server to contact.

–xrm *resourcestring*

This option specifies a resource string to be used. This is espe-cially useful for setting resources that do not have separate com-mand line options.

X DEFAULTS

It understands all of the core resource names and classes as well as:

width (class **Width**)

Specifies the width of the clock.

height (class **Height**)

Specifies the height of the clock.

foreground (class **Foreground**)

Specifies the color for the tic marks. Using the class specifies the color for all things that normally would appear in the fore-ground color. The default is "black" since the core default for background is "white."

bell (class **Boolean**)

Specifies whether or not a bell should be rung on the hour and half hour.

font (class **Font**)

Specifies the font to be used for the date.

reverseVideo (class **ReverseVideo**)

Specifies that the foreground and background colors should be reversed.

scroll (class **Boolean**)

Specifies whether the digits should scroll or not.

seconds (class **Boolean**)

Specifies whether the seconds should be displayed or not.

bell (class **Boolean**)

Specifies whether the bell should sound on the half hour and on the hour.

ENVIRONMENT
DISPLAY

to get the default host and display number.

XENVIRONMENT
>to get the name of a resource file that overrides the global resources stored in the RESOURCE_MANAGER property.

SEE ALSO
>X(1), xrdb(1), time(3C).

BUGS

Dclock believes the system clock.

Scrolling from 9 to 10 O'Clock seems weird, but chances are you won't notice it.

If the window is too small, the seconds are tough to read. This should be recognized by the program and should display seconds using a font rather than the bitmaps used by the clock itself.

Color has been untested.

COPYRIGHT
>Copyright (c) 1988, Dan Heller.

AUTHOR
>Dan Heller -- <island!argv@sun.com> or <dheller@cory.berkeley.edu>

NAME

   dirb – X11 directory browser

SYNOPSIS

   dirb [[**–topdir path**] **–mkdir –rmdir –rmfile**]

DESCRIPTION

   Dirb is a graphically oriented directory browser that runs under the MIT X
   Window System. The browser generates a horizontally oriented directory
   tree which allows selection of an arbitary directory node for Unix directory operations. Operations are made available by pressing the LEFT
   mouse button after positioning the pointer inside a NODE button in the
   graph window. This activates a popup menu of the available commands
   (at present these consist of list {*ls*},rmdir, mkdir and rmfiles {*rm*}). Dirb
   with no arguments generates a directory graph consisting of the users
   current working directory and its subtree with list as the only directory
   operation available. The dirb can be destroyed by selecting the CANCEL
   button in the Command Bar at the top of the browser.

   The browser consists of a Command Bar and a scrollable graph window.
   A directoryis selected by moving the mouse pointer into a NODE button
   and pressing the LEFT mouse button. This activates the *dirop* popup
   menu. Items on the popup menu are selectable by sliding the pointer over
   the items (while keeping the LEFT button down) and releasing the button
   at the desired item. Selection of a popup menu item generates a dialog
   box (for entering new directory names) in the case of mkdir or a file
   selection box in the case of list, rmdir and rmfiles.

   The Dirop popup items rmdir and rmfiles generates a file window which
   can be used to select objects (rmdir = directories, rmfiles = files) contained
   in the selected directory. One or more objects can be selected at a time.
   After selecting an object(s) [again by clicking the LEFT mouse button on
   an object name] select the ACCEPT Button on the file windows command
   bar. Selections can be cancelled or reset by selecting one of the other
   command buttons. The list item generates a file window with unselectable
   buttons.

   Dirb has several options:

   -topdir *path*   - sets root node for the subtree to be browsed.

   -mkdir   - actives mkdir item in popup menu (allows user to
                           create subdirectories).

   -rmdir   - activates rmdir item in popup menu (allows user to
                           remove empty subdirectories).

   -rmfile   - activates remove file item in popup menu (allows
                           user to remove files from directories).

FILES

   /usr/local/lib/xgsh/dirb
   /usr/local/lib/xgsh/dirb.hlp

BUGS

   Dirb ignores secondary hard links and any symbolic links encountered as
   it traverses the subtree. Envoking dirb on a very large subtree results in a
   substantial wait (for amusement we ran it from / and came back 20 mins
   later to see the result). Related to the above, you have to scroll down the
   graph window to find the beginnings of the tree, the viewport does not

auto position the window. Also related to the above, redisplay events
cause the whole tree to redraw, this is not so bad in relation to drawing
the links but the buttons take a long time. Removing multiple directories
results in a little dance on the window since dirb recalcs the positions of
the nodes and redraws the tree for each dir removed.

3

NAME
>   dviselect – extract pages from DVI files

SYNOPSIS
>   **dviselect** [**−s**] [**−i** *infile*] [**−o** *outfile*] *list of pages* [*infile* [
>   *outfile*]]

DESCRIPTION
>   *Dviselect* selects pages from a DVI file produced by TeX, creating a new
>   DVI file usable by any of TeX's conversion program (e.g., iptex), or even
>   by dviselect itself.
>
>   A *range* is a string of the form *first:last* where both *first* and *last* are
>   optional numeric strings, with negative numbers indicated by a leading
>   underscore character " _ ". If both *first* and *last* are omitted, the colon
>   may also be omitted, or may be replaced with an asterisk "*". A *page
>   range* is a list of ranges separated by periods. A *list of pages* is described
>   by a set of page ranges separated by commas and/or white space.
>
>   *Dviselect* actually looks at the ten *count* variables that TeX writes; the first
>   of these (\count0) is the page number, with \count1 through \count9 hav-
>   ing varied uses depending on which macro packages are in use. (Typi-
>   cally \count1 is a chapter or section number.) A page is included in
>   *dviselect*'s output if all its \count values are within any one of the ranges
>   listed on the command line. For example, the command "dviselect
>   *.1,35:" might select everything in chapter 1, as well as pages 35 and up.
>   "dviselect 10:30" would select pages 10 through 30 (inclusive). ":43"
>   means everything up to and including page 43 (including negative-
>   numbered pages). If a Table of Contents has negative page numbers,
>   ": _1" will select it. "*.4 ....1" might mean everything in every
>   chapter 4 and an index, presuming \count9 was set to 1 in the index.
>   ("*" must be quoted from the shell; the null string is more convenient to
>   use, if harder to read.)
>
>   Instead of \count values, *dviselect* can also select by "absolute page
>   number", where the first page is page 1, the second page 2, and so forth.
>   Absolute page numbers are indicated by a leading equal sign "=".
>   Ranges of absolute pages are also allowed: "dviselect =3:7" will extract
>   the third through seventh pages. Dot separators are not legal in absolute
>   ranges, and there are no negative absolute page numbers.
>
>   More precisely, an asterisk or a null string implies no limit; an equal sign
>   means absolute pages rather than \counts; a leading colon means every-
>   thing up to and including the given page; a trailing colon means every-
>   thing from the given page on; and a period indicates that the next \count
>   should be examined. If fewer than 10 ranges are specified, the remaining
>   \counts are left unrestricted (that is, "1:5" and "1:5.*" are equivalent).
>   A single number *n* is treated as if it were the range *n:n*. An arbitrary
>   number of page selectors may be given, separated by commas or whi-
>   tespace; a page is selected if any of the selectors matches its \counts or
>   absolute page number.
>
>   Dviselect normally prints the page numbers of the pages selected; the *−s*
>   option suppresses this.

AUTHOR
>   Chris Torek, University of Maryland

SEE ALSO
>   dvipr(1), iptex(1), tex(1), *The TeXbook*

BUGS

A leading "-" ought to be allowed for negative numbers, but it is currently used as a synonym for ":", for backwards compatibility.

Section or subsection selection will sometimes fail, for the DVI file lists only the \count values that were active when the page ended. Clever macro packages can alleviate this by making use of other "free" \count registers. Chapters normally begin on new pages, and do not suffer from this particular problem.

Dviselect does not adjust the parameters in the postamble; however, since these values are normally used only to size certain structures in the output conversion programs, and the parameters never need to be adjusted upward, this has not proven to be a problem.

3

NAME

 f2p – translates fig output into pic language

SYNOPSIS

 f2p [-s font_size] [input_file [output_file]]

DESCRIPTION

 F2p translates fig objects in the named *input_file* into pic language and put them in *output_file*. If only one file name is presented, it is assumed to be the input file (fig output file). The output file *(pic_file)*, if not presented, will be the stdout. If the *input_file* is not presented, input will be assumed to come from the stdin. The output from f2p can be edited to change font sizes/types.

 The unit of *font_size* is point. There are 72 points in an inch. The upper limit of font_size is 300 points (about 4 inches). The default size is 11 points. The position of text on the hard copy is depended on the specified font size.

SEE ALSO

 fig(1), pic(1).

AUTHOR

 Supoj Sutanthavibul (supoj@sally.UTEXAS.EDU),
 University of Texas at Austin,
 January 29, 1985.

NAME

f2ps – Fig to Postscript translator

SYNOPSIS

f2ps [**-f** font] [**-s** size] [**-e** scale] [**-N**][**-c**] [input_file [
output_file]]

DESCRIPTION

F2ps translates fig output format (in *input_file* into the postscript language
(in *output_file*). The default *input_file* and *output_file* are standard input
and standard output.

The *font* should be font that your printer knows about. The unit of *size*
(font size) is point. There are 72 points in an inch. The upper limit for
size is 300 points (about 4 inches). *Scale* will also be applied to *size*. The
default value of *font, size* and *scale* are Times-Roman, 11 points and 1
respectively. The -c option tells f2ps to center the figure on the page.
The centering may not be accurate if there are texts in the *input_file* that
extends too far to the right of other objects. The option -N indicates that
no page printing command (showpage) is to be appended after the figure.
This ensures that when the output is used as an included illustration, it
won't untimely skip the rest of the page. However you can not print it by
itself on the printer.

Objects (except text) which are created in *fig* while the dash-line mode
was on will be produced with dashed line even though they may be drawn
with solid line in *fig*.

SEE ALSO

fig(1).

AUTHOR

Supoj Sutanthavibul (supoj@sally.UTEXAS.EDU),
University of Texas at Austin,
November 13, 1986.

FIG(1)   FIG(1)

NAME
  fig – Facility for Interactive Generation of figures
SYNOPSIS
  fig [**-r**] [*file*]
DESCRIPTION
  Fig is a menu-driven tool that allows the user to draw and manipulate
  objects interactively on the screen of a Sun Workstation. It can only be
  run within the SunWindows environment and requires a three-button
  mouse. *File* specifies the name of a file to be edited. The description of
  objects in the file will be read at the start of *fig*.

  The output from *fig* can be printed by first using *f2p* (*fig* to *pic*(1) translator, also known by its previous name *ftop*(1L)) to translate it into *pic*(1)
  language. The *pic*(1) file can be saved and edited like ordinary text file.
  To print the file one should issue the command:
  pic file l troff
  *adding any required options to the invocation of troff(1). The file may be
  used in conjunction with any other troff(1) preprocessors.*

  Another way to produce a hrad copy is to use *f2ps* (the fig to postscript
  translator) to produce a postscript file from *fig* file. The postscript file can
  be sent directly to a postscript printer via *lpr*(1).

OPTIONS
  -r   Change the position of the panel window to the right of the can-
              vas window (default: left).

GRAPHICAL OBJECTS
  The objects in *fig* are divided into **primitive objects** and **compound
  object**. The primitive objects are: *ARC, CIRCLE, CLOSED SPLINE,
  ELLIPSE, POLYLINE, POLYGON, SPLINE,* and *TEXT*. A primitive can
  be moved, rotated, flipped, copied or erased. A compound object is com-
  posed of primitive objects. The primitive objects that constitute a compound can not be individually modified, but they can be manipulated as an
  entity; a compound can be moved, rotated, flipped, copied or erased. An
  extra function that can be applied to a compound object is **scaling**, which
  is not available for primitive objects.

DISPLAY WINDOWS
  Three windows comprise the display area of *fig*: the panel window the
  message window, and the canvas window. The message window always
  appears below the others; it is the area in which messages are sent and
  received. from the The menu window can be placed to the left or right of
  the the canvas window (default: left).

POP-UP MENU
  The pop-up menu appears when the right mouse button is pressed with the
  cursor positioned within the canvas window. Positioning the cursor over
  the desired menu entry and releasing the button selects a menu entry.

  There are a number of file accessing functions in the pop-up menu. Most
  of the time when one of these functions is selected, the user will be asked
  for a file name. If the specified file can be located and the access permission are granted, *fig* will carry out the function. However in case things
  go wrong, *fig* will abort the function and printed the causes on the message window.

  Undo   Undo the last object creation or modification.

  Redisplay
            Redraw the canvas.

FIG(1)   FIG(1)

Remove all
Remove all objects on the canvas window (can be undone).

Edit file ...
The current contents of the canvas are cleared and objects are read from the specified file. The user will be asked for a file name. This file will become the current file.

Save   Save the current contents of the canvas in the current file. If no file is being edited, the user will be asked for a file name as in the "Save in ..." function.

Read file ...
Read objects from the specified file and merge them with objects already shown on the canvas. (The user will be asked for a file name.)

Save as ...
Save objects on the screen into a file specified by the user. (The user will be asked for a file name.)

Status   Show the name of the current file and directory.

Change Directory
Change the working directory. Any file name without a full path name will employ the current working directory.

Save & Exit
Save the objects in the current file and exit from *fig*. If there is no current file, the user will be asked for a file name. No confirmation will be asked.

Quit   Exit from *fig*, discarding all objects. The user will be asked to confirm the action, by clicking the left button.

Save as BITMAP ...
Create a bitmap picture of the drawings for use with other tools (for example, for use as an icon). The smallest rectangular area of pixels that encompasses the figure is written to the named file (the user will be asked for a file name) from top row to bottom and left to right (in Sun raster format). Only *TEXT* objects that are parts of compound objects will be treated as parts of the picture; other texts are saved as objects in *fig* format following the bitmap data. The coordinates of these text objects can be used to identify locations on the bitmap.

MENU WINDOW MANIPULATION FUNCTIONS
Icons in the menu window represent object manipulation functions, modes and other drawing or modification aids. Manipulation functions are selected by positioning the cursor over it and clicking the left mouse button. The selected icon is highlighted, and a message describing its function appears in the message window.

The left and middle buttons are used to creat and modify objects in the canvas window. Most actions start with clicking of the left button and end with clicking of the right button. There is no need to hold down a button while positioning the cursor.

MENU WINDOW COMMAND DESCRIPTIONS
Entries in the panel window can be classified into two categories: object creation/modification/removal commands (only one of which may be active at any one time), and drawing aids (which act as toggle switches). There are two ways for drawing circles, two for ellipses, two for splines

FIG(1)   FIG(1)

and two for closed splines. There are two basic splines. One is the interpolated spline in which the spline pass thorough the entered points (knots). The other is the normal spline in which on control points are passed by the spline (except for the two end points in the open spline).

OBJECT CREATION/MODIFICATION/REMOVAL

Multiple commands are grouped thematically in the following descriptions (which is listed alphabetically).

ADD/DELETE ARROWS
> Add or delete arrow heads for *POLYLINE, POLYGON, SPLINE* or *CLOSED SPLINE* objects (points of a *BOX* can not be added or deleted).

ADD/DELETE POINTS
> Add or delete points for *POLYLINE, POLYGON, SPLINE* or *CLOSED SPLINE* objects (points of a *BOX* can not be added or deleted).

ARC   Create an arc. Specify three points using the left button.

BOX   Create rectangular boxes. Start with the left button and terminate with the right button.

BREAK COMPOUND
> Break a compound object to allow manipulation of its component parts. Click the left button on the bounding box of the compound object.

CIRCLE
> Create circles by specifying their radii or diameters. Click the left button on the canvas window, move the cursor until the desired radius or diameter is reached, then click the middle button to terminate. The circle will be drawn after the pressing of the middle button.

CLOSED INTERPOLATED SPLINE
> Create closed or periodic splines. The function is similar to *POLYGON* except that a closed interpolated spline is drawn. The spline will pass through the points (knots).

CLOSED SPLINE
> Create closed or periodic spline objects. The function is similar to *POLYGON* except that a closed spline will be drawn instead of polygon. The entered points are just control points; i.e., the spline will not pass any of these points.

COPY   Copy object. Click the left button over part of the object to be copied (for *CIRCLE* and *ELLIPSE* objects, position on their circumferences). Drag the object to the desired position and click the middle button. This function as well as the following three functions (*MOVE, MOVE POINT, REMOVE*) will cause point markers (manipulation aids) to be shown on the canvas window. There are no markers for *CIRCLE* or *ELLIPSE* objects.

ELLIPSE
> Create ellipses using the same procedure as for the drawing of circles.

GLUE   Glue the primitive objects within a bounding box into a compound object (the bounding box itself is not part of the figure; it is a visual aid for manipulating the compound).

FIG(1)   FIG(1)

INTERPOLATED SPLINE
Create (cubic spline) spline objects. Enter control vectors in the same way as for creation of a *POLYLINE* object. At least three points (two control vectors) must be entered. The spline will pass through the entered points.

MOVE   Move objects in the same way as in *COPY*.

MOVE POINT
Modify the position of points of *POLYLINE, BOX, POLYGON, ELLIPSE, ARC and SPLINE objects. Click the left button over the desired point, reposition the point, and click the middle button. Note that BOX and POLYGON objects are internally stored as POLYLINE objects, and therefore moving certain points may open these objects.*

POLYGON
Same as *POLYLINE* except that a line segment is drawn connecting the first and last points entered.

POLYLINE
Create polylines (line segments connecting a sequence of points). Enter points by clicking the left button at the desired positions on the canvas window. Click the middle button to terminate.

REMOVE
Remove (or delete) objects.

SCALE COMPOUND
Only compound objects can be scaled. Click the left button on a corner of the bounding box, stretch the bounding box to the desired size, and click the middle button.

SPLINE Create (quadratic spline) spline objects. Enter control vectors in the same way as for creation of a *POLYLINE* object. At least three points (two control vectors) must be entered. The spline will pass only the two end points.

TEXT   Create text strings. Click the left button at the desired position on the canvas window, then enter text from the keyboard. Terminate by clicking the middle button or typing the return key.

TURN   Turn *POLYGON* into a *CLOSED INTERPOLATED SPLINE* object, or turn *POLYLINE* into a *INTERPOLATED SPLINE* object.

DRAWING AIDS
Drawing aids act as toggle switches. More than one can be selected at a time (except for *GRID* and the line drawing modes).

AUTO FORWARD/BACKWARD ARROW
Automatically add forward/backward arrow heads to *POLYLINE, SPLINE* or *ARC* objects.

FLIP   Invert the object (middle button) or produce a mirror-image copy of an object (left button). Point to part of the object ("the handle"), click the appropriate button.

GRID   Display either the quarter- or half-inch grids (left button).

MAGNET
Round points to the nearest 1/16 of an inch. This affects every function, and is provided as an alignment aid.

FIG(1)   FIG(1)

UNRESTRICTED
Allow lines to be drawn with any slope.

MANHATTAN
Enforce drawing of lines in the horizontal and vertical direction only. Both *MANHATTAN* and *MOUNTAIN* can be turned on simultaneously. The creations of *POLYGON*, *POLYLINE* and *SPLINE* objects are affected by these two modes.

MOUNTAIN
Enforce drawing of only diagonal lines. Both *MANHATTAN* and *MOUNTAIN* can be turned on simultaneously. The creations of *POLYGON*, *POLYLINE* and *SPLINE* objects are affected by these two modes.

MANHATTAN MOUNTAIN
Allow lines to be drawn at any slope allowed when in MOUNTIAIN or MANHATTAN modes.

LATEX LINE
Allow lines to be drawn only at slopes which can be handled by LaTeX picture environment lines: slope = x/y, where x,y are integers in the range [-6,6].

LATEX VECTOR
Allow lines to be drawn only at slopes which can be handled by LaTeX picture environment vectors: slope = x/y, where x,y are integers in the range [-4,4].

ROTATE
Rotate the object (middle button) or copy (left button) +90 degrees.

SOLID/DASHED LINE STYLE
Toggle between solid and dashed line styles. The dash length is fixed at 0.05 inch.

BUGS

Text strings will appear differently on hard copy, because the display fonts are fixed-width fonts while the fonts used by *pic*(1) are variable-width fonts.

A double quote in a text string should be preceded by a back slash if the it is to be printed through *pic*(1).

Objects that extend beyond the canvas window may cause image shrinkage in hard copy printed by *pic*(1), since it will try to fit every object onto a single 8.5" x 11" page.

Ellipses which are too narrow may cause *fig* to loop forever.

Objects which are created while one of the *grids* is on may appear ragged. This can be corrected by selecting *Redisplay* from the pop-up menu.

The X11 cursors are not the original ones but chosen from X11's cursor font.

Righthand panel is not supported. It should be possible to do that but Ken was too lazy.

SEE ALSO

Brian W. Kernighan *PIC - A Graphics Language for Typesetting User Manual*
col(1) ditroff(1), eqn(1), f2p(1), f2ps(1), man(7), me(7), ms(7), pic(1), tbl(1), troff(1),

FIG(1)   FIG(1)

ACKNOWLEDGEMENT
Many thanks goes to Professor Donald E. Fussell who inspired the creation of this tool.

AUTHOR
Supoj Sutanthavibul
University of Texas at Austin
(supoj@sally.UTEXAS.EDU)
Manual page modified by R. P. C. Rodgers, UCSF School of Pharmacy, San Francisco, CA 94118
Frank Schmuck of Cornell contributed the LaTeX line drawing modes.

3

NAME
>   gfto – convert MetaFont generic file to other formats

SYNOPSIS
>   **gfto** [*flags*] *gffile*

DESCRIPTION
>   *Gfto* converts Generic Font files, typically produced by MetaFont (TM Addison Wesley Publishing Company), to other formats as indicated by the flags argument.

OPTIONS
>   **–b**   Produce an Adobe BDF file format. In an X11 context this can be processed by the standard X11 font compiler to produce an SNF file which the server can then use.
>
>   **–c**   Produce a character dump of the glyph images as asterisks and dashes.
>
>   **–d**   Enable debugging output.
>
>   **–F**   Followed by a string which is used as a Family name in a BDF output file, currently ignored by other formats.
>
>   **–f**   Followed by a string which is used as a face name in a BDF output file, currently ignored by other formats.
>
>   **–C**   Followed by a string which is used as a Copyright field in a BDF output file, currently ignored by other formats.

>   The *gffile* is searched for in the user's current directory, a directory specified by the environment variable GFDIR if present and a system supplied directory which is compiled into the program when installed in that order (unless the pathname begins with a slash in which case it is simply taken literally.)

>   The result is sent to the standard output.

NOTES
>   Conversion to a postscript bitmap font download format is forthcoming.

>   The MetaFont program is available as part of the TeX82 source distribution for a nominal charge. Contact the TeX user's group (401-272-9500) for details, where your get it from depends upon what system you need it for.

SEE ALSO
>   Knuth, Donald E., *The METAFONTbook*, Addison Wesley Publishing Company, Reading, Massachusetts, 1986.

>   The gftype and other programs and documents provided with the MetaFont distribution which made this program possible.

AUTHOR
>   Barry Shein, Boston University.

>   Copyright (c) 1988 by the author, a complete copyright notice is enclosed with the source distribution.

NAME

giftopbm - convert GIF files into portable bitmaps

SYNOPSIS

giftopbm [giffile]

DESCRIPTION

Reads a GIF file as input. Produces a portable bitmap as output.

Note that there is currently no pbmtogif tool.

Also note that, since PBM only supports monochrome, this tool is useless for 99% of the GIF files out there.

BUGS

This tool has not been tested in its PBM form AT ALL. However, in the original gif2ras form, it worked fine.

SEE ALSO

pbm(5)

AUTHOR

Trivial modifications to produce PBM by Jef Poskanzer. Otherwise:

Copyright (c) 1988 by Patrick J. Naughton (naughton@wind.sun.com)

Permission to use, copy, modify, and distribute this software and its documentation for any purpose and without fee is hereby granted, provided that the above copyright notice appear in all copies and that both that copyright notice and this permission notice appear in supporting documentation.

NAME
     gs – get a text string from a dialogue box

SYNOPSIS
     gs [–z] [–r width height] [–t timeout] [–n title] [–standard X Toolkit options ...] [text to be displayed]

DESCRIPTION
     Gs is a utility designed for use in shell scripts for obtaining short text responses from users.

     Gs opens a window containing a box to display the text passed on the command line. If the –r option is present, another box is created into which the user may enter a reply (the maximum number characters that may be entered is given by *widthxheight* fields from the –r option). The reply box allows simple character editing (such as cursor movement, character insertion and deletion). The window can be closed and any text typed by the user sent to standard output by clicking the 'Finished' button with the mouse. The window is also closed and any text sent if a timeout has been specified (see the –t option) and this has been exceeded.

     Gs can take the following options:

     –z   No Zoom. *Gs* will attempt to bypass the window manager and appear immediately, rather than going through the window manager's placement and sizing scheme.

     –r *width height*
               A reply box of *width* characters wide and *height* characters high will be created (if the window manager or screen size allows). The maximum number of characters the user may enter is always *widthxheight* characters. The text in the reply box may be scrolled if the box cannot be made large enough or lots of short lines have been entered.

     –n *title* or –title *title*
               Specifies the title for the *gs* window. The default, if this option is not supplied, is 'Get string'.

     –t *number*
               Specifies a timeout value (in seconds) in which the user must enter a reply. If the time limit is exceeded, any text already typed will be sent to s' standard output and *gs* will exit.

     Gs additionally recognizes the following standard X Toolkit command line arguments:

     –bg *colour* or –background *colour*
               This option specifies the colour to use for the background of the window and widgets. The default is 'white.'

     –bd *colour* or –bordercolor *colour*
               This option specifies the colour to use for the border of the main window. The default is 'black.'

     –bw *number* or –borderwidth *number*
               This option specifies the width in pixels of the border surrounding the main window.

     –fg *colour* or –foreground *colour*
               This option specifies the colour to use for the text. The default is 'black'.

     –fn *font* This option specifies the font to be used for displaying the text warning message. The default is 'serif10'.

–name *name*

> This option specifies the application name under which resources are to be obtained, rather than the default executable file name, 'gs'.

–geometry *geometry*

> This option specifies the preferred size and position of the gs window; see *X(1)*;

–display *display*

> This option specifies the X server to contact; see *X(1)*.

–xrm *resourcestring*

> This option specifies a resource string to be used. This is especially useful for setting resources that do not have separate command line options.

X DEFAULTS

> *Gs* is implemented using the Athena widgets. Each widget can individually or in groups have various visual and operational aspects changed via a '.Xdefaults' file on the client machine or the 'RESOURCE_MANAGER' property on the server. All widgets have a common set of resources (background, backgroundPixmap, etc.) and resources unique to each type of widget; a 'command button' widget, for example, also has a cursor resource. For a full list see the document *X Toolkit Widgets - C Language X Interface*.

> The path names and types of all widgets used by *gs* are as follows:

XXX.**gsbox**

> The widget that is a child of root. All the other widgets used by the gs box are children or grand children of this widget.

XXX.**gsbox.contents**

> A form widget that manages the layout of the gs box. Normally completely covers the 'gsbox' widget.

XXX.**gsbox.contents.message**

> A widget to display and format the text message.

XXX.**gsbox.contents.Finished**

> A command button widget that when clicked causes *gs* to write any text entered by the user to standard output and exit.

XXX.**gsbox.contents.reply**

> A text widget where the user can type a reply.

> Additionally, the following item is also fetched from the resource database:

backgroundPixmap.foreground

> One of two colours (the other is the widget's background colour) required when converting a bitmap file into a pixmap for use as the widget's background pixmap.

RETURN CODES

> 0 – Termination via the tick box or the timeout value being exceeded.

> 2 – Termination due to some internal error.

ENVIRONMENT

> DISPLAY - the default host and display number of the X server.

> XENVIRONMENT - the name of the Xdefaults file to use (normally $HOME/.Xdefaults).

EXAMPLES

        gs -r 40 1 Please enter the name of a file to edit

Will open an gs box with the title *Get string* and containing a box displaying the text *Please enter the name of a* and another box where the user
may type upto 40 characters.

FILES

    $HOME/.Xdefaults /usr/lib/X11/app-defaults/Xopentop

SEE ALSO

    alert(1), yorn(1)

BUGS

If the font is too large or the message too long, the text will be clipped
and the window will have to be scrolled before the whole message may be
read.

The title may not be displayed if the window manager does not provide
title bars around windows or the –z option is used.

AUTHOR

    Gary Henderson & Mark E. Howells, Torch Computers Ltd.

NAME
> ico – animate an icosahedron or other polyhedron

SYNOPSIS
> **ico** [-display display] [-geometry geometry] [-r] [-d pattern] [-i] [-dbl]
> [-faces] [-noedges] [-sleep n] [-obj object] [-objhelp] [-colors color-list]

DESCRIPTION
> *Ico* displays a wire-frame rotating polyhedron, with hidden lines removed,
> or a solid-fill polyhedron with hidden faces removed. There are a number
> of different polyhedra available; adding a new polyhedron to the program
> is quite simple.

OPTIONS
> **-r**   Display on the root window instead of creating a new window.
>
> **-d pattern**
> > Specify a bit pattern for drawing dashed lines for wire frames.
>
> **-i**   Use inverted colors for wire frames.
>
> **-dbl**   Use double buffering on the display. This works for either wire
> > frame or solid fill drawings. For solid fill drawings, using this
> > switch results in substantially smoother movement. Note that this
> > requires twice as many bit planes as without double buffering.
> > Since some colors are typically allocated by other programs, most
> > eight-bit-plane displays will probably be limited to eight colors
> > when using double buffering.
>
> **-faces**   Draw filled faces instead of wire frames.
>
> **-noedges**
> > Don't draw the wire frames. Typically used only when -faces is
> > used.
>
> **-sleep** *n* Sleep n seconds between each move of the object.
>
> **-obj** *object*
> > Specify what object to draw. If no object is specified, an
> > icosahedron is drawn.
>
> **-objhelp**
> > Print out a list of the available objects, along with information
> > about each object.
>
> **-colors** *color color* ...
> > Specify what colors should be used to draw the filled faces of the
> > object. If less colors than faces are given, the colors are reused.

ADDING POLYHEDRA
> If you have the source to ico, it is very easy to add more polyhedra. Each
> polyhedron is defined in an include file by the name of objXXX.h, where
> XXX is something related to the name of the polyhedron. The format of
> the include file is defined in the file polyinfo.h. Look at the file objcube.h
> to see what the exact format of an objXXX.h file should be, then create
> your objXXX.h file in that format.
>
> After making the new objXXX.h file (or copying in a new one from else-
> where), simply do a 'make depend'. This will recreate the file allobjs.h,
> which lists all of the objXXX.h files. Doing a 'make' after this will
> rebuild ico with the new object information.

COPYRIGHT
> Copyright 1988, Massachusetts Institute of Technology.
> See *X(1)* for a full statement of rights and permissions.

NAME
    icontopbm - convert Sun icons into portable bitmaps
SYNOPSIS
    icontopbm [iconfile]
DESCRIPTION
    Reads a Sun icon as input. Produces a portable bitmap as output.
SEE ALSO
    pbmtoicon(1), pbm(5)
AUTHOR
    Copyright (C) 1988 by Jef Poskanzer.

    Permission to use, copy, modify, and distribute this software and its docu-
    mentation for any purpose and without fee is hereby granted, provided that
    the above copyright notice appear in all copies and that both that copy-
    right notice and this permission notice appear in supporting documenta-
    tion. This software is provided "as is" without express or implied war-
    ranty.

NAME
    imake – C preprocessor interface to the make utility

SYNOPSIS
    imake [**–Ddefine**] [**–Idirectory**] [**–T**] [**–f** *imakefile*] [**–s** [
    makefile]] [**–v**] [make options or arguments]

DESCRIPTION
    Imake takes a template and an Imakefile and runs the C preprocessor on it
    producing a temporary makefile in /usr/tmp. It then runs *make* on this
    pre-processed makefile. See IMPLEMENTATION DETAIL below.

    By default, *Imake* looks first for the file named *Imakefile* and if that fails,
    looks for the file named *imakefile,* both in the current working directory.

OPTIONS
    –Ddefine
        Define. This argument is passed on to the preprocessor, cpp. This
        can also be accomplished with the environment variable, IMAKEIN-
        CLUDE.

    –Idirectory
        Include directory. This argument is passed on to the preprocessor,
        cpp. This can also be accomplished with the environment variable,
        IMAKEINCLUDE.

    –T template
        Template file. Specifies the template file to be initially included by
        cpp, instead of the default file *Imake.template.*

    –f imakefile
        File. Specifies an alternate imakefile for *imake to use.*

    –s [filename]
        Show. *Imake* will preprocess the imakefile, and direct it to the stan-
        dard output. The *make* program will not be invoked. If the
        filename argument is present the output will be directed instead to
        the named file. Typically, this is *–s Makefile.*

    –v   Verbose. *Imake* will display the command line it uses to invoke the
        C preprocessor before actually doing so.

ENVIRONMENT VARIABLES
    Imake consults its environment for three variables:

    IMAKEINCLUDE
        If defined, this should be a valid include argument for the C prepro-
        cessor. E.g. ''-I/usr/include/local''. Actually, any valid *cpp* argu-
        ment will work here.

    IMAKECPP
        If defined, this should be a valid path to a preprocessor program.
        E.g. ''/usr/local/cpp''. By default, *imake* will use /lib/cpp.

    IMAKEMAKE
        If defined, this should be a valid path to a make program. E.g.
        ''/usr/local/make''. By default, *imake* will use whatever *make* pro-
        gram is found using *execvp(3).*

IMPLEMENTATION DETAIL
    Imake first determins the name of the imakefile from the command line –f
    flag or from the content of the current directory, depending on whether
    Imakefile or imakefile exist. We shall call this *<imakefile>.* It also deter-
    mines the name of the template from the command line –T flag or the
    default, Imake.template. Call this *<template>.*

The program then examines the imakefile looking for any lines that begin with a '#' character. If it finds one, it checks to see if it is a valid C preprocessor directive from the set *#include, #define, #undef, #ifdef, #else, #endif* or *#if.* If it is, *imake* leaves it unchanged. If not, it pads the beginning of the line with a null C comment ''/**/'' so that the line will by untouched by the preprocessor. This is usefull for preserving the use of *make* style ''#'' comments. If any lines needed to be changed, a temporary file named /tmp/tmp-imake.* will receive the "padded" imakefile. Call this file, whether it needed to be changed or not, *<input-imakefile>*.

Then the program starts up the C preprocessor with the command line

/lib/cpp -I. -I/usr/lib/local/imake.includes -Uunix

perhaps prepending the argument list with the IMAKEINCLUDE environment variable, the *–I*, and the *–D* command line arguments; or changing the preprocessor program to the IMAKECPP environment variable. Standard input is from the *imake* program and standard output is directed to a temporary file in /usr/tmp/tmp-make.*; unless there was an argument to the –s flag, in which case output is directed there. Call this file *<makefile>*. The first three lines provided as input to the preprocessor will be

```
#define IMAKE_TEMPLATE        "<template>"
#define INCLUDE_IMAKEFILE     "<input-imakefile>"
#include IMAKE_TEMPLATE
```

Note that this implies that the template must have, at a bare minimum, the line

#include INCLUDE_IMAKEFILE

Next, *imake* reads the entire output of the preprocessor into memory, stripping off any double '@' signs encountered in the input. This is very useful for writing cpp multi-line macros that won't be coalesced into a single line the way *cpp* normally does. In addition, trailing white space on any line is thrown away to keep *make* from getting upset; and most blank lines are thrown away. For example, the macro

```
#define   program_target(program, objlist)              @@\
program:  objlist                                        @@\
          $(CC) -o $@ objlist $(LDFLAGS)
```

when called with *program_target(foo, foo1.o foo2.o)* will expand to

```
foo:      foo1.o foo2.o
          $(CC) -o $@ foo1.o foo2.o $(LDFLAGS)
```

Finally, if the **-s** option has not been specified, *imake* calls the program

make   MAKE=*<program>*   MAKEFILE=*<imakefile>*   -f *<makefile>* makeargs

where ''makeargs'' is replaced with any arguments found on the command line.

FILES

/usr/tmp/tmp-imake.*nnnnnn*	temporary input file for cpp
/usr/tmp/tmp-make.*nnnnnn*	temporary input file for make
/lib/cpp	default C preprocessor
/usr/lib/local/imake.includes	default directory for include files.

SEE ALSO

make(1)

S. I. Feldman *Make – A Program for Maintaining Computer Programs*

AUTHOR

Todd Brunhoff; Tektronix, inc. and Project Athena, MIT.

BUGS

The C-preprocessor, Cpp, on a Sun compresses all tabs in a macro expansion to a single space. It also replaces an escaped newline with a space instead of deleting it. There is a kludge in the code to try to get around this but it depends on the fact that all targets have a ':' somewhere in the line and all actions for a target do not have a ':'.

You can use *make*-style '#' comments in the Imakefile, but not in the template or any other included files. If you want them, you must preceed them with a C null comment, /**/.

NAME

iptex – print DVI files on the Imagen

SYNOPSIS

iptex [**–c**] [**–d** *maxdrift*] [**–l**] [**–m** *magnification*] [**–p**] [**–r**
resolution] [**–s**] [**–X** *x-offset*] [**–Y** *y-offset*] *filename*

DESCRIPTION

Iptex takes a DVI file produced by TeX and converts it to a format suitable for the Imagen series printers. *filename* should be the name of a **.dvi**
file, or ''–'' for standard input (useful for reading the output of the
dviselect program). By default, *iptex* produces output for a 300 dpi printer
(the 8/300) but this may be overridden with the *–r* flag: **–r 240** produces
output suitable for the Imprint-10 (a.k.a. the 10/240).

To get landscape mode (rather than portrait mode) output, use the **–l** flag.
However, this has not been extensively tested.

The *–m* flag applies a global magnification to the output. If you have
slides that are to be reduced, you can fiddle with the output size using –m.
(By the way, –r is really –m in disguise.)

Normally, iptex will print the page number of each page (actually the
value in \count0) as it runs, to demonstrate its blinding speed. If this is
not desired, use the *–s* option to suppress unnecessary verbiage. (And yes,
it really *is* supposed to count down from the last page.)

Iptex is actually a shell script that invokes the conversion program and
feeds its output to Imagen's *ipr* command. By default, this is done by
creating a file in /tmp, so that missing fonts can be caught before ipr runs
away with the output. However, if desired, you can force the output to be
piped directly to ipr with the *–c* flag.

The *maxdrift* parameter controls **iptex**'s behaviour under certain obscure
conditions. Because it is so rarely needed, and because 2 is such a
wonderful default, I am not going to tell you exactly what it really does.
(Besides, I have not yet figured out how to describe it.)

There are three options that are normally only useful to people installing
iptex which are quickly summarized here: **–p** prevents page reversal (useful with the Ricoh engine); **–X** and **–Y** set an offset to apply to every page
(useful with the LBP-10, for example, where output starts a few tenths of
an inch away from the upper left hand corner of the page). The offsets
are in thousandths of an inch and may be negative. It is important to note
that the offsets are **relative** to the standard offsets. Default offsets should
be set in the *iptex* shell script; they will be overridden by explicit **–X** and
–Y arguments.

DIAGNOSTICS

Most of these should be self explanatory. The message ''unable to copy
input to temp file'' should only occur when reading standard input, and
indicates that the temporary file required when reading pipes is too large
for wherever it is being stored. The environment variable ''TMPDIR''
defines which file system is used for this temporary file; the default is
/tmp. Either put the intermediate DVI file in a real disk file, or set
TMPDIR, in such cases.

AUTHOR

Chris Torek, University of Maryland
Mike Urban (TRW) added the –p, –X, and –Y options.

FILES

imagen1 - conversion program

ipr - Imagen spooler

SEE ALSO

dvipr(1), dviselect(1), tex(1)

BUGS

Still needs to handle more "\special"s.

NAME
>   kbd_mode – recover the Sun console keyboard

SYNOPSIS
>   **kbd_mode** [-a -e -n -u]

DESCRIPTION
>   *Kbd_mode* resets the Sun console keyboard to a rational state.

OPTIONS
>   The following options are supported, see *kb(4S)* for details:

>   **–a**   Causes ASCII to be reported.

>   **–e**   Causes *Firm_events* to be reported.

>   **–n**   Causes up/down key codes to be reported.

>   **–u**   Causes undecoded keyboard values to be reported.

SEE ALSO
>   kb(4S)

NAME

kterm – terminal emulator for X

SYNOPSIS

kterm [-*toolkitoption* ...] [-option ...]

DESCRIPTION

The *kterm* program is a Kanji terminal emulator for the X Window System. It provides DEC VT102 and Tektronix 4014 compatible terminals for programs that can't use the window system directly. It comes from *xterm* in the core programs of the distribution of the X Window System. The most of the functions are the same as original *xterm*'s, however, it has capabilities of displaying Kanji strings and handling of the status line, if compiled with -DKANJI or -DSTATUSLINE compile time options.

OPTIONS

The *kterm* terminal emulator accepts all of the standard *xterm* command line options along with the additional options listed below (if the option begins with a '+' instead of a '−', the option is restored to its default value):

−fk *kanji-font*

This option specifies a Kanji font to be used when displaying Kanji text. This font must be the same height and width as the ascii font. The default is "a14."

−fkb *kanji-font*

This option specifies a Kanji bold font to be used when displaying bold text. This font must be the same height and width as the kanji font. If no Kanji bold font is specified, it will be used as the normal font and the bold font will be produced by overstriking this font. The default is not specified.

This option specifies a Kana font, which may be used as GR in 8bit environment. This font is used if "ESC (I" is appeared in JIS Kanji mode, SS2 (0x8e) is appeared in EUC Kanji mode, and not used so frequntly in normal Japanese text. The default is "kana14."

b *kana-font*

This option specifies a Kana bold font.

−km kanji-mode

This option specifies the Kanji code from the pty output. If kanji-mode is "jis", then it assumes the output is coded by JIS code, i.e., each Kanji string is proceeded by ESC-$-B or ESC-$-@ and each ascii string is proceeded by ESC-(-B or ESC-(-J. This mode does not require 8 bit passing tty modele because 7 bit encoding with appropriate escape sequences is used. If kanji-mode is "euc", then it assumes the output is coded by EUC. If kanji-mode is "sjis", then it assumes the output is coded by Shift-JIS code (which is the same as MicroSoft Kanji code). The default mode is "jis."

−sn

By default, the status line is in reverse-video (relative to the rest of the window). This option causes the status line to be in normal video (the status line is still enclosed in a box).

−st

This option causes the status line to be displayed on startup.

X DEFAULTS

The program understands all of the core xterm resource names and classes as well as:

kanjiFont (class **KanjiFont**)
> Specifies the name of the kanji font. The default is "a14."

kanjiboldFont (class **KanjiFont**)
> Specifies the name of the bold font. The default is not specified.

kanaFont (class **KanaFont**)
> Specifies the name of the kana font. The default is "kana14."

kanaboldFont (class **KanaFont**)
> Specifies the name of the bold font. The default is not specified.

kanjiMode (class **KanjiMode**)
> Specifies the Kanji code of pty output. The default is "jis."

statusLine (class **StatusLine**)
> Causes the status line to be displayed on startup.

statusNormal (class **StatusNormal**)
> Specifies whether or not the last column bug in cursor should be worked around. The default is "false."

EMULATIONS

The VT102 emulation is fairly complete, but does not support the blinking character attribute nor the double-wide and double-size character sets. *Termcap*(5) entries that work with *xterm* include "kterm", "xterm", "vt102", "vt100" and "ansi", and *xterm* automatically searches the termcap file in this order for these entries and then sets the "TERM" and the "TERMCAP" environment variables.

POINTER USAGE

Kterm converts the specified text by the cut operation into JIS code regardless of the Kanji mode and then saves it to the Xserver. This convention allows us to cut and paste between different kterm's with differecnt Kanji mode.

SEE ALSO

xterm(1), resize(1), X(1), pty(4), tty(4)
"Xterm Control Sequences"

BUGS

Xterm will hang forever if you try to paste too much text at one time. It is both producer and consumer for the pty and can deadlock.

Variable-width fonts are not handled reasonably.

This program still needs to be rewritten. It should be split into very modular sections, with the various emulators being completely separate widgets that don't know about each other. Ideally, you'd like to be able to pick and choose emulator widgets and stick them into a single control widget.

The focus is considered lost if some other client (e.g., the window manager) grabs the pointer; it is difficult to do better without an addition to the protocol.

There needs to be a dialog box to allow entry of log file name and the COPY file name.

Many of the options are not resettable after *xterm* starts.

All programs should be written to use X directly; then we could eliminate this program.

Current *kterm* does not support the designate sequence of KANJI as "ESC $ (B" but "ESC $ B" which is still valid sequence in ISO 2022 (even if it seems to be historical reason :-)

COPYRIGHT
Copyright 1988, XXI working group in Japan Unix Society Japan.
See *X(1)* for a full statement of rights and permissions.

AUTHORS
Far too many people, including:

Katsuya Sano (Tokyo Inst. of Tech.), Michael Irie (Sony Corp.), Akira
Kato (Tokyo Inst. of Tech.), Michiharu Ariza (Software Research Associates), Makoto Ishisone (Software Research Associates)

3

NAME

macptopbm - convert MacPaint files into portable bitmaps

SYNOPSIS

macptopbm [macpfile]

DESCRIPTION

Reads a MacPaint file as input. Produces a portable bitmap as output.

SEE ALSO

pbmtomacp(1), pbm(5)

AUTHOR

Copyright (C) 1988 by Jef Poskanzer.

Permission to use, copy, modify, and distribute this software and its documentation for any purpose and without fee is hereby granted, provided that
the above copyright notice appear in all copies and that both that copyright notice and this permission notice appear in supporting documentation. This software is provided "as is" without express or implied warranty.

The MacPaint-reading code is Copyright (c) 1987 by Patrick J. Naughton
(naughton@wind.sun.com)

Permission to use, copy, modify, and distribute this software and its documentation for any purpose and without fee is hereby granted, provided that
the above copyright notice appear in all copies and that both that copyright notice and this permission notice appear in supporting documentation.

NAME

makedepend – create dependencies in makefiles

SYNOPSIS

makedepend [**–D**name=def] [**–D**name] [**–I**includedir] [
–fmakefile] [**–o**objsuffix] [**–s**string] [**–w**width] [– – **otherop-
tions** – –] sourcefile ...

DESCRIPTION

Makedepend reads each *sourcefile* in sequence and parses it like a C-
preprocessor, processing all *#include, #define, #undef, #ifdef, #ifndef,
#endif, #if* and *#else* directives so that it can correctly tell which *#include,*
directives would be used in a compilation. Any *#include,* directives can
reference files having other *#include* directives, and parsing will occur in
these files as well.

Every file that a *sourcefile* includes, directly or indirectly, is what **makedepend** calls a "dependency". These dependencies are then written to a
makefile in such a way that **make(1)** will know which object files must be
recompiled when a dependency has changed.

By default, **makedepend** places its output in the file named *makefile* if it
exists, otherwise *Makefile*. An alternate makefile may be specified with the
-f option. It first searches the makefile for the line

DO NOT DELETE THIS LINE -- make depend depends on it.

or one provided with the *-s* option, as a delimiter for the dependency output. If it finds it, it will delete everything following this to the end of the
makefile and put the output after this line. If it doesn't find it, the program will append the string to the end of the makefile and place the output following that. For each *sourcefile* appearing on the command line,
makedepend puts lines in the makefile of the form

sourcefile.o: dfile ...

Where "sourcefile.o" is the name from the command line with its suffix
replaced with ".o", and "dfile" is a dependency discovered in a *#include*
directive while parsing *sourcefile* or one of the files it included.

EXAMPLE

Normally, **makedepend** will be used in a makefile target so that typing
"make depend" will bring the dependencies up to date for the makefile.
For example,
SRCS = file1.c file2.c ...
CFLAGS = -O -DHACK -I../foobar -xyz
depend:
          makedepend -- $(CFLAGS) -- $(SRCS)

OPTIONS

Makedepend will ignore any option that it does not understand so that
you may use the same arguments that you would for **cc(1).**

–Dname=def or **–D**name

Define. This places a definition for *name* in **makedepend's** symbol
table. Without =*def* the symbol becomes defined as "1".

–Iincludedir

Include directory. This option tells **makedepend** to prepend *includedir* to its list of directories to search when it encounters a *#include*
directive. By default, **makedepend** only searches /usr/include.

–fmakefile

Filename. This allows you to specify an alternate makefile in which **makedepend** can place its output.

–oobjsuffix

Object file suffix. Some systems may have object files whose suffix is something other than ".o". This option allows you to specify another suffix, such as ".b" with *-o.b* or ":obj" with *-o:obj* and so forth.

–sstring

Starting string delimiter. This option permits you to specify a different string for **makedepend** to look for in the makefile.

–wwidth

Line width. Normally, **makedepend** will ensure that every output line that it writes will be no wider than 78 characters for the sake of readability. This option enables you to change this width.

– – options – –

If **makedepend** encounters a double hyphen (– –) in the argument list, then any unrecognized argument following it will be silently ignored; a second double hyphen terminates this special treatment. In this way, **makedepend** can be made to safely ignore esoteric compiler arguments that might normally be found in a CFLAGS **make** macro (see the **EXAMPLE** section above). All options that **makedepend** recognizes and appear between the pair of double hyphens are processed normally.

ALGORITHM

The approach used in this program enables it to run an order of magnitude faster than any other "dependency generator" I have ever seen. Central to this performance are two assumptions: that all files compiled by a single makefile will be compiled with roughly the same *-I* and *-D* options; and that most files in a single directory will include largely the same files.

Given these assumptions, **makedepend** expects to be called once for each makefile, with all source files that are maintained by the makefile appearing on the command line. It parses each source and include file exactly once, maintaining an internal symbol table for each. Thus, the first file on the command line will take an amount of time proportional to the amount of time that a normal C preprocessor takes. But on subsequent files, if it encounter's an include file that it has already parsed, it does not parse it again.

For example, imagine you are compiling two files, *file1.c* and *file2.c,* they each include the header file *header.h,* and the file *header.h* in turn includes the files *def1.h* and *def2.h.* When you run the command

    makedepend file1.c file2.c

makedepend will parse *file1.c* and consequently, *header.h* and then *def1.h* and *def2.h.* It then decides that the dependencies for this file are

    file1.o: header.h def1.h def2.h

But when the program parses *file2.c* and discovers that it, too, includes *header.h,* it does not parse the file, but simply adds *header.h, def1.h* and *def2.h* to the list of dependencies for *file2.o.*

SEE ALSO
     cc(1), make(1)

BUGS
     If you do not have the source for cpp, the Berkeley Unix C preprocessor,
     then **makedepend** will be compiled in such a way that all *#if* directives
     will evaluate to "true" regardless of their actual value. This may cause the
     wrong *#include* directives to be evaluated. **Makedepend** should simply
     have its own parser written for *#if* expressions.

     Imagine you are parsing two files, say *file1.c* and *file2.c,* each includes the
     file *def.h.* The list of files that *def.h* includes might truly be different when
     def.h is included by *file1.c* than when it is included by *file2.c*. But once
     makedepend arrives at a list of dependencies for a file, it is cast in con-
     crete.

AUTHOR
     Todd Brunhoff; Tektronix, inc. and Project Athena, MIT.

3

NAME

maze - an automated maze program... [demo][X11]

SYNTAX

maze [**–S**] [**–r**] [**–g** *geometry*] [**–d** *display*]

DESCRIPTION

The *maze* program creates a "random" maze and then solves it with graphical feedback.

Command Options

–S   Full screen window option...

–r   Reverse video option...

–g *geometry*
          Specifies the window geometry to be used...

–d *display*
          Specifies the display to be used...

The following lists the current functionality of various mouse button clicks;

LeftButton
          Clears the window and restarts maze...

MiddleButton
          Toggles the maze program, first click -> *stop*, second click -> *continue*...

RightButton
          Kills maze...

LIMATIONS

No color support...

Expose events force a restart of maze...

Currently, mouse actions are based on "raw" values [Button1, Button2 and Button3] from the ButtonPress event...

[doesn't use pointer mapping]

COPYRIGHT

Copyright 1988 by Sun Microsystems, Inc. Mountain View, CA.

CONNECTION WITH THE USE OR PERFORMANCE OF THIS
SOFTWARE.

AUTHOR(s)
Richard Hess   [X11 extensions]   {...}!uunet!cimshop!rhess
  Consilium, Mountain View, CA
Dave Lemke   [X11 version]   lemke@sun.COM
  Sun MicroSystems, Mountain View, CA
Martin Weiss   [SunView version]
  Sun MicroSystems, Mountain View, CA

3

NAME
        mazefind – discover current MazeWar games
SYNTAX
        /usr/games/mazefind
DESCRIPTION
        Mazefind broadcasts a query on the net to discover what MazeWar games
        are being played, and prints out useful information about them. It's useful
        for discovering what games might be interesting to connect to on a distant
        network.
SEE ALSO
        mazewar(6)

NAME

MazeWar – distributed rats in a maze

SYNTAX

/usr/games/mw [*window system options*]

DESCRIPTION

This program implements the age-old game of MazeWar. MazeWar first appeared at MIT in the early 1970s, using IMLAC displays and the ArpaNet network. Legend has it that, at one point during that period, MazeWar was banned by DARPA from the ArpaNet because half of all the packets in a given month were MazeWar packets flying between Stanford and MIT.

MazeWar appeared again at the Xerox Palo Alto Research Center in the late 1970's on the Alto, the first personal computer. This version has subsequently been ported to many personal machines, and forms the basis for this Unix version.

Mw attempts to be as faithful to the original Alto version as possible. The shape and pictures of the maze are as in the original, and there are no embellishments such as teleport traps or robot amanuenses.

PLAY

You, the player, are a rat in a maze, and the objective is to find your opponents and shoot them before they shoot you.

Each of the (up to eight) players in a game may be on a different host. Upon startup, you are asked for the name by which you wish to be known for the duration of the game, and the name of the "Duke host". If you type a bare carriage return to this query, *mw* will find a game by broadcasting on the local network, and join any game it finds. If you wish to join a specific game, or a game on another network, or your network doesn't support broadcasting, type in the name of one of the hosts involved in that game. The program *mazefind* will aid you in finding out what games are currently being played.

Once in a game, you are presented with the game window. This window is made up of three sections. The upper section is a perspective view of your view forward. By pressing the left or right mouse buttons, you may peek to the left or right around corners.

The middle section of the window is a top view of the maze, showing your current position and heading in the maze. You move around the maze by using the following keys:

A   About face; flip end–for–end
S   Turn 90 degrees left
D   Move forward one cell
F   Turn 90 degrees right
<space> Move backward one cell
Q   Quit

For left–handers, there are equivalents on the numeric keypad. On the DEC LK201 keyboard, the '4', '5', '6', ',', and right cursor arrow keys perform the equivalent operations.

The lower section of the window shows the names and scores of the other players in the game. When you sight another rat, that rat's score line is highlighted. Shoot by pressing the middle mouse button. When you are shot at, the mouse cursor changes from a rat to a dead rat, and you have one second to move out of the way of the shot or shoot back or both. A shot costs one point; getting hit costs five points; hitting someone adds ten points. When you are hit, the screen flashes and you are transported to another section of the maze.

If your window system supports it, when you iconify the game window, it will let you know when someone joins the game or shoots at you (by flashing, in most cases). This way, you can be notified whenever someone else is interested in wasting some time, by always leaving a game around.

SEE ALSO
    mazefind(6)

AUTHOR
    Christopher A. Kent

NAME
    mkfontdir - create fonts.dir file from directory of font files.

SYNOPSIS
    mkfontdir [directory-names]

DESCRIPTION
    Mkfontdir For each directory argument, mkfontdir reads all of the font files in the directory searching for properties named "FONT", or (failing that) the name of the file stripped of its suffix. These are used as font names, which are written out to the file "fonts.dir" in the directory along with the name of the font file.

    The kinds of font files read by mkfontdir depends on configuration parameters, but typically include SNF (suffix ".snf"), compressed SNF (suffix ".snf.Z"), BDF (suffix ".bdf"), and compressed BDF (suffix ".bdf.Z"). If a font exists in multiple formats, the most efficient format will be used.

FONT NAME ALIAES
    The file "fonts.alias" which can be put in any directory of the font-path is used to map new names to existing fonts, and should be edited by hand. The format is straight forward enough, two white-space separated columns, the first containing aliases and the second containing font-name patterns.

    When a font alias is used, the name it references is search for in the normal manner, looking through each font directory in turn. This means that the aliases need not mention fonts in the same directory as the alias file.

    To embed white-space in either name, simply enclose them in double-quote marks, to embed double-quote marks (or any other character), preceed them with back-slash:

    "magic-alias with spaces" "\"font\name\" with quotes"
    regular-alias   fixed

    If the string "FILE_NAMES_ALIASES" stands alone on a line, each file-name in the directory (stripped of it's .snf suffix) will be used as an alias for that font.

USAGE
    Xserver(1) looks for both "fonts.dir" and "fonts.alias" in each directory in the font path each time it is set (see xset(1)).

SEE ALSO
    X(1), Xserver(1), xset(1)

NAME
   muncher – draw interesting patterns in an X window

SYNOPSIS
   muncher [-option ...]

OPTIONS
   –r   display in the root window

   –s *seed*   seed the random number seed

   –v   run in verbose mode

   –q   run in quite mode

   –geometry *geometry*
          define the initial window geometry; see *X(1)*.

   –display *display*
          specify the display to use; see *X(1)*.

DESCRIPTION
   Muncher draws some interesting patterns in a window.

SEE ALSO
   X(1)

BUGS
   There are no known bugs. There are lots of lacking features.

COPYRIGHT
   Copyright 1988, Massachusetts Institute of Technology.
   See *X(1)* for a full statement of rights and permissions.

NAME

pbm - portable bitmap file format

DESCRIPTION

The portable bitmap format is a lowest common denominator. It was originally designed to make it reasonable to mail bitmaps between different types of machines using the typical stupid network mailers we have today. Now it serves as the common language of a large family of bitmap conversion filters. The definition is as follows:

- A "magic number" for identifying the file type. A pbm file's magic number is the two characters "P1".
- Whitespace (blanks, TABs, CRs, LFs).
- A width, formatted as ASCII characters in decimal.
- Whitespace.
- A height, again in ASCII decimal.
- Whitespace.
- Width * height bits, each either '1' or '0', starting at the top-left corner of the bitmap, proceding in normal English reading order.
- The character '1' means black, '0' means white.
- Whitespace in the bits section is ignored.
- Characters from a "#" to the next end-of-line are ignored (comments).
- No line may be longer than 70 characters.

Here is an example of a small bitmap in this format:

```
P1
# feep.pbm
24 7
0 0 0 0 0 0 0 0 0 0 0 0 0 0 0 0 0 0 0 0 0 0 0 0
0 1 1 1 1 0 0 1 1 1 1 0 0 1 1 1 1 0 0 1 1 1 1 0
0 1 0 0 0 0 0 1 0 0 0 0 0 1 0 0 0 0 0 1 0 0 1 0
0 1 1 1 0 0 0 1 1 1 0 0 0 1 1 1 0 0 0 1 1 1 1 0
0 1 0 0 0 0 0 1 0 0 0 0 0 1 0 0 0 0 0 1 0 0 0 0
0 1 0 0 0 0 0 1 1 1 1 0 0 1 1 1 1 0 0 1 0 0 0 0
0 0 0 0 0 0 0 0 0 0 0 0 0 0 0 0 0 0 0 0 0 0 0 0
```

Programs that read this format should be as lenient as possible, accepting anything that looks remotely like a bitmap.

SEE ALSO

brushtopbm(1), cbmtopbm(1), giftopbm(1), icontopbm(1), macptopbm(1), pbmcatlr(1), pbmcattb(1), pbmcrop(1), pbmcut(1), pbmenlarge(1), pbmfliplr(1), pbmfliptb(1), pbminvert(1), pbmmake(1), pbmpaste(1), pbmtoascii(1), pbmtocbm(1), pbmtoicon(1), pbmtolj(1), pbmtomacp(1), pbmtops(1), pbmtoptx(1), pbmtorast(1), pbmtox10bm(1), pbmtox10wd(1), pbmtoxbm(1), pbmtoxwd(1), pbmtrnspos(1), rasttopbm(1), xbmtopbm(1), xwdtopbm(1), xxxtopbm(1)

AUTHOR

NAME
  pbmcatlr - concatenate portable bitmaps left to right

SYNOPSIS
  pbmcatlr [-0]/[-w]/[-1]/[-b] pbmfile pbmfile ...

DESCRIPTION
  Reads portable bitmaps as input. Concatenates them left to right and produces a portable bitmap as output. If the bitmaps are not all the same
  height, the shorter ones are centered vertically with the edges filled in.
  The -0/-w and -1/-b flags specify what color to use for this fill -- if neither
  is specified, the program makes a guess as to which would look better.

SEE ALSO
  pbmcattb(1), pbm(5)

AUTHOR
  Copyright (C) 1988 by Jef Poskanzer.

  Permission to use, copy, modify, and distribute this software and its documentation for any purpose and without fee is hereby granted, provided that
  the above copyright notice appear in all copies and that both that copyright notice and this permission notice appear in supporting documentation. This software is provided "as is" without express or implied warranty.

NAME
  pbmcattb - concatenate portable bitmaps top to bottom

SYNOPSIS
  pbmcattb [-0]/[-w]/[-1]/[-b] pbmfile pbmfile ...

DESCRIPTION
  Reads portable bitmaps as input. Concatenates them top to bottom and
  produces a portable bitmap as output. If the bitmaps are not all the same
  width, the narrower ones are centered horizontally with the edges filled in.
  The -0/-w and -1/-b flags specify what color to use for this fill -- if neither
  is specified, the program makes a guess as to which would look better.

SEE ALSO
  pbmcatlr(1), pbm(5)

AUTHOR
  Copyright (C) 1988 by Jef Poskanzer.

  Permission to use, copy, modify, and distribute this software and its documentation for any purpose and without fee is hereby granted, provided that
  the above copyright notice appear in all copies and that both that copyright notice and this permission notice appear in supporting documentation. This software is provided "as is" without express or implied warranty.

NAME
pbmcrop - crop a portable bitmap

SYNOPSIS
pbmcrop [-0]/[-w]/[-1]/[-b] [pbmfile]

DESCRIPTION
Reads a portable bitmap as input. Removes edges that are the background color, and produces a portable bitmap as output. By default, it makes a guess as to what the background color is. You can override the default with the -0/-w and -1/-b flags.

SEE ALSO
pbmcut(1), pbm(5)

AUTHOR
Copyright (C) 1988 by Jef Poskanzer.

3

NAME
pbmcut - cut a rectangle out of a portable bitmap

SYNOPSIS
pbmcut x y width height [pbmfile]

DESCRIPTION
Reads a portable bitmap as input. Extracts the specified rectangle, and produces a portable bitmap as output.

SEE ALSO
pbmcrop(1), pbmpaste(1), pbm(5)

AUTHOR
Copyright (C) 1988 by Jef Poskanzer.

NAME
pbmenlarge - read a portable bitmap and enlarge it N times

SYNOPSIS
pbmenlarge [-N] [pbmfile]

DESCRIPTION
Reads a portable bitmap as input. Replicates its bits N times, and produces a portable bitmap as output. The default enlargement is two.

# SEE ALSO
pbm(5)

AUTHOR
Copyright (C) 1988 by Jef Poskanzer.

NAME
pbmfliplr - flip a portable bitmap left for right

SYNOPSIS
pbmfliplr [pbmfile]

DESCRIPTION
Reads a portable bitmap as input. Flips it left for right and produces a portable bitmap as output.

# SEE ALSO
pbmfliptb(1), pbmtrnspos(1), pbm(5)

AUTHOR
Copyright (C) 1988 by Jef Poskanzer.

NAME
    pbmfliptb - flip a portable bitmap top for bottom
SYNOPSIS
    pbmfliptb [pbmfile]
DESCRIPTION
    Reads a portable bitmap as input. Flips it top for bottom and produces a
    portable bitmap as output.
SEE ALSO
    pbmfliplr(1), pbmtrnspos(1), pbm(5)
AUTHOR
    Copyright (C) 1988 by Jef Poskanzer.

    Permission to use, copy, modify, and distribute this software and its docu-
    mentation for any purpose and without fee is hereby granted, provided that
    the above copyright notice appear in all copies and that both that copy-
    right notice and this permission notice appear in supporting documenta-
    tion. This software is provided "as is" without express or implied war-
    ranty.

NAME
    pbminvert - invert a portable bitmap
SYNOPSIS
    pbminvert [pbmfile]
DESCRIPTION
    Reads a portable bitmap as input. Inverts it black for white and produces
    a portable bitmap as output.
SEE ALSO
    pbm(5)
AUTHOR
    Copyright (C) 1988 by Jef Poskanzer.

    Permission to use, copy, modify, and distribute this software and its docu-
    mentation for any purpose and without fee is hereby granted, provided that
    the above copyright notice appear in all copies and that both that copy-
    right notice and this permission notice appear in supporting documenta-
    tion. This software is provided "as is" without express or implied war-
    ranty.

NAME
     pbmmake - create a blank bitmap of a specified size
SYNOPSIS
     pbmmake [-0]/[-w]/[-1]/[-b]/[-g] <width> <height>
DESCRIPTION
     Produces a portable bitmap of the specified width and height. The color
     defaults to 0/white.

     In addition to the usual -w/-0 for white and -b/-1 for black, this program
     implements -g for gray. This gives a simple 50% gray pattern with 1's
     and 0's alternating.
SEE ALSO
     pbm(5)
AUTHOR
     Copyright (C) 1988 by Jef Poskanzer.

     Permission to use, copy, modify, and distribute this software and its docu-
     mentation for any purpose and without fee is hereby granted, provided that
     the above copyright notice appear in all copies and that both that copy-
     right notice and this permission notice appear in supporting documenta-
     tion. This software is provided "as is" without express or implied war-
     ranty.

NAME
     pbmpaste - paste a rectangle into a portable bitmap
SYNOPSIS
     pbmpaste [-r]/[-o]/[-a]/[-x] frompbmfile x y [intopbmfile]
DESCRIPTION
     Reads two portable bitmaps as input. Inserts the first bitmap into the
     second at the specified location, and produces a portable bitmap the same
     size as the second as output. If the second bitmap is not specified, it is
     read from stdin.

     The -r/-o/-a/-x flags specify the logical operation to use when doing the
     paste. They stand for Replace, Or, And, and Xor, respectively. The
     default is replace.

     This tool is most useful in combination with pbmcut(1). For instance, if
     you want to edit a small segment of a large bitmap, and your bitmap edi-
     tor is TOO STUPID to edit the large bitmap, you can cut out the segment
     you are interested in, edit it, and then paste it back in.
SEE ALSO
     pbmcut(1), pbm(5)
AUTHOR
     Copyright (C) 1988 by Jef Poskanzer.

     Permission to use, copy, modify, and distribute this software and its docu-
     mentation for any purpose and without fee is hereby granted, provided that
     the above copyright notice appear in all copies and that both that copy-
     right notice and this permission notice appear in supporting documenta-
     tion. This software is provided "as is" without express or implied war-
     ranty.

NAME

    pbmtoascii - convert portable bitmaps into ASCII graphics

SYNOPSIS

    pbmtoascii [pbmfile]

DESCRIPTION

    Reads a portable bitmap as input. Produces a somewhat crude ASCII graphic as output.

    Note that there is no asciitopbm tool - this transformation is one-way.

SEE ALSO

    pbm(5)

AUTHOR

    Copyright (C) 1988 by Jef Poskanzer.

3

NAME

    pbmtocbm - convert portable bitmaps into compact bitmaps

SYNOPSIS

    pbmtocbm [pbmfile]

DESCRIPTION

    Reads a portable bitmap as input. Produces a compact bitmap as output.

SEE ALSO

    cbmtopbm(1), pbm(5)

AUTHOR

    Copyright (C) 1988 by Jef Poskanzer.

NAME
pbmtoicon - convert portable bitmaps into Sun icons

SYNOPSIS
pbmtoicon [pbmfile]

DESCRIPTION
Reads a portable bitmap as input. Produces a Sun icon as output.

SEE ALSO
icontopbm(1), pbm(5)

AUTHOR
Copyright (C) 1988 by Jef Poskanzer.

Permission to use, copy, modify, and distribute this software and its documentation for any purpose and without fee is hereby granted, provided that the above copyright notice appear in all copies and that both that copyright notice and this permission notice appear in supporting documentation. This software is provided "as is" without express or implied warranty.

NAME
pbmtolj - convert portable bitmaps into HP LaserJet

SYNOPSIS
pbmtolj [-r <resolution>] [<pbmfile>]

DESCRIPTION
Reads a portable bitmap as input. Produces HP LaserJet data as output.

The -r flag specifies the resolution of the output device, in dpi. Typical values are 75, 100, 150, 300. The default is 75.

Note that there is no ljtopbm tool.

SEE ALSO
pbm(5)

AUTHOR
Copyright (C) 1988 by Jef Poskanzer and Michael Haberler.

Permission to use, copy, modify, and distribute this software and its documentation for any purpose and without fee is hereby granted, provided that the above copyright notice appear in all copies and that both that copyright notice and this permission notice appear in supporting documentation. This software is provided "as is" without express or implied warranty.

NAME
pbmtomacp - convert portable bitmap into MacPaint

SYNOPSIS
pbmtomacp [-l left] [-r right] [-b bottom] [-t top] [pbmfile]

DESCRIPTION
Reads a portable bitmap as input. If no input-file is given, standard input is assumed. Produces a MacPaint file as output.

Left, right,bottom & top let you define a square into the pbm file, that must be converted. Default is the whole file. If the file is too large for a MacPaint-file, the bitmap is cut to fit from (left, top).

BUGS
The source code contains comments in a language other than English.

SEE ALSO
macptopbm(1), pbm(5)

AUTHOR
Copyright (C) 1988 by Douwe van der Schaaf. USENET: ..!mcvax!uvapsy!vdschaaf

NAME
pbmtops - convert portable bitmaps into PostScript

SYNOPSIS
pbmtops [-s <scale>] [<pbmfile>]

DESCRIPTION
Reads a portable bitmap as input. Produces PostScript as output.

The -s flag controls the scale of the result. The default scale is 1, which results in one pbm pixel producing a 3x3 square of PostScript pixels. On a 300 dpi printer such as the Apple Laserwriter, this makes the output look about the same size as the input would if it was displayed on a typical 72 dpi screen. To get one pbm pixel per PostScript pixel, use "-s 0.333333".

Note that there is no pstopbm tool - this transformation is one-way, because a pstopbm tool would be a full-fledged PostScript interpreter, which is beyond the scope of this package.

SEE ALSO
pbm(5)

AUTHOR
Copyright (C) 1988 by Jef Poskanzer.

NAME
pbmtoptx - convert portable bitmaps into Printronix printer graphics

SYNOPSIS
pbmtoptx [pbmfile]

DESCRIPTION
Reads a portable bitmap as input. Produces a file of Printronix printer graphics as output.

Note that there is no ptxtopbm tool - this transformation is one way.

SEE ALSO
pbm(5)

AUTHOR
Copyright (C) 1988 by Jef Poskanzer.

pbmtorast(1)   pbmtorast(1)

NAME
pbmtorast - convert portable bitmaps into Sun rasters

SYNOPSIS
pbmtorast [pbmfile]

DESCRIPTION
Reads a portable bitmap as input. Produces a Sun raster file as output. NOTE: since it uses Sun-specific include files, pbmtorast will compile only on Suns.

SEE ALSO
rasttopbm(1), pbm(5)

AUTHOR
Barry Klawans

Copyright (C) 1988 by Jef Poskanzer.

NAME
pbmtox10bm - convert portable bitmaps into X10 bitmaps
SYNOPSIS
pbmtox10bm [pbmfile]
DESCRIPTION
Reads a portable bitmap as input. Produces an X10 bitmap as output. This older format is maintained for compatibility.

Note that there is no x10bmtopbm tool, because xbmtopbm can read both X11 and X10 bitmaps.
SEE ALSO
pbmtoxbm(1), xbmtopbm(1), pbm(5)
AUTHOR
Copyright (C) 1988 by Jef Poskanzer.

Permission to use, copy, modify, and distribute this software and its documentation for any purpose and without fee is hereby granted, provided that the above copyright notice appear in all copies and that both that copyright notice and this permission notice appear in supporting documentation. This software is provided "as is" without express or implied warranty.

NAME
pbmtox10wd - convert portable bitmaps into X10 window dumps
SYNOPSIS
pbmtox10wd [pbmfile]
DESCRIPTION
Reads a portable bitmap as input. Produces an X10 window dump as output.
SEE ALSO
pbmtoxwd(1), xwdtopbm(1), pbm(5)
AUTHOR
Copyright (C) 1988 by Jef Poskanzer.

Permission to use, copy, modify, and distribute this software and its documentation for any purpose and without fee is hereby granted, provided that the above copyright notice appear in all copies and that both that copyright notice and this permission notice appear in supporting documentation. This software is provided "as is" without express or implied warranty.

NAME
pbmtoxbm - convert portable bitmaps into X11 bitmaps
SYNOPSIS
pbmtoxbm [pbmfile]
DESCRIPTION
Reads a portable bitmap as input. Produces an X11 bitmap as output.
SEE ALSO
pbmtox10bm(1), xbmtopbm(1), pbm(5)
AUTHOR
Copyright (C) 1988 by Jef Poskanzer.

Permission to use, copy, modify, and distribute this software and its documentation for any purpose and without fee is hereby granted, provided that
the above copyright notice appear in all copies and that both that copyright notice and this permission notice appear in supporting documentation. This software is provided "as is" without express or implied warranty.

NAME
pbmtoxwd - convert portable bitmaps into X11 window dumps
SYNOPSIS
pbmtoxwd [pbmfile]
DESCRIPTION
Reads a portable bitmap as input. Produces an X11 window dump as output. This window dump can be displayed using the xwud tool.
SEE ALSO
pbmtox10wd(1), xwdtopbm(1), pbm(5)
AUTHOR
Copyright (C) 1988 by Jef Poskanzer.

Permission to use, copy, modify, and distribute this software and its documentation for any purpose and without fee is hereby granted, provided that
the above copyright notice appear in all copies and that both that copyright notice and this permission notice appear in supporting documentation. This software is provided "as is" without express or implied warranty.

NAME

pbmtrnspos - transpose a portable bitmap x for y

SYNOPSIS

pbmtrnspos [pbmfile]

DESCRIPTION

Reads a portable bitmap as input. Transposes it x for y and produces a portable bitmap as output.

Note that transposition is not rotation, but can be used to produce it. For example, if you wanted a 90 degree clockwise rotation, perhaps for printing a landscape bitmap on a laser printer, you could do 'pbmtrnspos | pbmfliplr' or 'pbmfliptb | pbmtrnspos'. For counter-clockwise rotation, you would use the opposite flips.

SEE ALSO

pbmfliplr(1), pbmfliptb(1), pbm(5)

AUTHOR

Copyright (C) 1988 by Jef Poskanzer.

NAME
    pixedit – pixel color editor for X11
SYNTAX
    /usr/bin/X11/pixedit
DESCRIPTION
    Pixedit makes temporary changes to the installed colormap, allowing the
    user to observe the effects. It's useful for trying to pick that perfect color
    or find the appropriate color combination for an application.

    When pixedit first starts, the cursor changes to a crosshair. Click on the
    screen pixel whose color and whose colormap you wish to edit. Then, in
    the upper right there will be a box containing the current color along with
    a label showing the current RGB values in X11 hex format.

    To adjust the current color you can use one of the nine sliders, each con-
    trolling one of the RGB, HSV, or CMY values for the current color. Or
    you can click on a cell displayed in the palette to use its color. The but-
    ton underneath the hex label switches between the three palettes: range,
    narrow, and wide.

    The "select" button allows you to choose another cell to edit, the "cancel"
    button restores the current color to its original value, the "restore" button
    restores all the cells of the colormap to their original value, and the "quit"
    button exits out of pixedit.

SEE ALSO
    cpicker(1)
AUTHOR
    Mike Yang

NAME

> plaid – paint some plaid-like patterns in an X window

SYNOPSIS

> **plaid** [-option ...]

OPTIONS

> **–b**   enable backing store for the window
>
> **–fg** *color*
> > This option specifies the color to use for the foreground of the window. The default is "white."
>
> **–bg** *color*
> > This option specifies the color to use for the background of the window. The default is "black."
>
> **–bd** *color*
> > This option specifies the color to use for the border of the window. The default is "white."
>
> **–bw** *number*
> > This option specifies the width in pixels of the border surrounding the window.
>
> **–geometry** *geometry*
> > define the initial window geometry; see *X(1)*.
>
> **–display** *display*
> > specify the display to use; see *X(1)*.

DESCRIPTION

> *Plaid* displays a continually changing plaid-like pattern in a window.

SEE ALSO

> X(1)

BUGS

> There are no known bugs. There are lots of lacking features.

COPYRIGHT

> Copyright 1988, Massachusetts Institute of Technology.
> See *X(1)* for a full statement of rights and permissions.

NAME
   puzzle – 15-puzzle game for X

SYNOPSIS
   puzzle [-option ...]

OPTIONS
   –display *display*
         This option specifies the display to use; see *X(1)*.

   –geometry *geometry*
         This option specifies the size and position of the puzzle window;
         see *X(1)*.

   –size *WIDTHxHEIGHT*
         This option specifies the size of the puzzle in squares.

   –speed *num*
         This option specifies the speed in tiles per second for moving
         tiles around.

   –picture *filename*
         This option specifies an image file containing the picture to use
         on the tiles. Try "mandrill.cm." This only works on 8-bit
         pseudo-color screens.

   –colormap
         This option indicates that the program should create its own
         colormap for the picture option.

DESCRIPTION
   Puzzle with no arguments plays a 4x4 15-puzzle. The control bar has two
   boxes in it. Clicking in the left box scrambles the puzzle. Clicking in the
   right box solves the puzzle. Clicking the middle button anywhere else in
   the control bar causes puzzle to exit. Clicking in the tiled region moves
   the empty spot to that location if the region you click in is in the same
   row or column as the empty slot.

SEE ALSO
   X(1)

BUGS
   The picture option should work on a wider variety of screens.

COPYRIGHT
   Copyright 1988, Don Bennett.

AUTHOR
   Don Bennett, HP Labs

NAME

qix – play a game of qix

SYNOPSIS

qix [-r]

DESCRIPTION

Qix was originally a video game written owned by Taito Corporation. I spent enough money learning to get good at this game that it's been embedded in my head for years. Now that this game is written, I've got *centipedes* to deal with. When *Qix* starts up, it is running in demo mode to show the user how to play it. You will probably figure it out much more easily than reading this silly man page. After all, you don't get man pages for the games you play in an arcade, do you?

The -r command line option specifies reverse video for X11 only.

RULES

Since you're still with me, I'll tell you the rules of the game. The object is to use the *pen* to draw lines which will enclose a region which will give you points. If you enclose more than 75% of the board, then the board is cleared and the level of difficulty increases. When drawing lines, you can't cross over lines that are not already part of a region; that is to say, you can't self-intersect a line. You may move around the board freely without drawing lines as long as you remain on lines that have already been drawn. Once you start drawing, you *cannot stop* drawing until you have completed a region. See, you're already getting confused, I can tell.

Things to watch out for (enemies). When moving about the board, the *Qix* will try to kill you. This is an object with 7 lines that moves (seemingly) randomly bouncing off things everywhere. You are safe from the qix while you are not drawing any lines. If you are drawing lines, the qix may hit you or any part of your unconnected line.

While you're trying to avoid the qix, you might get zapped by *sparx*. These are electical pulses of something-or-other which has yet to be defined, so it's best to stay away from them. Sparx are always released in pairs at the top of the playing board during play. Sparks can zap you even though you're not drawing lines. In fact, normal sparx can't zap you if you're drawing lines (hint: this is a way to escape sparx, but then there's that damn qix you gotta avoid). If you start taking too much time, sparx will become *aggressive* and will follow you along your new lines if you're drawing. You will be informed when sparx become aggressive.

If that's not enough to avoid, there is the the *fuse.* A fuse is a special case type of spark. If you are drawing a line and you stop drawing before establishing an enclosed region, a fuse will start at the beginning of your line and follow it till it zaps you. You can stop the fuse by resuming drawing. If you stop again, the fuse will start where it left off before.

As you progress to each level, the game gets more difficult. The qix will follow you more closely, it will go faster, it will drive you *nuts.* Sparx won't change; they remain as annoying as they do in the beginning. If you progress to level 3, then there will be two qix to deal with. If you split the two qix by drawing a line which separates them, then you proceed to the next screen and all new points are doubled. Each screen after this repeats this. You go from 2-times values to 3-times, and so on.

PLAYING THE GAME

Actually moving the joystick is indeed the most difficult, frustrating and bothersome part about learning this game. But that's the price *you* pay for the number of blisters *I* got on my first $50 with the coin-op version of *Qix*. Since this games runs under two different windowing systems, how easy it is to use is very dependent on which windowing system your particular computer is using. If it's *Sunview*, you'll do ok. If it's *X11*, then plan on spending some time with it.

There are two different ways to move the pen. The mouse and the keyboard. The keyboard is much easier than the mouse, so I suggest you put the mouse away. At the bottom of the board there is an icon of the joystick which shows which direction the mouse is moving (or wants to move). To start the game, send me a quarter in the mail and click the right mouse button or press the spacebar. To move the pen around, move the mouse in the direction you want to go. To draw a line, do as above, but press the left mouse button to draw a fast line, or the middle button to draw a slow line. Slow lines go twice the speed as fast lines, but you get twice the points for the area you cover. You can change speeds from slow to fast, but not from fast to slow. To stop the pen, press the spacebar once or the right mouse button once. To suspend the game (that is, stop all movement and free the mouse to move about the console), press the spacebar or right mouse button a second time (from a *stop* state). To terminate the game, acheive this state, move the mouse to the window which started this thing and hit ^C. Or, you could just unplug the computer; both are effective.

To use the keyboard to move the pen around, the letters h, j, k, and l, are used to move left, down, up and right respectively. To draw a line, use a capital letter of each direction. You'll find that the game will respond more quickly to keyboard input than mouse input. The game **will** respond to mouse movement, there is a delay and it's hard to get used to. There used to be a method of drawing slow lines using the keyboard only, but it doesn't seem to work anymore, so I won't tell you about it. If you need to draw a slow line, use the mouse.

You are given 5 (lives) chances and then you have to send me another quarter to play again.

SOURCE CODE AND AUTHOR INFORMATION

This program was written for the Sun Workstation by Dan Heller with some added help by Sky Schultz for his interesting method of polygon fills. A completely non-intuitive, but effective, method of polygon fill is found in auxiliary files distributed with the source. This stuff was written by Don Hatch who happens to be working at Ardent Computer right now, but they had nothing to do with it.

A port to X11 was done in July, 1988 by Dan Heller in an attempt to make an X11 program out of a Sunview program. If you don't know X already, I highly discourage using the source to this program as an example. If you know Sunview, then you might find it quite helpful since virtually all of it is in Sunview; the X port is mostly defines and stuff to get it to work. The X version does not use the toolkit at all. It is implemented using the raw Xlib libraries only.

Please send comments, bug reports and quarters to: Dan Heller

<island!argv@sun.com>

NAME
rasttopbm - convert Sun rasters into portable bitmaps

SYNOPSIS
rasttopbm [rastfile]

DESCRIPTION
Reads a Sun raster as input. Produces a portable bitmap as output.
NOTE: since it uses Sun-specific include files, pbmtorast will compile
only on Suns.

Using this program you can convert anything you can see on a Sun screen
into a pbm bitmap. Just display whatever you're interested in, do a
screendump, run it through rasfilter8to1 if you're on a color Sun, run it
through rasttopbm, and then use pbmcut to select the part you want.

SEE ALSO
pbmtorast(1), pbm(5)

AUTHOR
Barry Klawans

Copyright (C) 1988 by Jef Poskanzer.

NAME

rcmd - run a remote command in the background, without stdout and stderr.

SYNOPSIS

rcmd remotehost command

DESCRIPTION

Rcmd runs the given *command* on the specified *remotehost* via *rsh* but by redirecting stdout and stderr to /dev/null, and running command in the background, it results in the rsh exiting and closing the connection, leaving the command as a daemon on the remote machine. This is useful only for commands that have no use for stdout and stderr like most X Windows applications.

EXAMPLE

rcmd godzilla /local/bin/X11/xterm -display ${HOST}:0 -geometry 80x50+3-3 -ls

will run xterm on the remote machine *godzilla* with the display on the current HOST (assuming the environment variable HOST is set to 'hostname').

BUGS

The remote command has no way of notifying the user about error conditions, except through logs.

NAME

remapbdf – change the glyph positions in a BDF file

SYNOPSIS

remapbdf mapfile

DESCRIPTION

Remapbdf reads BDF from stdin and writes BDF to stdout, changing the positions of the glyphs according to the pairs of numbers in *mapfile*. The first number of the pair is the old position and the second number is the new position. There is only one level of mapping, No loops can happen.

BUGS

Yes I know it can be done with awk/sed, but took little time to write the C code.

AUTHOR

Ken Yap

3

NAME
        resize - utility to set TERMCAP and terminal settings to current window
        size
SYNOPSIS
        resize [-u] [–s [row col]]
DESCRIPTION
        Resize prints a shell command for setting the TERM and TERMCAP
        environment variables to indiciate the current size of *xterm* window from
        which the command is run. For this output to take effect, *resize* must
        either be evaluated as part of the command line (usually done with a shell
        alias or function) or else redirected to a file which can then be read in.
        From the C shell (usually known as */bin/csh*), the following alias could be
        defined in the user's *.cshrc*:

                % alias rs 'set noglob; 'eval resize''

        After resizing the window, the user would type:

                % rs

        Users of versions of the Bourne shell (usually known as */bin/sh*) that don't
        have command functions will need to send the output to a temporary file
        and the read it back in with the "." command:

                $ resize >/tmp/out
                $. /tmp/out

OPTIONS
        The following options may be used with *resize*:

        –u   This option indicates that Bourne shell commands should be
                    generated even if the user's current shell isn't */bin/sh*.

        –c   This option indicates that C shell commands should be generated
                    even if the user's current shell isn't */bin/csh*.

        –s [*rows columns*]
                    This option indicates that that Sun console escape sequences will
                    be used instead of the special *xterm* escape code. If *rows* and
                    columns are given, *resize* will ask the *xterm* to resize itself.
                    However, the window manager may choose to disallow the
                    change.

FILES
        /etc/termcap   for the base termcap entry to modify.
        ~/.cshrc user's alias for the command.
SEE ALSO
        csh(1), tset(1), xterm(1)
AUTHORS
        Mark Vandevoorde (MIT-Athena), Edward Moy (Berkeley)
        Copyright (c) 1984, 1985 by Massachusetts Institute of Technology.
        See *X*(1) for a complete copyright notice.
BUGS
        The *-u* or *-c* must appear to the left of *-s* if both are specified.

        There should be some global notion of display size; termcap and terminfo
        need to be rethought in the context of window systems. (Fixed in
        4.3BSD, and Ultrix-32 1.2)

NAME
>   showsnf - print contents of an SNF file

SYNOPSIS
>   **showsnf** [-v] [-g] [-m] [-M] [-l] [-L] [-p#] [-u#]

DESCRIPTION
>   The *showsnf* utility displays the contents of font files in the Server Natural
>   Format produced by *bsdtosnf*. It is usually only to verify that a font file
>   hasn't been corrupted or to convert the individual glyphs into arrays of
>   characters for proofreading or for conversion to some other format.

OPTIONS

−v	This option indicates that character bearings and sizes should be printed.
−g	This option indicates that character glyph bitmaps should be printed.
−m	This option indicates that the bit order of the font is MSBFirst (most significant bit first).
−l	This option indicates that the bit order of the font is LSBFirst (least significant bit first).
−M	This option indicates that the byte order of the font is MSBFirst (most significant bit first).
−L	This option indicates that the byte order of the font is LSBFirst (least significant bit first).
−p#	This option specifies the glyph padding of the font (# is a number).
−u#	This option specifies the scanline unit of the font (# is a number).

SEE ALSO
>   X(1), Xserver(1), bdftosnf(1)

BUGS
>   There is no way to just print out a single glyph.

COPYRIGHT
>   Copyright 1988, Massachusetts Institute of Technology.
>   See *X(1)* for a full statement of rights and permissions.

NAME
       spaceout – animated space display

SYNOPSIS
       spaceout [–frCc] [host:display]

DESCRIPTION
       Spaceout is an X11 version of the program for Xerox XDE workstaions.
       Spaceout displays a star field, which moves as if you were traveling
       throught space (simalar to the begining of old Star Trek tv shows).

       Spaceout options include:

       –f   tries to fill the entire screen.

       –r   ´reverse video´.

       –C   Color Spaceout.

       –c   The stars move down the middle of the screen.

       If a host is not specify the enviroment variable DISPLAY is used.

FILES
       /usr/lib/X11/rgb*

AUTHOR
       John H. Pochmara
       hoyt@polyslo.CalPoly.EDU

NAME
:   texx – view DVI files on your X-11 display

SYNOPSIS
:   **texx [many options] filename**

DESCRIPTION

Texx allows you to preview a DVI file produced by *TeX82, LaTeX,* etc., under the X-11 windowing system. You may specify a number of options via the commandline or your **.defaults** file. Here is a list of all the options and what they do. The name in the **.defaults** file is shown in parentheses:

OPTIONS

−rv (ReverseVideo)
:   Toggle reverse video.

−rvOn Force reverse video on.

−tvOff Force reverse video off.

−ns (NormalShrink)
:   Specifies the integer shrink size used at the Normal display size.

−ls (LargeShrink)
:   Specifies the integer shrink size used in the Large display mode.

−bl (Blackness)
:   Specifies an integer blackness threshold for shrunken fonts.

−l (Leaves)
:   Specifies the number of leaves to be used in displaying normal text. The number must be either 1 or 2.

−tm (TopMargin)
:   Specifies the floating point top margin in inches.

−sm (SideMargin)
:   Specifies the floating point side margin in inches.

−pg Specifies the page number to start viewing.

−dpi (Dpi)
:   Specifies the desired integer font resolution in dots per inch.

By now, you're probably wondering what a lot of these options do. *Texx* can display your document at two different sizes, *Normal* and *Large*. These two sizes are used for viewing the overall structure of the document and checking detailed structure, respectively. In Normal mode, you will normally have two *leaves* on your display simultaneously. Two adjacent pages of your DVI file are displayed in these leaves. To make the image so small, *texx* shrinks the fonts and scales everything down to size. This is where the blackness parameter comes in---you can control the shrinking algorithm to some extent. The default values for NormalShrink and LargeShrink are determined by the size of your display and the number of leaves you specify (2 is the default, unless the DVI file contains only one page), so you normally don't need to specify them yourself. Similarly, TopMargin, SideMargin, and Dpi will default to reasonable values, so you normally don't need to worry about any of these options except perhaps **−rv.**

COMMANDS

Texx precomputes each page's image before displaying it. This means that you can obscure parts of the *texx* window, or move it around, without having to wait for the display to be recomputed. It takes about a second on a 3/50 to compute the image when only text is present, though heavy graphics take a little longer.

When *texx* starts up, it will be in Normal mode, and you'll normally see two leaves of your document, containing the first two pages of your DVI file. To go to the next page, just type Return. This will move page 2 to the left leaf, and put page 3 in the right leaf. Typing "-Return", or Delete, or Backspace, will move back one page. Typing a number followed by one of these keys will go that many pages in the indicated direction.

To see one of the pages in Large mode, put the mouse on top of the text to be displayed and hold down any mouse button. The cursor will turn to an clock while the enlarged image is being computed. Once it has been completely computed, the enlarged image will be displayed, taking up the entire *texx* window (or only one leaf, if two leaves are in use). Release the button to go back to Normal mode. Once the enlarged image for the pages on display have been computed, they are retained, so you can switch quickly between the Normal and Large modes. Once a page is not being displayed in either leaf, however, its enlarged image is also discarded, so if you come back to it, its normal and enlarged images will have to be recomputed.

To move around in the DVI file, you can also go to absolute page numbers by typing the number of the page followed by the letter "g". Typing "q" will exit *texx*.

You can "reload" the DVI file by pressing R. This saves time when you're intensively editing a document.

BUGS

Although *texx* understands most *tpic* graphical commands, it is unable to display shading, because Dirk was too lazy to finsih it. All other graphics commands are supported, however.

AUTHOR

Dirk Grunwald, at the University of Illinois wrote *TeXx* based using a DVI-library written by Chris Torek at UMD. Tim Morgan, at the University of Calif, Irvine, wrote the enhanced *tpic* support.

NAME
>   todm – switch from X back to the Apollo DM

SYNOPSIS
>   **todm**

DESCRIPTION
>   *Todm* will switch from the X server back to the Apollo DM. While "switched away" from X, the X server is blocked.

SEE ALSO
>   *tox (1),* which switches from the DM to X.

3

NAME

tox – switch from Apollo DM environment back to X

SYNOPSIS

tox

DESCRIPTION

Tox will switch from the Apollo DM environment back to the already running X server.

SEE ALSO

todm (1), which switches from X to the DM.

NAME
>   twm - a window manager for X11 (Tom's Window Manager)

SYNTAX
>   **twm** [-display *display*]

DESCRIPTION
>   The *twm* program is a window manager client application of the window
>   server.

>   The *twm* program was written to incorporate some of the desirable
>   features of both the **wm** and **uwm** window managers. *Twm* puts a title
>   bar on and re-parents each window. The title bar contains the window's
>   name and three "buttons". When a pointer button press event is detected
>   in any of these title bar "buttons" a certain action is performed. The left-
>   most title bar button that looks like a window pane causes the window to
>   be iconified. The right-most title bar button with the right-angles is the
>   re-size button. The resize function is identical to the window resize func-
>   tion of the **wm** window manager. The other title bar button represents a
>   keyboard; a button click here causes the input focus to stay directed to this
>   window until the **f.unfocus** function is executed or another window is
>   selected to get input focus (by default, the input focus follows the mouse
>   or other pointing device). The title bar also becomes highlighted on the
>   window that currently has the input focus.

>   When *twm* is invoked, it attempts to read a *twm* startup file. The name of
>   the *twm* startup file is:

> $HOME/.twmrc

>   The *twm* startup file has three logical sections: the variables section, the
>   buttons section, and the menus section. The variables section must come
>   first, followed by either the buttons section or the menus section.

>   All variables and keywords may be entered in any combination of upper
>   and lower case letters. Functions must be entered in lower case. A pound
>   sign (#) character in the startup file indicates a comment which is ter-
>   minated by the newline character. A *string* in the startup file is a series of
>   characters enclosed by double quotes.

VARIABLES SECTION
>   Variables must be entered first, at the top of the startup file. Variables are
>   initialized only once, when *twm* begins execution. They will not be
>   affected when a subsequent **f.twmrc** function is executed. It is probably a
>   good idea to initialize the color variables first.

>   Several variables take filenames as arguments. Filenames are processed as
>   follows. *Twm* checks to see if the first character in the filename is a tilde
>   (~), if it is, *twm* prepends the user's **HOME** environment variable to the
>   filename. In the case of variables requiring bitmap files, if the above
>   expansion does not produce a path to a valid bitmap file, the following
>   steps are taken. If the **IconDirectory** variable has been set, and the
>   filename does not start with a slash (/), the **IconDirectory** variable is
>   prepended to the filename. If that path does not produce a valid bitmap
>   file, the string "/usr/include/X11/bitmaps/" is prepended to the original
>   filename.

>   The following describes the *twm* variables:

>   **AutoRaise** { *list* }   This variable is a list of window names that will
>   automatically raise to the top of the stacking order
>   whenever the pointer enters the window. The

window names in the list are the first characters in the window name to check for. For example:

AutoRaise
{
    "xterm"
    "xclock"
}

The above list contains two names which will match window names beginning with the string "xterm" or "xclock". The following window names will match and be in auto-raise mode: "xterm", "xterm_iguana", "xclock".

BorderColor *string*   This variable sets the color of the border to placed around all non-iconified windows. It can only be specified inside of a **Color** or **Monochrome** list. The default is "black".

BorderTileForeground *string*
This variable sets the foreground color of the "grey" bitmap used in non-highlighted borders. It can only be specified inside of a **Color** or **Monochrome** list. The default is "black".

BorderTileBackground *string*
This variable sets the background color of the "grey" bitmap used in non-highlighted borders. It can only be specified inside of a **Color** or **Monochrome** list. The default is "white".

BorderWidth *pixels*   This variable specifies the width in pixels of of the border surrounding all windows. The default is 2.

Color { *colors* }   This variable is a list of color assignments to be made if the default display has a depth greater than one, or in other words, has the ability to display more than black and white. For example:

Color
{
    BorderColor "red"
    TitleForeground "yellow"
    TitleBackground "blue"
}

The various color variables may be found in this section of the manual page. There is also a **Monochrome** list of colors that may be specified. This enables you to use the same initialization file on a color or monochrome display.

DecorateTransients   This variable causes *twm* to put a title bar on transient windows. By default, transient windows will not be re-parented.

DefaultFunction *function*
This variable defines a default window manager function to be performed if no function is assigned to a combination of modifier keys and

mouse buttons. A useful function to execute might be **f.beep**.

DontIconifyByUnmapping { *list* }

This variable is a list of windows to not iconify by simply unmapping the window. This may be used when specifying **IconifyByUnmapping** to selectively choose windows that will iconify by mapping an icon window.

DontMoveOff
If this variable is set, windows will not be allowed to be moved off the display.

ForceIcons
This variable is only meaningful if a **Icons** list is defined. It forces the icon bitmaps listed in the **Icons** list to be used as window icons even if client programs supply their own icons. The default is to not force icons.

Icons { *list* }
This variable is a list of window names and bit-map filenames to be used as icons. For example:

> **Icons**
> {
>   "xterm"   "xterm.icon"
>   "xfd" "xfd_icon"
> }

The names "xterm" and "xfd" are added to a list that is searched when the client window is reparented by *twm*. The window names specified are just the first portion of the name to match. In the above example, "xterm" would match "xtermfred" and also "xterm blob". The client window names are checked against those specified in this list in addition to the class name of the client if it is specified. By using the class name, all xterm windows can be given the same icon by the method used above even though the names of the windows may be different.

IconBackground *string*
This variable sets the background color of icons. It can only be specified inside of a **Color** or **Monochrome** list. The default is "white".

IconBorderColor *string*
This variable sets the color of the border around icons. It can only be specified inside of a **Color** or **Monochrome** list. The default is "black".

IconDirectory *string*
This variable names the directory in which to search for icon bitmap files. This variable is described under the **VARIABLES SECTION** heading. The default is to have no icon directory.

IconFont *string*
This variable names the font to be displayed within icons. The default is "8x13".

IconForeground *string* This variable sets the foreground color of icons. It can only be specified inside of a **Color** or **Monochrome** list. The default is "black".

IconifyByUnmapping This variable causes *twm* to iconify windows by simply unmapping them. The icon window will not be made visible. This variable can be used in conjunction with the **DontIconifyByUnmapping** list. The default is to iconify by unmapping the window and mapping a seperate icon window.

IconManagerDontShow { *list* }
This variable is a list of window names that will not be displayed in the icon manager window. This may be useful in specifying windows that are rarely iconified such as "xclock."

IconManagerBackground *string*
This variable sets the background color of the icon manager window. It can only be specified inside of a **Color** or **Monochrome** list. The default is "white".

IconManagerForeground *string*
This variable sets the foreground color of the icon manager window. It can only be specified inside of a **Color** or **Monochrome** list. The default is "black".

IconManagerGeometry *string*
This variable sets the geometry of the icon manager window. The *string* is of the form:
    =*<width>*x*<height>*{+-}*<xoffset>*{+-}*<yoffset>*
The height of the icon manager window is not vrey important because the height of the window will be changing as windows are created and destroyed.

MenuBackground *string*
This variable sets the background color of menus. It can only be specified inside of a **Color** or **Monochrome** list. The default is "white".

MenuFont *string*   This variable names the font to be displayed within menus. The default is "8x13".

MenuForeground *string*
This variable sets the foreground color of menus. It can only be specified inside of a **Color** or **Monochrome** list. The default is "black".

MenuShadowColor *string*
This variable sets the color of the shadow behind pull-down menus. It can only be specified inside of a **Color** or **Monochrome** list. The default is "black".

MenuTitleBackground *string*
This variable sets the background color for **f.title** entries in menus. It can only be specified inside of a **Color** or **Monochrome** list. The default is "white".

MenuTitleForeground *string*
This variable sets the foreground color for **f.title** entries in menus. It can only be specified inside

of a **Color** or **Monochrome** list. The default is "black".

Monochrome { *colors* }

This variable is a list of color assignments to be made if the default display has a depth equal to one, or in other words can only display black and white pixels. For example:

> **Monochrome**
> {
>   BorderColor "black"
>   TitleForeground "black"
>   TitleBackground "white"
> }

The various color variables may be found in this section of the manual page. There is also a **Color** list of colors that may be specified. This enables you to use the same initialization file on a color or monochrome display.

NoBackingStore

Twm menus attempt to use backing store to minimize menu repainting. If your server has implemented backing store but you would rather not use this feature, this variable will disable *twm* from using backing store.

NoHighlight [{ *list* }]

This variable turns off border highlighting. An optional list may be specified with window names to selectively turn off border highlighting. The default is to highlight the borders of all windows when the cursor enters the window. When the border is highlighted, it will be drawn in the current **BorderColor**. When the border is not highlighted, it will be rendered with a "grey" bitmap using the current **BorderTileForeground** and **BorderTileBackground** colors.

NoSaveUnder

Twm menus attempt to use save unders to minimize window repainting following menu selections. If your server has implemented save unders but you would rather not use this feature, this variable will disable *twm* from using save unders.

NoTitle [{ *list* }]

This variable is a list of window names that will NOT have a title bar created for them. If **NoTitle** is specified with no window name list, *twm* will not put title bars on any windows. The list of windows and how they match window names is exactly like the **AutoRaise** variable described above.

NoRaiseOnDeiconify

If this variable is specified, windows will not be raised to the top of the stacking order when de-iconified.

NoRaiseOnMove

If this variable is specified, windows will not be raised to the top of the stacking order following a move.

NoRaiseOnResize   If this variable is specified, windows will not be raised to the top of the stacking order following a resize.

NoTitleFocus   If this variable is specified, input focus will not be directed to windows when the pointer is in the title bar. The default is to focus input to a client when the pointer is in the title bar.

RandomPlacement   This causes windows with no specified geometry to be placed on the display in a random (kind of) position when they are created. The default is to allow the user to position the window interactively.

ResizeFont *string*   This variable names the font to be displayed in the dimensions window during window resize operations. The default is "fixed".

TitleFont *string*   This variable names the font to be displayed within the window title bar. Note that the title bar is only 17 pixels in height, so the largest practical font would be something like "9x15". The default is "8x13".

ReverseVideo   This variable causes *twm* to display white characters on a black background, rather than black characters on white. This variable doesn't really do much now that you can specify individual colors.

ShowIconManager   This variable causes the icon manager window to be displayed when twm is started. The default is to not display the icon manager window.

TitleBackground *string*
    This variable sets the background color for the title bars. It can only be specified inside of a **Color** or **Monochrome** list. The default is "white".

TitleForeground *string*
    This variable sets the foreground color for the title bars. It can only be specified inside of a **Color** or **Monochrome** list. The default is "black".

UnknownIcon *string*   This variable specifies the file name of a bitmap format file to be used as the default icon. This bitmap will be used for the icon of all clients which do not provide an icon bitmap and are not listed in the **Icons** list. The default is to use no bitmap.

WarpCursor   This variable causes the pointer cursor to be warped to a window which is being deiconified. The default is to not warp the cursor.

WindowFunction *function*
    This variable is the function to perform when a window is selected from the **TwmWindows** menu. If this variable is not set, a window selected from the **TwmWindows** menu will be deiconified (if it is an icon) and then raised to the

top of the window stacking order.

Zoom [*count*]   This variable causes a series of outlines to be drawn when a window is iconified or deiconified. The optional count is a number which will be the number of outlines to be drawn. The default is to not draw the outlines. The default outline count is 8.

BUTTONS SECTION

The buttons section of the startup file contains definitions of functions to perform when pointer buttons or specific keyboard keys are pressed. Functions are assigned either to a pointer button, a keyboard key, or a menu entry. Functions are assigned to pointer buttons as follows:

Button*n* = *keys* : *context* : *function*

The *n* following **Button** can be a number between 1 and 5 to indicate which pointer button the function is to be tied to. The **keys** field is used to specify which modifier keys must be pressed in conjunction with the pointer button. The **keys** field may contain any combination of the letters **s**, **c**, and **m**, which stand for Shift, Control, and Meta, respectively. The **context** field specifies the context in which to look for the button press. Valid contexts are: **icon**, **root**, **title**, **frame**, **window**, and **iconmgr**. The **function** field specifies the window manager function to perform. It is important to note that the **iconmgr** context is only used when a pointer button is pressed in an icon manager window and the window is an icon. By default, a button press in an icon manager window while the window is not iconic, will turn the window into an icon. Now for some examples:

```
Button2 =     : title  : f.move           # 1
Button1 =     : root   : f.menu "menu 1"      # 2
Button1 = m   : icon   : f.menu "icon menu 1"  # 3
Button3 = msc : window : f.menu "menu3 1"      # 4
```

Line 1 specifies that when pointer button 2 is pressed in the title bar with no modifier keys pressed, the **f.move** function is to be executed. Line 2 specifies that when pointer button 1 is pressed in the root window with no modifier keys pressed, the menu "menu 1" is popped up. Line 3 specifies that when pointer button 1 is pressed in an icon window with the meta key pressed, the menu "icon menu 1" is popped up. Line 4 specifies that when pointer button 3 is pressed in a client window with the shift, control, and meta keys pressed, the menu "menu 3" is popped up.

Function Key Specifications

Twm allows you execute functions when any key on the keyboard is pressed. The specification of a function key is exactly like the button specification described above, except instead of **Button[1-5]**, a function key name in double quotes is used. In addition to the normal contexts that may be specified, a window name may be used, and the function will be applied to all windows matching the name. For example:

```
"F1"  =     : window : f.iconify
"F2"  = m   : root   : f.refresh
"F3"  = m   : "window_name" : f.iconify
```

Keyboard key names can be found in /usr/include/X11/keysymdef.h. Simply remove the **XK_** and you have the name that the X server will recognize.

TWM Functions

! *string* — This function causes *string* to be sent to /bin/sh for execution.

^ *string* — This function causes *string* followed by a new line character to be placed in the window server's cut buffer.

f.beep — This function causes the bell of the workstation to be sounded.

f.circledown — This function causes the top window that is obscuring another window to drop to the bottom of the stack of windows.

f.circleup — This function raises the lowest window that is obscured by other windows.

f.cutfile — This function takes the contents of the window server's cut buffer and uses it as a filename to read into the server's cut buffer.

f.deiconify — This function deiconifies a window. If the window is not an icon, this function does nothing. If executed from a menu, the cursor is changed to a dot and the next window that receives a button press will be the window that is deiconified.

f.destroy — This function allows you to destroy a window client. If executed from a menu, the cursor is changed to a skull and crossbones and the next window to receive a button press will be destroyed.

f.file *string* — This function assumes *string* is a file name. This file is read into the window server's cut buffer.

f.focus — This function implements the same function as the keyboard focus button in the title bar. If executed from a menu, the cursor is changed to a dot and the next window to receive a button press will gain the input focus.

f.forcemove — This function allows you to move a window. If **DontMoveOff** is set, **f.forcemove** allows you to move a window partially off the display. If executed from a menu, the cursor is changed to a double arrow and the next window that receives a button press will be the window that is moved.

f.fullzoom — This function resizes the current window to the full size of your display. It is a toggle function so it is really a fullzoom/unfullzoom function. In order to undo the fullzoom, you invoke f.fullzoom again - similar to **f.iconify**. If executed from a menu, the cursor is changed to a dot and the next window that receives a button press will be the window that is fullzoomed/unfullzoomed.

f.function *string* — This function executes the user defined function stream specified by *string*. A function stream is zero or more *twm* functions that will be executed in order as if they were a single function. To define a function stream the syntax is:

Function *"function name"*
{
    function
    function
       .
       .
       .
    function
}

for example:

Function "raise-n-focus"
{
    f.raise
    f.focus
}

f.hideiconmgr   This function causes the icon manager window to become unmapped (not visible).

f.iconify   This function implements the same function as the iconify button in the title bar. If executed from a menu, the cursor is changed to a dot and the next window to receive a button press will be iconified or de-iconified depending on the current state of the window.

f.lower   This function lowers the window to the bottom of the stacking order. If executed from a menu, the cursor is changed to a dot and the next window that receives a button press will be the window that is lowered.

f.menu *string*   This function assigns the pull-down menu named *string* to a pointer button. If this function is used as an entry in a pull-down menu a pull-right menu will be assigned to the menu entry.

f.move   This function allows you to move a window. If executed from a menu, the cursor is changed to a double arrow and the next window that receives a button press will be the window that is moved. Double clicking the pointer button tied to this function causes a constrained move function to be executed. The pointer will be warped to the center of the grid. Moving the pointer to one of the grid lines will cause the window to begin moving in either an up-down motion or a left-right motion depending on which grid line the pointer was moved across.

f.nop   This function does nothing.

f.quit   This function causes *twm* to exit. There is no function to exit the X Window System from a window manager; at present you must save the X Server's PID in a variable and send it "kill -TERM". This can easily be done in TWM by the ! function (see example below).

f.raise   This function raises the window to the top of the stacking order. If executed from a menu, the cursor is changed to a dot and the next window that receives a button press will be the window that is raised.

f.raiselower   This function raises the window to the top of the stacking order if it is obscured in any way. If the window is unobscured, the window is lowered to the bottom of the stacking order. If executed from a menu, the cursor is changed to a dot and the next window that receives a button press will be the window that is raised or lowered.

f.refresh   This function causes all windows to be refreshed.

f.resize   This function implements the window resize function of the resize button in the title bar. If executed from a menu, the cursor is changed to a double arrow and the next window that receives a button press will be the window that is resized.

f.showiconmgr   This function causes the icon manager window to become mapped (visible).

f.source *string*   This function assumes *string* is a file name. The file is read and parsed as a *twm* startup file. This function is intended to be used only to re-build pull-down menus. None of the *twm* variables are changed.

f.title   This function is to be used as an entry in a pull-down menu. It centers the menu entry string in a menu entry and outlines it with a border. This function may be used more than once in a pull-down menu.

f.twmrc   This function causes the *$HOME/.twmrc* file to be re-read. This function is exactly like the **f.source** function without having to specify the filename.

f.unfocus   This function assigns input focus to the root window.

f.version   This function causes the *twm* version window to be displayed. This window will be displayed until a pointer button is pressed or the pointer is moved from one window to another.

f.winrefresh   This function is similar to the **f.refresh** function, but allows you to refresh a single window. If executed from a menu, the cursor is changed to a dot and the next window that receives a button press will be the window that is refreshed.

f.zoom   This function is similar to the **f.fullzoom** function, but resizes the height to the maximum height of your screen, not the width. It is also a toggle function like **f.iconify** and **f.fullzoom**. If executed from a menu, the cursor is changed to a dot and the next window that receives a button press will be the window that is zoomed/unzoomed.

MENUS SECTION

The menus section is where pull-down menus are defined. Entries in menus consist of functions as described in the Buttons Section. The syntax to define a menu is:

Menu *"menu name"*
{
    string   function
    string   function
    .
    .
    string function
}

The *menu name* should be an identical string to one being used with an **f.menu** function. Note that the *menu name* is case sensitive. The *string* portion of each menu entry will be the text which will appear in the menu. The *function* portion of the menu entry is one of the functions described in the previous section.

There is a special menu called **TwmWindows**. When this menu is pulled down, a list of all window names is displayed in the menu. Selecting one of these window names will cause the **WindowFunction** to be executed. If **WindowFunction** has not been set, the window will be deiconified (if it is an icon) and then raised to the top of the window stacking order.

ICON MANAGER

The icon manager is a window that contains names of selected or all windows currently on the display. In addition to the window name, a small "window-pane" iconify button will be displayed to the left of the name when the window is in an iconic state. If the window is not currently an icon, a pointer button press when the pointer is on the window name will cause the window to be iconified. If the window is iconic, a pointer button press when the pointer is either on the window name or on the iconify button will by default, cause the window to be deiconified. If however, a button function was specified with a context of **iconmgr**, theat function will be executed instead.

WINDOW STARTUP

When a client is started, *twm* does one of twm things. If the **Random-Placement** variable has been set and the window has not specified an intial geometry, the window will be placed in a random (kind of) position the display. If the **RandomPlacement** variable has not been set and the client has not specified both **User Specified Size** hints and **User Specified Position** hints, *twm* will put up a rubberband box indicating the initial window size. If pointer button one is pressed, the client window is created with the window position equal to the current pointer position. If pointer button two is pressed, *twm* allows the window to be resized. The resizing operation takes place until button two is released. While the initial positioning of the window is taking place, *twm* will place a window in the upper-left corner of the display showing the window's name. If resizing is taking place, *twm* will also place a window in the upper-left corner, indicating the current window size.

EXAMPLES

```
#***********************************************************
#
#    .twmrc
#
#***********************************************************

WarpCursor
BorderWidth     2
TitleFont       "8x13"
MenuFont        "8x13"
IconFont        "8x13"

Color
{
    BorderColor "red"
    BorderTileForeground "blue"
    BorderTileBackground "yellow"
    TitleForeground "white"
    TitleBackground "blue"
    MenuForeground "yellow"
    MenuBackground "darkgreen"
    MenuTitleForeground "red"
    MenuTitleBackground "blue"
    IconForeground "darkgreen"
    IconBackground "cadetblue"
    IconBorderColor "green"
}

#Button = KEYS : CONTEXT : FUNCTION
#---------------------------------
Button1 =       : root  : f.menu "button1"
Button2 =       : root  : f.menu "button2"
Button3 =       : root  : f.menu "button3"
Button1 = m  : window : f.menu "button1"
Button2 = m  : window : f.menu "button2"
Button3 = m  : window : f.menu "button3"
Button1 = m  : title  : f.menu "button1"
Button2 = m  : title  : f.menu "button2"
Button3 = m  : title  : f.menu "button3"
Button1 =       : title  : f.raise
Button2 =       : title  : f.move
Button3 =       : title  : t.lower

ForceIcons
IconDirectory   "~/icons"
Icons
{
  "xterm"       "xterm.icon" # obtained from IconDirectory
  "xfd"         "xfd_icon"   # obtained from /usr/include/X11/bitmaps
}
UnknownIcon     "default.icon"

NoTitle
{
  "xclock"      # don't need a title bar on this ...
  "xckmail"     # or this
```

```
        }

        menu "button1"
        {
        "Sun Systems"   f.title
        "iguana"        !"xterm -T iguana =80x24+100+100 -e rlogin iguana &"
        "worm"          !"xterm -T worm =80x24+100+100 &"
        "shiva"         !"xterm -T shiva =80x24+200+200 -e rlogin shiva &"
        "tegus"         !"xterm -T tegus =80x24+200+200 -e rlogin tegus &"
        "Vax Systems"   f.title
        "shade"         !"xterm -T shade =80x24+200+200 -e rlogin shade &"
        "bilbo"         !"xterm -T bilbo =80x24+250+250 -e rlogin bilbo &"
        "frodo"         !"xterm -T frodo =80x24+300+300 -e rlogin frodo &"
        "esunix"        !"xterm -T esunix =80x24+350+350 -e rlogin esunix &"
        "lynx8"         !"xterm -T lynx8 =80x24+390+390 -e rlogin lynx8 &"
        }

        menu "button2"
        {
        "Window Ops"            f.title
        "Refresh"               f.refresh
        "Focus on Root"         f.unfocus
        "Re-read .twmrc"f.twmrc
        "Source something"      f.source "something"
        "twm Version"           f.version
        "(De)Iconify"      f.iconify
        "Move Window"           f.move
        "Resize Window"         f.resize
        "Raise Window"          f.raise
        "Lower Window"          f.lower
        "Focus on Window"       f.focus
        "Destroy Window"        f.destroy
        "Exit TWM (only)"       f.quit
        "Exit X Windows"        !"kill -TERM $XTOOLSPID"
        }

        menu "button3"
        {
        "Cut Buffer"            f.title
        "Procedure Header"      f.file "/usr/ias_soft/tlastrange/src/proc.twm"
        "File Header"           f.file "/usr/ias_soft/tlastrange/src/file.twm"
        "pull right"            f.menu "blob"
        }

        menu "blob"
        {
        "pull right"            f.menu "final"
        "another"               ^"some text"
        }

        menu "final"
        {
        "entry 1"               f.nop
        "entry 2"               f.nop
        "entry 3"               f.nop
        "entry 4"               f.nop
```

3

```
    }
```

BUGS

Pull-right menus may still have some problems. They may sometimes stay around when all pointer buttons have been released.

Double clicking very fast to get the constrained move function will sometimes cause the window to move, even though the pointer is not moved.

The window auto-raise feature does not work consistently when the mouse is moved very fast over auto-raise windows.

FILES

$HOME/.twmrc

SEE ALSO

X(1), Xserver(1)

COPYRIGHT

AUTHOR

Thomas E. LaStrange

Hewlett Packard Company
Graphics Technology Division
Fort Collins, Colorado

ARPA: toml%hpfcla@hplabs.hp.com
UUCP: hplabs!hpfcla!toml

NAME
>   uwm - a window manager for X

SYNTAX
>   **uwm** [-display *display*] [-f *filename*]

DESCRIPTION
>   The *uwm* program is a window manager for X.
>
>   When *uwm* is invoked, it searches a predefined search path to locate any
>   *uwm* startup files. If no startup files exist, *uwm* initializes its built-in
>   default file.
>
>   If startup files exist in any of the following locations, it adds the variables
>   to the default variables. In the case of contention, the variables in the last
>   file found override previous specifications. Files in the *uwm* search path
>   are:
>
>> */usr/lib/X11/uwm/system.uwmrc*
>> *$HOME/.uwmrc*
>
>   To use only the settings defined in a single startup file, include the vari-
>   ables **resetbindings, resetmenus, resetvariables** at the top of that specific
>   startup file.

OPTIONS
>   -f *filename*
>>   Names an alternate file as a *uwm* startup file.

STARTUP FILE VARIABLES
>   Variables are typically entered first, at the top of the startup file. By con-
>   vention, **resetbindings, resetmenus**, and **resetvariables** head the list.

>   **autoselect/noautoselect**
>>   places the menu cursor in the first menu item. If
>>   unspecified, the menu cursor is placed in the menu
>>   header when the menu is displayed.

>   **background=***color*
>>   specifies the default background color for popup sizing
>>   windows, menus, and icons. The default is to use the
>>   WhitePixel for the current screen.

>   **bordercolor=***color*
>>   specifies the default border color for popup sizing win-
>>   dows, menus, and icons. The default is to use the
>>   BlackPixel for the current screen.

>   **borderwidth=***pixels*
>>   specifies the default width in pixels for borders around
>>   popup sizing windows, menus, and icons. The default
>>   is 2.

>   **delta=***pixels*   indicates the number of pixels the cursor is moved
>>   before the action is interpreted by the window manager
>>   as a command. (Also refer to the **delta** mouse action.)

>   **foreground=***color*
>>   specifies the default foreground color for popup sizing
>>   windows, menus, and icons. The default is to use the
>>   BlackPixel for the current screen.

>   **freeze/nofreeze**   locks all other client applications out of the server dur-
>>   ing certain window manager tasks, such as move and
>>   resize.

grid/nogrid   displays a finely-ruled grid to help you position an icon or window during resize or move operations.

hiconpad=*pixels* indicates the number of pixels to pad an icon horizontally. The default is five pixels.

hmenupad=*pixels*

indicates the amount of space in pixels that each menu item is padded to the left and to the right of the text.

borderwidth=*pixels*

indicates the width in pixels of the border surrounding icons.

iconfont=*fontname*

names the font that is displayed within icons. Font names for a given server can be obtained using *xlsfonts(1)*.

maxcolors=*number*

limits the number of colors the window manager can use in a given invocation. If set to zero, or not specified, *uwm* assumes no limit to the number of colors it can take from the color map. **maxcolors** counts colors as they are included in the file.

mborderwidth=*pixels*

indicates the width in pixels of the border surrounding menus.

normali/nonormali

places icons created with **f.newiconify** within the root window, even if it is placed partially off the screen. With **nonormali** the icon is placed exactly where the cursor leaves it.

normalw/nonormalw

places window created with **f.newiconify** within the root window, even if it is placed partially off the screen. With **nonormalw** the window is placed exactly where the cursor leaves it.

push=*number*   moves a window *number* pixels or 1/*number* times the size of the window, depending on whether **pushabsolute** or **pushrelative** is specified. Use this variable in conjunction with **f.pushup, f.pushdown, f.pushright,** or **f.pushleft**.

pushabsolute/pushrelative

pushabsolute indicates that the number entered with push is equivalent to pixels. When an f.push (left, right, up, or down) function is called, the window is moved exactly that number of pixels.

pushrelative indicates that the number entered with the push variable represents a relative number. When an f.push function is called, the window is invisibly divided into the number of parts you entered with the push variable, and the window is moved one part.

resetbindings, resetmenus, and **resetvariables**

resets all previous function bindings, menus, and variable entries, specified in any startup file in the *uwm* search path, including those in the default environment. By convention, these variables are entered first in the startup file.

resizefont=*fontname*

identifies the font of the indicator that displays dimensions in the corner of the window as you resize windows. See *xlsfonts(1)* for obtaining font names.

resizerelative/noresizerelative

indicates whether or not resize operations should be done relative to moving edge or edges. By default, the dynamic rectangle uses the actual pointer location to define the new size.

reverse/noreverse

defines the display as black characters on a white background for the window manager windows and icons.

viconpad=*pixels*   indicates the number of pixels to pad an icon vertically. Default is five pixels.

vmenupad=*pixels*

indicates the amount of space in pixels that the menu is padded above and below the text.

volume=*number*   increases or decreases the base level volume set by the *xset(1)* command. Enter an integer from 0 to 7, 7 being the loudest.

zap/nozap   causes ghost lines to follow the window or icon from its previous default location to its new location during a move or resize operation.

BINDING SYNTAX

function=[*control key(s)*]:[*context*]:*mouse events*:" *menu name* "

Function and mouse events are required input. Menu name is required with the *f.menu* function definition only.

Function

f.beep   emits a beep from the keyboard. Loudness is determined by the volume variable.

f.circledown   causes the top window that is obscuring another window to drop to the bottom of the stack of windows.

f.circleup   exposes the lowest window that is obscured by other windows.

f.continue   releases the window server display action after you stop action with the **f.pause** function.

f.focus   directs all keyboard input to the selected window. To reset the focus to all windows, invoke *f.focus* from the root window.

f.iconify   when implemented from a window, this function converts the window to its respective icon. When implemented from an icon, f.iconify converts the icon to its respective window.

f.kill   kills the client that created a window.

f.lower   lowers a window that is obstructing a window below it.

f.menu	invokes a menu. Enclose 'menu name' in quotes if it contains blank characters or parentheses.

f.menu=[*control key(s)*]:[*context*]:*mouse events*:" *menu name* "

f.move	moves a window or icon to a new location, which becomes the default location.
f.moveopaque	moves a window or icon to a new screen location. When using this function, the entire window or icon is moved to the new screen location. The grid effect is not used with this function.
f.newiconify	allows you to create a window or icon and then position the window or icon in a new default location on the screen.
f.pause	temporarily stops all display action. To release the screen and immediately update all windows, use the **f.continue** function.
f.pushdown	moves a window down. The distance of the push is determined by the push variables.
f.pushleft	moves a window to the left. The distance of the push is determined by the push variables.
f.pushright	moves a window to the right. The distance of the push is determined by the push variables.
f.pushup	moves a window up. The distance of the push is determined by the push variables.
f.raise	raises a window that is being obstructed by a window above it.
f.refresh	results in exposure events being sent to the window server clients for all unobscured or partially obscured windows. The windows will not refresh correctly if the exposure events are not handled properly.
f.resize	resizes an existing window. Note that some clients, notably editors, react unpredictably if you resize the window while the client is running.
f.restart	causes the window manager application to restart, retracing the *uwm* search path and initializing the variables it finds.

Control Keys

By default, the window manager uses meta as its control key. It can also use ctrl, shift, lock, or null (no control key). Control keys must be entered in lower case, and can be abbreviated as: c, l, m, s for ctrl, lock, meta, and shift, respectively.

You can bind one, two, or no control keys to a function. Use the bar (l) character to combine control keys.

Note that client applications other than the window manager use the shift as a control key. If you bind the shift key to a window manager function, you can not use other client applications that require this key.

Context

The context refers to the screen location of the cursor when a command is initiated. When you include a context entry in a binding, the cursor must be in that context or the function will not be activated. The window manager recognizes the following four contexts: icon, window, root, (null).

The root context refers to the root, or background window, A (null) context is indicated when the context field is left blank, and allows a function to be invoked from any screen location. Combine contexts using the bar (|) character.

Mouse Buttons

Any of the following mouse buttons are accepted in lower case and can be abbreviated as l, m, or r, respectively: left, middle, right.

With the specific button, you must identify the action of that button. Mouse actions can be:

down   function occurs when the specified button is pressed down.

up   function occurs when the specified button is released.

delta   indicates that the mouse must be moved the number of pixels specified with the delta variable before the specified function is invoked. The mouse can be moved in any direction to satisfy the delta requirement.

MENU DEFINITION

After binding a set of function keys and a menu name to **f.menu**, you must define the menu to be invoked, using the following syntax:

> **menu** = " *menu name* " {
> "*item name*" : "*action*"
> .
> .
> .
>
> }

Enter the menu name exactly the way it is entered with the **f.menu** function or the window manager will not recognize the link. If the menu name contains blank strings, tabs or parentheses, it must be quoted here and in the f.menu function entry. You can enter as many menu items as your screen is long. You cannot scroll within menus.

Any menu entry that contains quotes, special characters, parentheses, tabs, or strings of blanks must be enclosed in double quotes. Follow the item name by a colon (:).

Menu Action

Window manager functions
> Any function previously described. E.g., **f.move** or **f.iconify**.

Shell commands
> Begin with an exclamation point (!) and set to run in background. You cannot include a new line character within a shell command.

Text strings
> Text strings are placed in the window server's cut buffer.
>
> Strings starting with an up arrow (ˆ) will have a new line character appended to the string after the up arrow (ˆ) has been stripped from it.
>
> Strings starting with a bar character (|) will be copied as is after the bar character (|) has been stripped.

Color Menus

Use the following syntax to add color to menus:

menu = "*menu name*" (*color1:color2:color3:color4*) {
"*item name*" : (*color5 :color6*) : " *action* "

.
.
.

}

color1   Foreground color of the header.

color2   Background color of the header.

color3   Foreground color of the highlighter, the horizontal band of color that moves with the cursor within the menu.

color4   Background color of the highlighter.

color5   Foreground color for the individual menu item.

color6   Background color for the individual menu item.

Color Defaults

Colors default to the colors of the root window under any of the following conditions:

1) If you run out of color map entries, either before or during an invocation of *uwm*.

2) If you specify a foreground or background color that does not exist in the RGB color database of the server (see */usr/lib/X11/rgb.txt* for a sample) both the foreground and background colors default to the root window colors.

3) If you omit a foreground or background color, both the foreground and background colors default to the root window colors.

4) If the total number of colors specified in the startup file exceeds the number specified in the *maxcolors* variable.

5) If you specify no colors in the startup file.

EXAMPLES

The following sample startup file shows the default window manager options:

```
# Global variables
#
resetbindings;resetvariables;resetmenus
autoselect
delta=25
freeze
grid
hiconpad=5
hmenupad=6
iconfont=oldeng
menufont=timrom12b
resizefont=9x15
viconpad=5
vmenupad=3
volume=7
```

```
#
# Mouse button/key maps
#
# FUNCTION    KEYS  CONTEXT  BUTTON    MENU(if any)
# ========    ====  =======  ======    ===========
f.menu =      meta :        :left down   :"WINDOW OPS"
f.menu =      meta :        :middle down :"EXTENDED WINDOW OPS"
f.move =      meta :wli     :right down
f.circleup =  meta :root    :right down
#
# Menu specifications
#
menu = "WINDOW OPS" {
"(De)Iconify":   f.iconify
Move:            f.move
Resize:          f.resize
Lower:           f.lower
Raise:           f.raise
}

menu = "EXTENDED WINDOW OPS" {
Create Window:                !"xterm &"
Iconify at New Position:  f.lowericonify
Focus Keyboard on Window:     f.focus
Freeze All Windows:           f.pause
Unfreeze All Windows:         f.continue
Circulate Windows Up:         f.circleup
Circulate Windows Down:           f.circledown
}
```

RESTRICTIONS

The color specifications have no effect on a monochrome system.

FILES

/usr/lib/X11/uwm/system.uwmrc
$HOME/.uwmrc

SEE ALSO

X(1), Xserver(1), xset(1), xlsfonts(1)

COPYRIGHT

AUTHOR

M. Gancarz, DEC Ultrix Engineering Group, Merrimack, New Hampshire, using some algorithms originally by Bob Scheifler, MIT Laboratory for Computer Science.

NAME

vf2bdf – convert vfont format to BDF format

SYNOPSIS

vf2bdf vffile pointsize

DESCRIPTION

Vf2bdf converts the vfont file to BDF on stdout.

AUTHOR

Ken Yap

NAME

vif – Configuration driven tty environment

SYNOPSIS

vif [-config config] [-e shell-cmd]

DESCRIPTION

Vif is a configuration defined interface built arround a terminal emulation window based on that provided by xterm(1). The configuration optionally defines a set of selection buttons, a scrollbar for generating up/down actions, actions related to input on the vt102 emulation window and lex(1) filters for the keyboard and tty data streams.

When any of these items are activated, there is an associated action performed that is defined in the configuration as the concatenation of the following:

VAC_PTYCHARS   - Send a char. string down the pty (ie. fake keyboard input)

VAC_VTCHARS   - Put a given char. string out onto the screen

VAC_SETSENSTV   - Modify the sensitivity of the other inputs (Buttons...)

VAC_DIALOGBOX   - Pop up a Dialog box to query for keyboard input

VAC_YESNOBOX   - Pop up a Box to query for a yes/no response via. Button selection

VAC_WARPPOINTER

                       - Warp the mouse pointer into a given widget on the vif

VAC_POPUPTEXT   - Pop up a text string in the top margin

VAC_POPUPICON   - Pop up an icon in the top margin

VAC_NEWMOUSE   - Change the mouse cursor

The filters recognize character sequences that match regular expressions on the I/O streams and invoke the associated action when matched. The Scrollbar is actually a 1D spring loaded joystick and generates the associated up or down actions a number of times, based on a defined acceleration. Although the up/down actions are arbitrary, they usually move to previous or further items. Button1 on the mouse may be configured to generate an appropriate number of arrow keystrokes to move the text cursor to the location of the mouse cursor. This only works if run with clients that understand the vt100 arrow keys. The other mouse buttons may be configured to activate arbitrary actions while on the vt102 emulation window. Mouse Button2 pops up help windows for the other widgets and they may be popped back down with a mouse press on a help window. An alternate configuration option sets the vt102 emulation window to page scroll and then requires a mouse press in the emulation window to continue output. Normally, vif should be run with the -e option followed by the shell command that the config is designed for.

FILES

/usr/local/lib/xgsh/*.vif
/usr/local/lib/xgsh/*vif.hlp

BUGS

A popup text string or icon sometimes doesn't get erased when its time expires. The mouse input on the vt102 emulation window is inconsistent with the rest of vif. There should be the option of multiple vt102 emulation windows and more state related information in the configuration. Button3 input cannot be used when run by xgsh(1), since xgsh grabs Button3 for the process control popup menu.

NAME
>   wm – a simple real-estate-driven window manager

SYNOPSIS
>   **wm** [-display *display*]

DESCRIPTION
>   *Wm* is a very primitive overlapping window manager for *X11*. It was
>   developed to help with the debugging of the *X11* server; we do not sug-
>   gest that the user interface presented here is a desired one, and we do not
>   suggest that you try to use this program on a regular basis.
>
>   *Wm* decorates each mapped appliction window with a banner. The banner
>   consists of four fields. Left-to-right, they are:
>
>   *Circulate button* - A command button which causes the window to change
>   its position in the stacking order.
>
>   *Title region* - An area in which an applications name or other specified
>   information is displayed. It is also used by the user to move the window.
>
>   *Iconize button* - A command button which causes the window to be
>   replaced by an icon.
>
>   *Resize button* - A command button which allows the user to change the
>   size of the window.
>
>   *Wm* supports the following user actions:
>
>   Raising or lowering a window in the stack of windows
>> Locating the pointer cursor in the Circulate box of a partially
>> obscured window and clicking with any pointer button will raise this
>> window to the top of the stack of windows so that it is no longer
>> obscured. Locating a pointer cursor in the Circulate box of a win-
>> dow which is currently on top of the window stack will send the
>> window to the bottom of the stack.
>
>   Iconizing a window
>> Locating the pointer cursor in the Iconize box and clicking any
>> pointer button will cause the window to be unmapped, and the asso-
>> ciated icon to become mapped. The icon will appear at its last loca-
>> tion, or, if this window has never been iconized, under the cursor.
>> However, if the client program initially set an icon position in the
>> WM_HINTS property, then that icon position will be used instead as
>> the initial icon position. To position an icon while iconizing the
>> window, locate the cursor in the Iconize box and press down any
>> pointer button. A rubber-band outline of the icon will appear under
>> the cursor. While holding down the pointer button, drag the cursor
>> to the desired location for the icon. The outline will follow the cur-
>> sor on the screen. When the outline moves to the desired location
>> for the icon, release the pointer button. The client window will be
>> unmapped, and its icon will appear at the desired location. To cancel
>> this operation while the pointer button is down, click another pointer
>> button.
>
>   Deiconizing an icon
>> Locating the pointer cursor in an icon and clicking any pointer but-
>> ton will cause the icon to be unmapped, and the associated window
>> to become mapped. To cancel this operation while the pointer button
>> is down, click another pointer button.
>
>   Moving a window on the screen
>> Locating pointer cursor in the area of the title region and pressing

any pointer button causes a "rubber-band" outline of the window to appear. As the user moves ("drags") the cursor (while holding down the pointer button), the outline moves accordingly. When the button is released, the window is repainted in the last location of the rubber-band outline. If the user presses another pointer button during the drag, the operation is cancelled, the rubber-band outline disappears, and the window is not moved. Note that a portion of the title region is constrained to remain on the screen.

Resizing a window.

Locating the pointer cursor in the resize box and pressing any pointer button initiates the spring-loaded resize mode. Then as soon a the cursor touches a border (while the pointer button is down), that border becomes a rubber-band line which follows the cursor until the button is released. If the cursor then touches an adjacent border, that border also becomes a rubber-band line, and the window can be resized in two dimensions at once. If the cursor touches a border after having touched the opposite border, the first border touched reverts to its original location, and the other one becomes a rubber-band line which follows the cursor. If the user presses another pointer button during the drag, the operation is cancelled, the rubber-band outline disappears, and the window does not change size. Note that the pointer cursor has to touch a border to initiate th resize action. As in the move operation, a protion of the title region is constrained to remain on the screen.

Moving an icon on the screen

To move an icon, press the Shift key and hold it, then position the pointer cursor in the icon, press any pointer button, and proceed dragging an outline of the icon around by moving the pointer cursor (with the pointer button down). When the outline moves to the desired position, release the pointer button and the Shift key. To cancel, click another pointer button during the drag; the icon will not move.

NOTES FOR CLIENT PROGRAMS

Wm uses the WM_ICON_NAME, WM_NAME, and WM_HINTS properties. It keeps the name in the Title region updated as the WM_NAME property changes. It keeps the name in the icon updated as the WM_ICON_NAME property changes; if a client does not set the WM_ICON_NAME property, *wm* will use the WM_NAME property for the icon name. *Wm* allows only text icons, and sets the icon sizes to accommodate the icon name. The maximum name length for both the icon name and the Title region name is 100 characters.

Of the WMHints, *wm* ignores all but icon_x and icon_y, which it uses for initial icon placement. These need to be set by the client before its window is mapped, because *wm* reads them only once, when it first encounters the window.

SEE ALSO

X(1), *Inter-Client Communication Conventions Manual*

BUGS

This program does not necessarily implement the current window manager protcols.

DIAGNOSTICS

If you try to run *wm* while you are already running a window manager, *wm* will let you know.

COPYRIGHT

AUTHOR
Hania Gajewska, DEC WSL Dave Rosenthal, Sun Microsystems

NAME
  worm – draw wiggly worms

SYNOPSIS
  worm [**–l** *length*] [**–s** *size*] [**–n** *number*] [**–d** *connection*] [**–g**
  geometry] [**–R**] [**–C**] [**–S**]

DESCRIPTION
  worm draws wiggly worms. It is adapted from a concept in the December
  1987 issue of Scientific American. Playing with the various parameters
  can create strange effects. Pressing any key in the worm window will
  cause them to freeze; pressing again will thaw.

OPTIONS
  –S   Screensaver. Takes over entire screen.

  –C   Chromocolor. Worms change colors as they crawl.

  –R   Rotate colormap. The colormap constantly changes.

  –n *number*
         Make *number* worms. Default is 50.

  –l *length*
         Worms are if length *length*. A negative value means infinite length.

  –size *size*
         Worms are *size* pixels wide.

  –display *connection*
         Connect to X server display, *connection*.

  –geometry *geomspec*
         Create window using *geomspec*.

SEE ALSO
  X(1)

COPYRIGHT
  Copyright (c) 1988 by Sun Microsystems, Inc.
  David Lemke (lemke@wirehead.sun.com)

NAME
>   x10tox11 – X version 10 to version 11 protocol converter

SYNOPSIS
>   **x10tox11** [-display host:display]

DESCRIPTION
>   *x10tox11* masquerades as an X Window System Version 10 server. It
>   enables an X Version 10 client to run unchanged under X Version 11 by
>   converting Version 10 requests into appropriate Version 11 requests, and
>   by converting all Version 11 events received from the server into Version
>   10 events. From the perspective of Version 10 clients, all Version 11
>   clients look like Version 10 clients; and from the perspective of Version
>   11 clients, all Version 10 clients just look like Version 11 clients. Hence,
>   a Version 11 window manager can manipulate Version 10 clients.
>
>   This program does NOT use the X10 *libnest* ddX library. It does actual
>   protocol translation, rather than simply using X11 graphics calls to imple-
>   ment X10 low level operations. As a result, it is both faster and more
>   robust than the X10 Xnest server.

TYPICAL USAGE
>   The protocol converter must be run after the X11 server is running and
>   should be run in the background:
>
>   *x10tox11* &
>
>   The program will continue to run until you intentionally kill it or the X11
>   server is shut down.

OPTIONS
>   -display host:display
>>   Standard option for specifying the X11 display to which you wish
>>   to be connected. By default, it uses unix:0.0. Note that *x10tox11*
>>   will always pretend to be an X10 server with the same display
>>   number as the X11 server to which it connects. For example, if
>>   the DISPLAY environment variable or the *-display* option specifies
>>   *fizzle:1.0*, then *x10tox11* will connect to the X11 server on host
>>   *fizzle* for display 1 and then will pretend to the the X10 server for
>>   display 1. Consequently, your X10 clients will expect to have the
>>   environment variable DISPLAY set to *fizzle:1* (but they should still
>>   work even if your X10 clients use *fizzle:1.0*).
>
>   MinimumTileSize=n
>>   Set minimum acceptable tile size to *n*. There is a difference in
>>   semantics between X10's XQueryShape and X11's XQueryBest-
>>   Size such that X11 will allow any tile size but will return the
>>   optimum whereas X10 enforced a minimum tile size. Usually this
>>   minimum tile size was 16 and this is the default for *x10tox11*. If
>>   you find that this makes your X10 clients break, then you can
>>   override it with this option.
>
>   help
>>   This prints out a usage message and exits.
>
>   NoOverrideRedirect
>>   This instructs *x10tox11* to make every effort not to use Overri-
>>   deRedirect when creating and mapping windows. Normally,
>>   *x10tox11* creates all windows with the OverrideRedirect attribute
>>   set to true. Placing this option on the command line will cause
>>   *x10tox11* not to use OverrideRedirect except for windows that look
>>   like they might be menus. This will allow window managers that

provide title bars to do so. Unfortunately, it is impossible to determine ahead of time what an X10 client intends to do with windows. In addition, X10 clients are known to spontaneously unmap their windows which upsets X11 window managers unless the OverrideRedirect attribute is true. Further, some X11 window managers may refuse to resize or move windows that are marked with OverrideRedirect. This may can be fixed to some extent when an Inter Client Communications Convention Manual (ICCCM) is adopted by the X11 community.

SEE ALSO

   X(1), Xserver(1)

BUGS

   There are limitations with respect to emulating Version 10 through a Version 11 server. See the file /usr/lib/X/x10tox11.help for more details.

   Some window managers may refuse to move, resize or perform any operations on X10 client windows because, by default,

   If the source is compiled with certain flags, there are significant debugging facilities available. Using the *help* option will tell you whether debugging facilities are available. *x10tox11* marks them with OverrideRedirect. See **OPTIONS** above.

COPYRIGHT

   Copyright 1988, Tektronix Inc.

   Permission to use, copy, modify, and distribute this software and its documentation for any purpose and without fee is hereby granted, provided that the above copyright notice appear in all copies and that both that copyright notice and this permission notice appear in supporting documentation.

AUTHOR

   Todd Brunhoff, Visual Systems Laboratory, Tektronix.

NAME

x11 - an easy way to start up the X windows system (Version 11)

SYNTAX

x11 [**-rv**] [*servername serveroptions*]

DESCRIPTION

x11 is a simple way to start up the X Windows system. It does this by let-
ting the X **server** initialize itself, and then executes a file called
x11startup.type in the user's home directory, which starts up the **window
manager** and various application programs. If this file is not present, then
it copies some default files there and starts up with those defaults. The
user can subsequently modify these files to select other preferences after
gaining the necessary familiarity with X. This manual tries to give the
user a working familiarity with X, but for more details, the user should
refer to the standard X documents.

The *.type* extension on the startup file name allows the user to have
different startup files for different types of displays - Locally, we have the
types *.bw2* for conventional Sun 3/50 and 3/60 monochrome displays,
bw2hires for high resolution Sun monochrome displays (like the one on
godzilla), *cg4* for the Sun 3/110 and 3/60 color displays, and *cg2* for the
Sun 3/260 color displays.

Startup

When X comes up, the screen fills with a patterned background, with a X
shaped cursor in the centre. This is the **Root Window** and all windows
created on the display are **descendants** of the Root Window. After the
Root Window comes up, a small **console window** appears at the top left
corner of the screen. This is where most messages will go (talk(1)
requests, biff(1) reminders etc.) On a *cg4* display, X uses the two available graphic planes as separate screens, side by side. You can move from
one screen to the other by sliding your mouse off the left or right edge of
either screen. The zero'th screen is a monochrome screen, and the first
screen is a color screen. They are referred to as 0.0 and 0.1 respectively
in the display numbering system. (if the machine is properly configured -
harass your system adminstartor if it isn't)
**To exit X Windows, hit Control-D or type "exit" in the console win-
dow**

Depending on the *x11startup* file found, various applications start up.
With the default file, there will be handy applications like a clock. Two
terminal emulator windows (*xterms*) will appear, which will behave
exactly like vt102 terminals, with shells in them. These can be used like
normal terminals, except that they are a lot bigger, and have a few bells
and whistles not found on the humble text terminal. To type into one of
these, move the mouse till the cursor is in the window (it changes shape
to a pillar-like symbol) and type away. (See *xterm*(x))

These *xterms* are what most people use most of the time, and familiarity
with their features is advised.

What is a window?

A *window* is a rectangular area on the screen, which has a background
color, a foreground color, and a border. Windows are created by the X
Windows server when asked for by various applications. An application
program sends all its output to its windows(s) and receives its input from
them. Windows may have child windows, forming a hierarchy, of which
the root is the Root Window.

What is X?
The X Windows server is a program which controls the display and takes requests from other application programs, called **clients** to draw text and graphics, and return **events** like mouse clicks and key presses back to the applications. These requests can come over a network, so it is possible to use a workstation running X to interact with a program running on another machine. (See *xhost*(x)) This allows the creation of windows by different client programs, and their manipulation and interaction, to form a multi-tasking desktop environment. X applications can be treated in most respects as ordinary UNIX® programs, and put in the background (as all the applications started up by *xstartup* are), suspended, etc. Most applications) not provide window management facilities for moving windows around, above and below one another, changing their size, and getting them out of the way. These functions are performed by another X application program - the window manager.

3

The Window Manager
There are several window managers for X, the more popular (around here) being *twm* and *awm*. The window manager makes such operations as resizing, moving, overlapping and iconification of application windows much easier, and most application programs will behave appropriately when such an action is taken. For example, when rescaling the clock, it redraws itself to the bigger/smaller scale.

The window manager and well-behaved X Windows applications decide between themselves what they'd like done about window management - usually, teh window manager will put a frame around the application's window, and throw on a *titlebar* on top. It highlights the titlebar when the mouse goes into the window, to indicate that that is the window that is going to receive the input *focus*. Sometimes, if you have the *Auto-Raise* attribute set, the window will also come to the top when it gets the focus. If not, clicking the LEFT mouse button on the titlebar raises the window. Clicking the RIGHT mouse button on the titlebar lowers the window, and clicking the MIDDLE mouse button on the titlebar, and holding it down will result in an outline appearing, which you can drag around, and place somewhere else on the screen by releasing the mouse button. The window will move there.

The titlebar also has *buttons* (or *gadgets*) on it. (Not to be confused with mouse buttons!). These are little square items, which can be used for other operations on the window. The button which looks like a window pane, on the left closes the window, and produces an *icon* in its place. Icons are small, and can be moved around the same way as windows can be - by holding down the MIDDLE mouse button over them and dragging. By keeping windows that you are not using closed, you can prevent them from cluttering the screen *desktop*. To reopen an icon, simply click on it with the RIGHT or LEFT mouse button. The window will reopen at its original locaation on the screen.

The button which shows boxes of several sizes is ro reshape the window. If you click a mouse button on it, and hold the mouse button down, and move around, a window outline will form. If you leave the window through any side, that side will start reshaping, and will now follow the mouse around. You can now go back into the window to reduce the size. When you release the mouse button, the window changes to the new shape.

A third, optional button, which may or may not appear, depending on what defaults you/your system adminstrator have selected, is a button with a small keyboard pattern on it will grab the *focus*. After that, even if you move out of the window, anything you type will still go into that window - this is indicated by its titlebar remaining highlighted, even when you leave. To restore the old behaviour (of focusing on the window the mouse cursor is in), you have to restore the focus to thr Root Window. Since the Root Window has no buttons on it, you have to use other means to set the focus - menus.

Menus

Clicking a mouse button in the Root Window and holding it down will produce a *menu* which *pops-up* at the mouse position. The menu has various items on it, like "Refresh", and "Focus on Root". As you move the mouse over them, they highlight to indicate that they can be selected. Releasing the mouse over one of them selects the item highlighted - for instance "Focus on Root" will restore the focus to the window the mouse wanders into.

Some items don't do anything when selected - they are pointers to other menus, and indicate this with an arrow pointing right on the right edge. If you move the mouse over the arrow of one of those, for instance, "New Windows", it will produce another window, with the entries "24 lines" and "48 lines". Selecting one of those will create a new *xterm* window on the screen. Such menus are called *walking menus*. (Menus have a whole taxonomy of their own!)

The behaviour of *twm,* its menus, its actions on buttons, and so on, can be extensively customized by editing the ˜/.twmrc file. (See *twm*(x)). To customize *awm,* you need to edit the *.awmrc* file and also your *defaults* file, described below. (See *awm*(x)). If you break anything drastically, so that things don't start up, or do really strange things, and want the good old defaults back, simply delete (rm) the *.twmrc/.awmrc* file - the next time you start up X with *x11,* you'll get another. Note that regardless of the window manager you choose to use eventually, you get default files for all of them.

Defaults, er, Resources

To permit users to specify defaults for applications (color, size, location, font etc.) without having to type long lists of command line options, X provides the facility of loading *resource databases* which are essentially files specifying default values. The files are simple, and as a local convention, we call them *X11defaults*.type where the extension .type is once again the display type, allowing the user to store different sets of defaults for the different displays. Initially, the *x11* command copies system default files for the user - these may be edited and changed as desired.

For example, the system defaults setup the *xterm* windows to be white characters on a black background on the *bw2* displays. To change that, edit the file ˜/X11defaults.bw2 and change the line

      xterm*reverseVideo: on

to

      xterm*reverseVideo: off

This example will only affect those terminal emulators whose *name* is xterm - for instance, the console window's name is not xterm, but 'console'. To affect ALL terminal emulators, you have to use the *class* rather than the name - the class for the *xterm* applications is *XTerm*. So to change all xterms to reverse video, use

      XTerm*reverseVideo: on

to

      XTerm*reverseVideo: off

Resources are usually as "program.name.subname.etc: value", one per line in resource files, or one per -xrm argument. Names are hierarchies, usually corresponding to major structures within an application (where structures are often objects like windows, panels, menus, scrollbars, etc.). The various subnames are called components and are specified left to right from most general to least general. Instead of names, classnames can be substituted - these are more general - typically all instances of a particular program would have the same classname (eg) XTerm for the xterm program.

See */usr/doc/resources.X11* for a fuller guide on how to set up resources, and the *X*(x) manual page for more information on resources and command line arguments.

Other X Applications
The list is growing rapidly enough to make this section obsolete. Further, since much of the software is distributed by anonymous ftp and Usenet, it varies from site to site. Very useful applications include the previewer for TeX, (*texx*(x)) the ditroff previewer, (*xtroff*(x)) the window dumper and printer, (*xwd*(x), *xwud*(x), *xpr*(x), *xdpr*(x)) which produce snapshots of windows, various editors for graphics and text, the *xmh* mail reader, the graph-plotting program (*gnuplot*(x)), the PostScript(tm) interpreter a bitmap editor (*bitmap*(x)), an access control program (*xhost*(x)), user preference setting programs (*xset*(x), *xsetroot*(x), and *xmodmap*(x)), a load monitor (*xload*(x)), clock (*xclock*(x)), a font displayer (*xfd*(x)), a protocol translator for running X10 programs (*x10tox11*(x)), various demos (*ico*(x), *muncher*(x)). and of course, games. (*xconq*(6), *xfish*(x), *xpuzzle*(x), *puzzle*(x)). Try looking in /usr/bin/X11, or /usr/man/manx.

Programming X Windows
The raw interface to the X Windows server is through the Xlib C Interface library. There is also a higher level X Toolkit C Interface library, and a library of **widgets** for the X Toolkit called the Athena Widgets. *(Xaw)* There's another set of widgets called the HP widgets, or *Xw*. There is also a toolkit in the C++ language called InterViews. There are also toolkits for Common Lisp. See the respective manuals, or the example programs in the X Windows source tree (stored locally in */csri3/X.V11R2*).

OPTIONS
(These options are for the x11 command - the previous section on options described the options which most applications provide)

-rv Starts the initial console xterm in reverse video.

server the name of the X Windows server to be started in place of the default Xsun. Useful for testing new servers. The server name may be followed by server options. If no server options are given, defaults are used. ("0 -a 4 -t 4 -c -fp *fontpath*" asking for display 0, an acceleration of 4 with a threshold of 4, no keyclick, and a default fontpath) If you change these, remember to specify the display.

SEE ALSO
Xsun(x), *Xserver*(x), *xinit*(x), *uwm*(x), *awm*(x), *twm*(x), *xtroff*(x), *texx*(x), *plotspice*(x), *bitmap*(x), *gnuplot*(x), *xrdb*(x), *xterm*(x) and many more. See section 'x' of the manual.

FILES
~/.X11defaults.*
    Resource files for different displays

~/.x11startup.*
>   Startup scripts for various displays. (Executable)

~/.twmrc
>   Window manager startup defaults

/usr/local/lib/x11/default.{X11defaults.*,x11startup.*,twmrc}
>   Defaults which get copied if the user has none.

AUTHOR
>   Mark Moraes. (University of Toronto)

BUGS
>   Really BAD things will happen if users set their paths in ~/.cshrc, and
>   don't make sure that /usr/bin/X11 (where most X11 programs are) is
>   **before** /usr/local and /usr/new. (where most X10 programs are) The right
>   path order is /usr/bin/X11:/usr/local:/usr/new.

NAME

x2pic - convert figures stored in *xpic* format to pic.

SYNOPSIS

x2pic [-s *scale*] [*filename*] ....

DESCRIPTION

X2pic takes the given *xpic* file (default is the standard input) and produces corresponding pic on the standard output. This can then be printed by passing it through the *pic* preprocessor and then through *ditroff* (or other variants of *troff*) to output devices like laser printers.

OPTIONS

-*s*scale scales the picture by *scale,* which is a floating point number. Text doesn't scale very well. (eg) -*s 0.5* will scale the picture to half its size.

SEE ALSO

xpic(L) is what generates the files for *x2pic* to convert.

x2ps(L) is another filter for converting *xpic* output to *PostScript(tm)* format.

tpic(L) is a preprocessor for *TeX* to permit inclusion of pic in *TeX* documents.

TRADEMARKS

PostScript is a registered trademark of Adobe Systems, Inc.

CAVEATS

Many versions of pic have a nasty bug in which the *scale* variable is not reset between consecutive pictures. Since xpic uses *scale* in its pictures, (eg) *scale = 80,* the next picture will start off at this scale, and will therefore be further shrunk if it is an xpic picture, or just shrunk if it is any other pciture, like a graph. Get someone to fix pic, or x2pic (which has a BROKENPIC ifdef to deal with this).

Pic does NOT do patterned splines, ellipses or circles - xpic does. This is a pic 'feature', not an xpic bug.

NAME
x2ps - convert figures stored in *xpic* format to PostScript(tm).

SYNOPSIS
x2ps [-r] [-x] [-s *scale*] [-p *prologuefile*] [-t *trailerfile*] [-h *hoffset*] [-v *voffset*] [*filename*] ....

DESCRIPTION
X2ps takes the given *xpic* file (default is the standard input) and produces corresponding PostScript on the standard output. This can then be printed on PostScript-supporting graphic output devices, like laser printers.

OPTIONS

-r   prints the figure in landscape mode, rotated by 90 degrees. It goes together with the -r option on xpic.

-x   suppresses the *showpage* emitted by *x2ps* - *LaTeX* used to need this. (Locally, we've fixed *LaTeX* by defining /*showpage* to be null in the *ecial* header).

-s scale   scales the picture by *scale,* which is a floating point number. (eg) -s *0.5* will scale the picture to half its size.

-p prologuefile

-t trailerfile
            specify the prologue and trailer to be used. The defaults are *LIBDIR/x2ps.pro* and *x2ps.tra*. Use these only if you know what you're doing. Typically, you'd take the default *x2ps.{pro,tra}* and modify them to change something you don't like - or you think is buggy. On your own head be it.

-h hoffset

-v voffset
            specify the horizontal and vertical offset to add to the figure, in inches. hoffset and voffset may be floats.

SEE ALSO
xpic(L) is what generates the files for *x2ps* to convert.
x2pic(L) is another filter for converting *xpic* output to *pic* format.
psfig(L) is a preprocessor for *ditroff* to permit inclusion of PostScript in *ditroff* documents. There is also a version for *TeX* apparently, which I haven't tried.
The other method I know of for including PostScript in TeX documents is *ecial* directive in some version of *LaTeX*. See the local guide for *LaTeX* and the examples in DOCDIR.

TRADEMARKS
PostScript is a registered trademark of Adobe Systems, Inc.

NAME
>   xbgsun – load a Sun rasterfile onto an X11 root window

SYNOPSIS
>   **xbgsun** [-display *dispname*] [-center] [-black] *rasterfile*

DESCRIPTION
>   *Xbgsun* loads a Sun monochrome rasterfile onto an X11 root window. If
>   the rasterfile name ends in .Z, the file will be uncompressed before loading
>   (this saves a lot of disk space).

OPTIONS
>   The following options are available with *xbgsun:*
>
>   -display dispname
>   X11 display name.
>
>   -center   If the raster image is smaller than the screen, this forces the
>   image to be centered on the screen instead of replicated.
>
>   -black   If the raster image is centered, this makes the border black.

AUTHOR
>   Jim Frost
>   madd@bu-it.bu.edu

BUGS
>   Only handles standard monochrome rasterfiles.

NAME
    xbiff - mailbox flag for X

SYNOPSIS
    xbiff [-*toolkitoption* ...] [-option ...]

DESCRIPTION
    The *xbiff* program displays a little image of a mailbox. When there is no
    mail, the flag on the mailbox is down. When mail arrives, the flag goes
    up and the mailbox beeps. By default, pressing any mouse button in the
    image forces *xbiff* to remember the current size of the mail file as being
    the "empty" size and to lower the flag.

    This program is nothing more than a wrapper around the Athena *Mailbox*
    widget.

OPTIONS
    Xbiff accepts all of the standard X Toolkit command line options along
    with the additional options listed below:

    –help   This option indicates that a brief summary of the allowed
            options should be printed on the standard error.

    –update *seconds*
            This option specifies the frequency in seconds at which *xbiff*
            should update its display. If the mailbox is obscured and then
            exposed, it will be updated immediately. The default is 60
            seconds.

    –file *filename*
            This option specifies the name of the file which should be moni-
            tored. By default, it watches /usr/spool/mail/*username*, where
            username is your login name.

    –volume *percentage*
            This option specifies how loud the bell should be rung when
            new mail comes in.

    The following standard X Toolkit command line arguments are commonly
    used with *xbiff*:

    –display *display*
            This option specifies the X server to contact.

    –geometry *geometry*
            This option specifies the prefered size and position of the mail-
            box window. The mailbox is 48 pixels wide and 48 pixels high
            and will be centered in the window.

    –bg *color*
            This option specifies the color to use for the background of the
            window. The default is "white."

    –bd *color*
            This option specifies the color to use for the border of the win-
            dow. The default is "black."

    –bw *number*
            This option specifies the width in pixels of the border surround-
            ing the window.

    –fg *color*
            This option specifies the color to use for the foreground of the
            window. The default is "black."

–rv   This option indicates that reverse video should be simulated by swapping the foreground and background colors.

–xrm *resourcestring*
This option specifies a resource string to be used. This is especially useful for setting resources that do not have separate command line options.

X DEFAULTS
This program uses the *Mailbox* widget in the X Toolkit. It understands all of the core resource names and classes as well as:

checkCommand (class **CheckCommand**)
Specifies a shell command to be executed to check for new mail rather than examining the size of **file**. The specified string value is used as the argument to a *system*(3) call and may therefore contain i/o redirection. A successful (zero) exit status should indicate that new mail is waiting.

file (class **File**)
Specifies the name of the file to monitor. The default is to watch /usr/spool/mail/*username*, where *username* is your login name.

onceOnly (class **Boolean**)
Specifies that the bell is only rung the first time new mail is found and is not rung again until at least one interval has passed with no mail waiting. The window will continue to indicate the presence of new mail until it has been retrieved.

width (class **Width**)
Specifies the width of the mailbox.

height (class **Height**)
Specifies the height of the mailbox.

update (class **Interval**)
Specifies the frequency in seconds at which the mail should be checked.

volume (class **Volume**)
Specifies how load the bell should be rung. The default is 33 percent.

foreground (class **Foreground**)
Specifies the color for the foreground. The default is "black" since the core default for background is "white."

reverseVideo (class **ReverseVideo**)
Specifies that the foreground and background should be reversed.

ACTIONS
The *Mailbox* widget provides the following actions for use in event translations:

check() This action causes the widget to check for new mail and display the flag appropriately.

unset() This action causes the widget to lower the flag until new mail comes in.

set()   This action causes the widget to raise the flag until the user resets it.

The default translation is

<ButtonPress>: unset()

ENVIRONMENT
> **DISPLAY**
>> to get the default host and display number.
>
> **XENVIRONMENT**
>> to get the name of a resource file that overrides the global resources stored in the RESOURCE_MANAGER property.

SEE ALSO
> X(1), xrdb(1), stat(2)

BUGS
> The mailbox bitmaps are ugly.

COPYRIGHT
> Copyright 1988, Massachusetts Institute of Technology.
> See *X(1)* for a full statement of rights and permissions.

AUTHOR
> Jim Fulton, MIT X Consortium
> Additional hacks by Ralph Swick, DEC/MIT Project Athena

NAME

xbmtopbm - convert X11 and X10 bitmaps into portable bitmaps

SYNOPSIS

xbmtopbm [bitmapfile]

DESCRIPTION

Reads an X11 or X10 bitmap as input. Produces a portable bitmap as output.

SEE ALSO

pbmtoxbm(1), pbmtox10bm(1), pbm(5)

AUTHOR

Copyright (C) 1988 by Jef Poskanzer.

Permission to use, copy, modify, and distribute this software and its documentation for any purpose and without fee is hereby granted, provided that the above copyright notice appear in all copies and that both that copyright notice and this permission notice appear in supporting documentation. This software is provided "as is" without express or implied warranty.

NAME
>   xcalc – scientific calculator for X

SYNOPSIS
>   **xcalc** [-display *display*]   [-bw *pixels*] [-stip] [-rv] [-rpn] [-analog] [-
>   geometry *geometry*]

DESCRIPTION
>   *Xcalc* is a scientific calculator desktop accessory that can emulate a TI-30,
>   an HP-10C, and a slide rule.

OPTIONS
>   **–display** *displayname*
>   >   This option specifies the X server to contact.
>
>   **–geometry** *geometry*
>   >   This option specifies the size and placement of the top level win-
>   >   dow. By default, the minimum size will be used. Note that
>   >   your window manager may require you to place it explicitly any-
>   >   way.
>
>   **–fg** *color*
>   >   This option specifies the foreground color to use.
>
>   **–bg** *color*
>   >   This option specifies the background color to use.
>
>   **–bw** *pixels*
>   >   This option specifies the border width in pixels.
>
>   **–stip**   This option indicates that the background of the calculator
>   >   should be drawn using a stipple of the foreground and back-
>   >   ground colors. On monochrome displays this makes for a nicer
>   >   display.
>
>   **–rv**   This option indicates that reverse video should be used.
>
>   **–rpn**   This option indicates that Reverse Polish Notation should be
>   >   used. In this mode the calculator will look and behave like an
>   >   HP-10C. Without this flag, it will emulate a TI-30.
>
>   **–analog** This option indicates that a slide rule should be used.

OPERATION
>   *Pointer Usage:* Most operations are done with the Button1 (usually left-
>   most button on the pointer). The only exception is that pressing the AC
>   key on the TI calculator with Button3 (usually on the right) will exit the
>   calculator.
>
>   *Key Usage (Normal mode):* The number keys, the +/- key, and the +, -, *,
>   /, and = keys all do exactly what you would expect them to. It should be
>   noted that the operators obey the standard rules of precedence. Thus,
>   entering "3+4*5=" results in "23", not "35". The parentheses can be used
>   to override this. For example, "(1+2+3)*(4+5+6)=" results in "6*15=90".
>   The non-obvious keys are detailed below.
>
>   **1/x** replaces the number in the display with its reciprocal.
>
>   **x^2** squares the number in the display.
>
>   **SQRT** takes the square root of the number in the display.
>
>   **CE/C** when pressed once, clears the number in the display without clear-
>   ing the state of the machine. Allows you to re-enter a number if you
>   screw it up. Pressing it twice clears the state, also.

AC clears everything, the display, the state, the memory, everything. Pressing it with the right button 'turns off' the calculator, in that it exits the program. Somewhat more equivalent to throwing the calculator in the trash, if we were to pursue the analogy.

INV inverts the meaning of the function keys. See the individual function keys for details.

sin computes the sine of the number in the display, as interpreted by the current DRG mode (see DRG, below). If inverted, it computes the arcsine.

cos computes the cosine, or arccosine when inverted.

tan computes the tangent, or arctangent when inverted.

DRG changes the DRG mode, as indicated by 'DEG', 'RAD', or 'GRAD' at the bottom of number window of the calculator. When in 'DEG' mode, numbers in the display are taken as being degrees. In 'RAD' mode, numbers are in radians, and in 'GRAD' mode, numbers are in gradians. When inverted, the DRG key has the nifty feature of converting degrees to radians to gradians and vice-versa. Example: put the calculator into 'DEG' mode, and type "45 INV DRG". The display should now show something along the lines of ".785398", which is 45 degrees converted to radians.

e the constant 'e'. (2.7182818...)

EE used for entering exponential numbers. For example, to enter "-2.3E-4" you'd type "2 . 3 +/- EE 4 +/-"

log calculates the log (base 10) of the number in the display. When inverted, it raises "10.0" to the number in the display. For example, typing "3 INV log" should result in "1000".

ln calcuates the log (base e) of the number in the display. When inverted, it raises "e" to the number in the display. For example, typing "e ln" should result in "1"

y^x raises the number on the left to the power of the number on the right. For example "2 y^x 3 =" results in "8", which is 2^3. For a further example, "(1+2+3) y^x (1+2) =" equals "6 y^x 3" which equals "216".

PI the constant 'pi'. (3.1415927....)

x! computes the factorial of the number in the display. The number in the display must be an integer in the range 0-500, though, depending on your math library, it might overflow long before that.

STO copies the number in the display to the memory location.

RCL copies the number from the memory location to the display.

SUM adds the number in the display to the number in the memory location.

EXC swaps the number in the display with the number in the memory location.

Key Usage (RPN mode): The number keys, CHS (change sign), +, -, *, /, and ENTR keys all do exactly what you would expect them to do. Many of the remaining keys are the same as in normal mode. The differences are detailed below.

<- is a backspace key that can be used while typing a number. It will erase digits from the display.

ON clears everything, the display, the state, the memory, everything. Pressing it with the right button 'turns off' the calculator, in that it exits the program. Somewhat more equivalent to throwing the calculator in the trash, if we were to pursue the analogy.

INV inverts the meaning of the function keys. This would be the "f" key on an HP calculator, but xcalc does not have the resolution to display multiple legends on each key. See the individual function keys for details.

10^x raises "10.0" to the number in the top of the stack. When inverted, it calculates the log (base 10) of the number in the display.

e^x raises "e" to the number in the top of the stack. When inverted, it calcuates the log (base e) of the number in the display.

STO copies the number in the top of the stack to a memory location. There are 10 memory locations. The desired memory is specified by following this key with pressing a digit key.

RCL pushes the number from the specified memory location onto the stack.

SUM adds the number on top of the stack to the number in the specified memory location.

x:y exchanges the numbers in the top two stack positions.

R v rolls the stack downward. When inverted, it rolls the stack upward.

blank these keys were used for programming functions on the HP11-C. Their functionality has not been duplicated here.

KEYBOARD EQUIVALENTS

If you have the pointer in the xcalc window, you can use the keyboard to speed entry, as almost all of the calculator keys have a keyboard equivalent. The number keys, the operator keys, and the parentheses all have the obvious equivalent. The less-obvious equivalents are as follows:

```
n: +/-          !: x!
p: PI           e: EE
l: ln           ^: y^x
i: INV          s: sin
c: cos          t: tan
d: DRG          BS, DEL:  CE/C ("<-" in RPN mode)
CR: ENTR        q: quit
```

COLOR USAGE

Xcalc uses a lot of colors, given the opportunity. In the default case, it will just use two colors (Foreground and Background) for everything. This works out nicely. However, if you're a color fanatic you can specify the colors used for the number keys, the operator (+-*/=) keys, the function keys, the display, and the icon.

X DEFAULTS

The program uses the routine *XGetDefault(3X)* to read defaults, so its resource names are all capitalized.

BorderWidth
Specifies the width of the border. The default is 2.

ReverseVideo
Indicates that reverse video should be used.

Stipple Indicates that the background should be stippled. The default is "on" for monochrome displays, and "off" for color displays.

Mode   Specifies the default mode. Allowable values are *rpn, analog.*

Foreground
          Specifies the default color used for borders and text.

Background
          Specifies the default color used for the background.

NKeyFore, NKeyBack
          Specifies the colors used for the number keys.

OKeyFore, OKeyBack
          Specifies the colors used for the operator keys.

FKeyFore, FKeyBack
          Specifies the colors used for the function keys.

DispFore, DispBack
          Specifies the colors used for the display.

IconFore, IconBack
          Specifies the colors used for the icon.

EXAMPLES
          If you're running on a monochrome display, you shouldn't need any .Xde-
          faults entries for xcalc. On a color display, you might want to try the fol-
          lowing in normal mode:

xcalc.Foreground:	Black
xcalc.Background:	LightSteelBlue
xcalc.NKeyFore:	Black
xcalc.NKeyBack:	White
xcalc.OKeyFore:	Aquamarine
xcalc.OKeyBack:	DarkSlateGray
xcalc.FKeyFore:	White
xcalc.FKeyBack:	#900
xcalc.DispFore:	Yellow
xcalc.DispBack:	#777
xcalc.IconFore:	Red
xcalc.IconBack:	White

SEE ALSO
          X(1), xrdb(1)

BUGS
          The calculator doesn't resize.

          The slide rule and HP mode may or may not work correctly.

          This application should really be implemented with the X Toolkit. It
          would make a very good example of a compound widget.

COPYRIGHT
          Copyright 1988, Massachusetts Institute of Technology.
          See *X(1)* for a full statement of rights and permissions.

AUTHORS
          John Bradley, University of Pennsylvania
          Mark Rosenstein, MIT Project Athena

NAME

xcalendar - calendar with a notebook for X11

SYNTAX

xcalendar [month [year]]

DESCRIPTION

The *xcalendar* is a simple interactive calendar program with a notebook capability. It is build on the X Toolkit and the Athena Widgets.

If month and year are not provided on the command line they are assumed to be current. To achieve pleasant visual effect you have to load a resource data base to the server. The default database is provided with this program and is also included in this text. Consult the man page for xrdb(1).

INTERACTIONS

Clicking the left mouse button on a day will start a text editor. You can edit and save a text.This text will be associated with the day. You can later on read and edit this text when you open the editor for the same day. The text is saved in a file in the directory ˜/Calendar. The editor lets you also clear an entry associated with a particular day.

You can highlight all entries in a month by invoking the function ShowEntries. By default this function is called when the left mouse button is pressed in the title window (where day, month and a year are displayed). Pressing again the same button will unhighlight the entries.

MISSING FEATURES

Currently, to view another month you have to start another process and specify the month and year on the command line. You can run several xcalendars at the same time. However, it would be nice to be able to scroll or browse through the calendar.

To remove all entries in a particular month you have to use your system's commands. The naming scheme for the files makes it easy : the command "rm ˜/Calendar/xc*sep1988 " on UNIX(TM) will remove all entries from september 1988. The facility to do that from the xcalendar should be provided.

One can imagine many other useful features. For example automatic parsing of the current day entry in search for appointments to trigger alarms (reminders) at the approriate time. Well, maybe one day...

RESOURCES

The resource data base lets you alter the visual appearance of the program. You can change fonts, border widths, labels, and other resources used by widgets. One use of this facility is to change names of week days and months.

Here are the names of widgets you can use to set various resources:

```
XCalendar    - class of the application
xcalendar    - top level form
controls     - control panel
quitButton   - quit button
helpButton   - help button
date         - date label
calendar     - calendar frame
daynumbers   - day numbers frame
1-49         - day number buttons
daynames     - day names frame
MON,TUE,WED,THU,FRI,SAT,SUN - day name buttons
```

```
            helpWindow   - help window
            dayEditor    - editor popup
            editorFrame  - editor frame
            editorTitle  - editor title
            editor       - editor
            editorControls- control panel
            doneButton   - done button
            saveButton   - save button
            clearEntry   - clear entry button
```

Application specific resources:

3

    reverseVideoMark - if True the entries are highlighted in reverse
        video; default True for black and white,
        and False for color displays;

    setMarkBackground - if True and reverseVideoMark is False the
        entries are highlighted by setting background
        to markBackground ;

    markBackground   - background color for highlighting entries;

    setMarkForeground - analogous to setMarkBackground;

    markForeground   - foreground color for highlighting entries;

    setMarkBackground and *setMarkForeground* can take any
combination of values.

    january,february,..,december - these resources can be used for
        changing names of months;
    firstDay - an integer between 1-7, indicating the day to start a
        week with, default: 1 (Monday);
    markOnStartup   - if True mark the entries upon startup,
        default: False;
    helpFile   - full pathname of the xcalendar.hlp file,
        default: /usr/lib/X11/xcalendar.hlp;
    textBufferSize - maximum size of the text buffer in the day editor
        default: 2048;

DEFAULT RESOURCE DATA BASE:
```
            XCalendar*Font: vtsingle
            XCalendar*Background: wheat
            XCalendar*BorderWidth:        2
            XCalendar*calendar*borderWidth: 0
            XCalendar*controls*borderWidth: 0
            XCalendar*date*font:          8x13bold
            XCalendar*date*borderWidth: 0
            XCalendar*daynames*font:               8x13bold

            XCalendar*daynames*Background: PaleGreen

            XCalendar*daynames.SUN*Foreground: Red
            XCalendar*daynames.SAT*Foreground: DarkGreen

            XCalendar*daynumbers.7*Foreground: Red
            XCalendar*daynumbers.14*Foreground: Red
```

```
XCalendar*daynumbers.21*Foreground: Red
XCalendar*daynumbers.28*Foreground: Red
XCalendar*daynumbers.35*Foreground: Red
XCalendar*daynumbers.42*Foreground: Red


XCalendar*controls*helpButton*Background: DarkGreen
XCalendar*controls*helpButton*Foreground: wheat
XCalendar*controls*quitButton*Background: DarkGreen
XCalendar*controls*quitButton*Foreground: wheat


XCalendar*daynumbers*Foreground: DarkGreen
XCalendar*editorTitle*Background: PaleGreen
XCalendar*editorTitle*Foreground: Red
XCalendar*editorControls*Background: PaleGreen
XCalendar*editorControls*doneButton*Background: Red
XCalendar*editorControls*doneButton*Foreground: wheat
XCalendar*editorControls*saveButton*Background: Red
XCalendar*editorControls*saveButton*Foreground: wheat
XCalendar*editorControls*clearEntry*Background: DarkGreen
XCalendar*editorControls*clearEntry*Foreground: wheat

XCalendar*dayEditor*geometry: 300x150
XCalendar*dayEditor*editorTitle*font: 8x13bold
XCalendar*dayEditor*editorTitle*Foreground: DarkGreen

XCalendar*helpWindow*geometry: 600x350
XCalendar*helpWindow*editorTitle*font: 8x13bold

XCalendar*doneButton*Label: done
XCalendar*editorTitle*Label: Help
XCalendar*helpButton*Label: help
XCalendar*quitButton*Label: quit
XCalendar*saveButton*Label: save

XCalendar*markBackground: PaleGreen
XCalendar*setMarkBackground: True
```

FILES

$HOME/Calendar/*

SEE ALSO

xrdb(1)

BUGS

Save button handler in the editor cannot detect when a text is pasted. Workaround : type something to the ditor to activate save button.

AUTHOR

Copyright 1988 by Massachusetts Institute of Technology Roman J. Budzianowski, MIT Project Athena

NAME

    xclipboard - X clipboard client

SYNOPSIS

    xclipboard [*-toolkitoption* ...] [-w] [-nw]

DESCRIPTION

    The *xclipboard* program is used to collect and display text selections that are sent to the CLIP_BOARD by other clients. It is typically used to gather together and hold a block of text that has been selected from a variety of different places.

    Since *xclipboard* uses a Text Widget to display the contents of the clipboard, text sent to the CLIP_BOARD may be re-selected for use in other applications.

    An *xclipboard* window has the following buttons across the top:

        quit   When this button is pressed, *xclipboard* exits.

        erase When this button is pressed, the contents of the text window are erased.

OPTIONS

    The *xclipboard* program accepts all of the standard X Toolkit command line options as well as the following:

    -w   This option indicates that lines of text that are too long to be displayed on one line in the clipboard should wrap around to the following lines.

    -nw   This option indicates that long lines of text should not wrap around.

SENDING TO CLIPBOARD

    Text is copied to the clipboard whenever a client asserts ownership of the **CLIP_BOARD** selection. Examples of event bindings that a user may wish to include in his/her resource configuration file to use the clipboard are:

```
*VT100.Translations: #override \
      Button1 <Btn2Down>:              select-end(CLIPBOARD) \n\
      Button1 <Btn2Up>:                ignore()

*Text.Translations: #override \
      Button1 <Btn2Down>:              extend-end(CLIPBOARD)
```

X DEFAULTS

    This program accepts all of the standard X Toolkit resource names and classes as well as:

    wordWrap (class **WordWrap**)

        This resource specifies whether or not lines of text should wrap around to the following lines. The default is *no*.

SEE ALSO

    X(1), xcutsel(1), xterm(1), individual client documentation for how to make a selection and send it to the CLIP_BOARD.

BUGS

    The erase button is not yet implemented.

    It would be nice to have a way of specifying the file in which the clipboard contents are saved.

FILES
    /usr/lib/X11/app-defaults/XClipboard - specifies required resources
COPYRIGHT
    Copyright 1988, Massachusetts Institute of Technology
    See *X(1)* for a full statement of rights and permissions.
AUTHOR
    Ralph R. Swick, DEC/MIT Project Athena

NAME
      xclock - analog / digital clock for X
SYNOPSIS
      xclock [-*toolkitoption* ...] [-option ...]
DESCRIPTION
      The *xclock* program displays the time in analog or digital form. The time
      is continuously updated at a frequency which may be specified by the
      user. This program is nothing more than a wrapper around the Athena
      Clock widget.

OPTIONS
      Xclock accepts all of the standard X Toolkit command line options along
      with the additional options listed below:

      –help   This option indicates that a brief summary of the allowed
                 options should be printed on the standard error.

      –analog This option indicates that a conventional 12 hour clock face with
                 tick marks and hands should be used. This is the default.

      –digital This option indicates that a 24 hour digital clock should be used.

      –chime   This option indicates that the clock should chime once on the
                 half hour and twice on the hour.

      –hd *color*
                 This option specifies the color of the hands on an analog clock.
                 The default is *black*.

      –hl *color*
                 This option specifies the color of the edges of the hands on an
                 analog clock, and is only useful on color displays. The default
                 is *black*.

      –update *seconds*
                 This option specifies the frequency in seconds at which *xclock*
                 should update its display. If the clock is obscured and then
                 exposed, it will be updated immediately. A value of less than
                 30 seconds will enable a second hand on an analog clock. The
                 default is 60 seconds.

      –padding *number*
                 This option specifies the width in pixels of the padding between
                 the window border and clock text or picture. The default is 10
                 on a digital clock and 8 on an analog clock.

      The following standard X Toolkit command line arguments are commonly
      used with *xclock:*

      –bg *color*
                 This option specifies the color to use for the background of the
                 window. The default is *white*.

      –bd *color*
                 This option specifies the color to use for the border of the win-
                 dow. The default is *black*.

      –bw *number*
                 This option specifies the width in pixels of the border surround-
                 ing the window.

      –fg *color*
                 This option specifies the color to use for displaying text. The
                 default is *black*.

-**fn** *font* This option specifies the font to be used for displaying normal text. The default is *6x10*.

-**rv** This option indicates that reverse video should be simulated by swapping the foreground and background colors.

-**geometry** *geometry*
This option specifies the prefered size and position of the clock window.

-**display** *host:display*
This option specifies the X server to contact.

-**xrm** *resourcestring*
This option specifies a resource string to be used.

X DEFAULTS

This program uses the *Clock* widget in the X Toolkit. It understands all of the core resource names and classes as well as:

width (class **Width**)
Specifies the width of the clock. The default for analog clocks is 164 pixels; the default for digital clocks is whatever is needed to hold the clock when displayed in the chosen font.

height (class **Height**)
Specifies the height of the clock. The default for analog clocks is 164 pixels; the default for digital clocks is whatever is needed to hold the clock when displayed in the chosen font.

update (class **Interval**)
Specifies the frequency in seconds at which the time should be redisplayed.

foreground (class **Foreground**)
Specifies the color for the tic marks. The default is *black* since the core default for background is *white*.

hands (class **Foreground**)
Specifies the color of the insides of the clock's hands.

highlight (class **Foreground**)
Specifies the color used to highlight the clock's hands.

analog (class **Boolean**)
Specifies whether or not an analog clock should be used instead of a digital one. The default is True.

chime (class **Boolean**)
Specifies whether or not a bell should be rung on the hour and half hour.

padding (class **Margin**)
Specifies the amount of internal padding in pixels to be used. The default is 8.

font (class **Font**)
Specifies the font to be used for the digital clock. Note that variable width fonts currently will not always display correctly.

reverseVideo (class **ReverseVideo**)
Specifies that the foreground and background colors should be reversed.

SEE ALSO

X(1), xrdb(1), time(3C), Athena Clock widget

BUGS

Xclock believes the system clock.

When in digital mode, the string should be centered automatically.

When specifying a time offset, the grammar requires an hours field but if only minutes are given they will be quietly ignored. A negative offset of less than 1 hour is treated as a positive offset.

Digital clock windows default to the analog clock size.

Border color has to be explicitly specified when reverse video is used.

COPYRIGHT

Copyright 1988, Massachusetts Institute of Technology.
See *X(1)* for a full statement of rights and permissions.

AUTHORS

Tony Della Fera (MIT-Athena, DEC)
Dave Mankins (MIT-Athena, BBN)
Ed Moy (UC Berkeley)

3

NAME
         xcolors - display all X11 color names and colors

SYNOPSIS
         xcolors [*X Toolkit option*] ...

DESCRIPTION
         xcolors reads in the rgb.txt file that defines symbolic names for RGB
         colors and displays all colors found. Accepts all standard toolkit options.

FILES
         X11 color names and values.

BUGS
         It requires every color to be defined twice or more. (It uses the last
         definition since that is usually the capitalized name).
         Dumps core if the server was started with different dbm databases.

AUTHOR
         Paul Vixie (vix@ubvax.ub.com)

NAME
        xcutsel - interchange between cut buffer and selection

SYNOPSIS
        xcutsel [*-toolkitoption* ...] [-selection *selection*] [-cutbuffer *number*]

DESCRIPTION
        The *xcutsel* program is used to copy the current selection into a cut buffer
        and to make a selection that contains the current contents of the cut
        buffer. It acts as a bridge between applications that don't support selec-
        tions and those that do.

        By default, *xcutsel* will use the selection named PRIMARY and the cut
        buffer CUT_BUFFER0. Either or both of these can be overridden by
        command line arguments or by resources.

        An *xcutsel* window has the following buttons:

        quit   When this button is pressed, *xcutsel* exits. Any selections held
                    by *xcutsel* are automatically released.

        copy PRIMARY to 0
                    When this button is pressed, *xcutsel* copies the current selection
                    into the cut buffer.

        copy 0 to PRIMARY
                    When this button is pressed, *xcutsel* converts the current contents
                    of the cut buffer into the selection.

        The button labels reflect the selection and cutbuffer selected by command
        line options or through the resource database.

        When the "copy 0 to PRIMARY" button is activated, the button will
        remain inverted as long as *xcutsel* remains the owner of the selection.
        This serves to remind you which client owns the current selection. Note
        that the value of the selection remains constant; if the cutbuffer is
        changed, you must again activate the copy button to retrieve the new
        value when desired.

OPTIONS
        Xcutsel accepts all of the standard X Toolkit command line options as
        well as the following:

        –selection *name*
                    This option specifies the name of the selection to use. The
                    default is PRIMARY. The only supported abbreviations for this
                    option are "-select", "-sel" and "-s", as the standard toolkit
                    option "-selectionTimeout" has a similar name.

        –cutbuffer *number*
                    This option specifies the cut buffer to use. The default is cut
                    buffer 0.

X DEFAULTS
        This program accepts all of the standard X Toolkit resource names and
        classes as well as:

        selection (class **Selection**)
                    This resource specifies the name of the selection to use. The
                    default is PRIMARY.

        cutBuffer (class **CutBuffer**)
                    This resource specifies the number of the cut buffer to use. The
                    default is 0.

WIDGET NAMES
> The following instance names may be used when user configuration of the labels in them is desired:

> **sel-cut** (class **Command**)
>> This is the "copy SELECTION to BUFFER" button.

> **cut-sel** (class **Command**)
>> This is the "copy BUFFER to SELECTION" button.

> **quit** (class **Command**)
>> This is the "quit" button.

SEE ALSO
> X(1), xclipboard(1), xterm(1), text widget documentation, individual client documentation for how to make a selection.

BUGS
> There is no way to change the name of the selection or the number of the cut buffer while the program is running.

COPYRIGHT
> Copyright 1988, Massachusetts Institute of Technology
> See *X(1)* for a full statement of rights and permissions.

AUTHOR
> Ralph R. Swick, DEC/MIT Project Athena

NAME
  xdm – X Display Manager
SYNOPSIS
  xdm [-config *configuration_file*] [-daemon] [-debug *debug_level*] [-error
  error_log_file]   [-nodaemon]   [-resources   *resource_file*]   [-server
  server_entry] [-session *session_program*] [-xrm *resource_specification*]
DESCRIPTION
  Xdm manages a collection of X displays, both local and possibly remote
  — the emergence of X terminals guided the design of several parts of this
  system. It is designed to provide services similar to that provided by init,
  getty and login on character terminals: prompting for login/password,
  authenticating the user and running a "session".

  A "session" is defined by the lifetime of a particular unix process; in the
  traditional character-based terminal world, it is the user's login shell process. In the *xdm* context, it is an arbitrary session manager. This is
  because in a windowing environment, a user's login shell process would
  not necessarily have any terminal-like interface with which to connect.

  Until real session managers become widely available, the typical *xdm* sub-
  stitute would be either a window manager with an exit option, or a terminal emulator running a shell - with the condition that the lifetime of the
  terminal emulator is the lifetime of the shell process that it is running -
  thus degenerating the X session to an emulation of the character-based terminal session.

  When the session is terminated, *xdm* resets the X server and (optionally)
  restarts the whole process.

  Because *xdm* provides the first interface that users will see, it is designed
  to be simple to use and easy to customize to the needs of a particular site.
  Xdm has many options, most of which have reasonable defaults. Browse
  through the various sections, picking and choosing the things you want to
  change. Pay particular attention to the **Xsession** section, which will
  describe how to set up the style of session desired.

OPTIONS
  First, note that all of these options, except **-config**, specify values which
  can also be specified in the configuration file as resources.

  -config *configuration_file*
          Specifies a resource file which specifies the remaining
          configuration parameters. If no file is specified and the file
          /usr/lib/X11/xdm/xdm-config exists, *xdm* will use it.

  -daemon
          Specifies   "true"   as   the   value   for   the
          DisplayManager.daemonMode resource. This makes *xdm* close
          all file descriptors, disassociate the controlling terminal and put
          itself in the background when it first starts up (just like the host
          of other daemons). It is the default behaviour.

  -debug *debug_level*
          Specifies the numeric value for the **DisplayManager.debugLevel**
          resource. A non-zero value causes *xdm* to print piles of debug-
          ging statements to the terminal; it also disables the
          DisplayManager.daemon Mode resource, forcing *xdm* to run syn-
          cronously.

  -error *error_log_file*
          Specifies   the   value   for   the   **DisplayManager.errorLogFile**

resource. This file contains errors from *xdm* as well as anything written to stderr by the various scripts and programs run during the progress of the session.

-nodaemon
  Specifies "false" as the value for the **DisplayManager.daemonMode** resource.

-resources *resource_file*
  Specifies the value for the **DisplayManager*resources** resource. This file is loaded using *xrdb (1)* to specify configuration parameters for the authentication widget.

-server *server_entry*
  Specifies the value for the **DisplayManager.servers** resource. See the section below which describes this resource in depth.

-xrm *resource_specification*
  This allows an arbitrary resource to be specified, just as most toolkit applications.

RESOURCES
  At many stages the actions of *xdm* can be controlled through the use of the configuration file, which is in the familiar X resource format. See Jim Fulton's article on resource files (*doc/tutorials/resources.txt*) for a description of the format. Some resources modify the behavior of *xdm* on all displays, while others modify its behavior on one single display. Where actions relate to a specific display, the display name is inserted into the resource name between "DisplayManager" and the final resource name segment. For example, **DisplayManager.expo.0.startup** is the name of the resource which defines the startup shell file on the "expo:0" display. Because the resource manager uses colons to separate the name of the resource from its value, *xdm* substitutes dots for the colons when generating the resource name.

DisplayManager.servers
  This resource lists the collection of servers (separated by newlines) which are local to this host. If the resource value begins with a slash, it is assumed to be the name of a Unix file containing the list. Each entry consists of three parts: a display name, a display type, and a type-dependent entry. A typical entry for local display number 0 would be:

  :0 local /usr/bin/X11/X :0

  The display types are:

  local   a local display which receives multiple sessions
  localTransient   a local display which has only one session run
  foreign   a remote display which receives multiple sessions
  transient   a remote display which has only one session run

  The display name must be something that can be passed in the **-display** option to any X program. This string is used in the display-specific resources to specify the particular display, so be careful to match the names (e.g. use ":0 local /usr/bin/X11/X :0" instead of "unix:0 local /usr/bin/X11/X :0" if your other resources are specified as "DisplayManager..0.session").

The type-dependent entry for local servers is a program name and its arguments. The program name should be an absolute Unix pathname as *xdm* does not search through the directories of the PATH environment variable.

For foreign servers, the type-dependent entry is ignored, but must contain at least one word. These servers are typically X terminals which want sessions run from a file server. In the future, it is expected that the X terminal will negotiate the session startup, but for now it is fixed by this resource specification.

DisplayManager.errorLogFile

Error output is normally directed at the system console. To redirect it simply set this resource to any file name. A method to send these messages to syslog should be developed for systems which support it; however the wide variety of "standard" interfaces precludes any system-independent implementation. This file also contains any output directed to stderr by *Xstartup, Xsession and Xreset*, so it will contain descriptions of problems in those scripts as well.

DisplayManager.DISPLAY.resources

This resource specifies the name of the file to be loaded by *xrdb (1)* as the resource data-base onto the root window of screen 0 of the display. This resource data base is loaded just before the authentication procedure is started, so it can control the appearance of the "login" window. See the section below on the authentication widget which describes the various resources which are appropriate to place in this file. There is no default value for this resource, but the conventional name is **Xresources**.

DisplayManager.DISPLAY.xrdb

Specifies the program used to load the resources. By default, *xdm* uses */usr/bin/X11/xrdb*.

DisplayManager.DISPLAY.startup

This specifies a program which is run (as root) after the authentication process succeeds. By default, no program is run. The conventional name for a file used here is *Xstartup*. See the **Xstartup** section below.

DisplayManager.DISPLAY.session

This specifies the session to be executed (not running as root). By default, */usr/bin/X11/xterm* is run. The conventional name is *Xsession*. See the **Xsession** session below.

DisplayManager.DISPLAY.reset

This specifies a program which is run (as root) after the session terminates. Again, by default no program is run. The conventional name is *Xreset*. See the **Xreset** section further on in this document.

DisplayManager.DISPLAY.openDelay

DisplayManager.DISPLAY.openRepeat

DisplayManager.DISPLAY.openTimeout

These numeric resources control the behavior of *xdm* when attempting to open intransigent servers. **openDelay** is the length of the pause (in seconds) between successive attempts. **openRepeat** is the number of attempts to make, and **openTimeout** is the amount of time to wait while actually attempting the open (i.e. the maximum time spent in the *connect (2)* syscall). After **openRepeat** attempts have been made, or if **openTimeout** seconds elapse in any particular attempt, *xdm* terminates and restarts the server, attempting to connect again. Although this behaviour may seem arbitrary, it has been empirically developed and works quite well on most systems. The default values are 5 for **openDelay**, 5 for **openRepeat** and 30 for **openTimeout**.

DisplayManager.DISPLAY.terminateServer

This boolean resource specifies whether the X server should be terminated when a session terminates (instead of resetting it). This option can be used when the server tends to grow without bound over time in order to limit the amount of time the server is run. The default value is "FALSE".

DisplayManager.DISPLAY.userPath

Xdm sets the PATH environment variable for the session to this value. It should be a colon separated list of directories, see *sh(1)* for a full description. The default value can be specified in the X system configuration file with DefUserPath, frequently it is set to ":/bin:/usr/bin:/usr/bin/X11:/usr/ucb".

DisplayManager.DISPLAY.systemPath

Xdm sets the PATH environment variable for the startup and reset scripts to the value of this resource. The default for this resource is specified with the DefaultSystemPath entry in the system configuration   file,   but   it   is   frequently "/etc:/bin:/usr/bin:/usr/bin/X11:/usr/ucb". Note the conspicuous absence of "." from this entry. This is a good practise to follow for root; it avoids many common trojan horse system penetration schemes.

DisplayManager.DISPLAY.systemShell

Xdm sets the SHELL environment variable for the startup and reset scripts to the value of this resource. By default, it is "/bin/sh".

DisplayManager.DISPLAY.failsafeClient

If the default session fails to execute, *xdm* will fall back to this program. This program is executed with no arguments, but executes using the same environment variables as the session would have had (see the section "Xsession" below). By default, */usr/bin/X11/xterm* is used.

CONTROLLING THE SERVER

Xdm controls local servers using Unix signals. SIGHUP is expected to reset the server, closing all client connections and performing other clean up duties. SIGTERM is expected to terminate the server. If these signals do not perform the expected actions, *xdm* will not perform properly.

To control remote servers, *xdm* searches the window heirarchy on the display and uses the protocol request KillClient in an attempt to clean up the terminal for the next session. This may not actually kill all of the clients, as only those which have created windows will be noticed. This is expected to change when better X terminal support is designed.

CONTROLLING XDM

Xdm responds to two signals: SIGHUP and SIGTERM. When sent a SIGHUP, *xdm* rereads the file specified by the **DisplayManager.servers** resource and notices if entries have been added or removed. If a new entry has been added, *xdm* starts a session on the associated display.

Entries which have been removed are disabled immediately, meaning that any session in progress will be terminated without notice, and no new session will be started.

When sent a SIGTERM, *xdm* terminates all sessions in progress and exits. This can be used when shutting down the system.

AUTHENTICATION WIDGET

The authentication widget is an application which reads a name/password pair from the keyboard. As this is a toolkit client, nearly every imaginable parameter can be controlled with a resource. Resources for this widget should be put into the file named by **DisplayManager.DISPLAY.resources**. All of these have reasonable default values, so it is not necessary to specify any of them.

xlogin.Login.width, xlogin.Login.height, xlogin.Login.x, xlogin.Login.y
> The geometry of the login widget is normally computed automatically. If you wish to position it elsewhere, specify each of these resources.

xlogin.Login.foreground
> The color used to display the typed-in user name.

xlogin.Login.font
> The font used to display the typed-in user name.

xlogin.Login.greeting
> A string which identifies this window. The default is "Welcome to the X Window System".

xlogin.Login.greetFont
> The font used to display the greeting.

xlogin.Login.greetColor
> The color used to display the greeting.

xlogin.Login.namePrompt
> The string displayed to prompt for a user name. *Xrdb* strips trailing white space from resource values, so to add spaces at the end of the prompt (usually a nice thing), add a character which is *not* a space or a tab, and doesn't have any bits drawn when displayed. In the default font, a control-A suffices. The default is "Login: "

xlogin.Login.passwdPrompt
> The string displayed to prompt for a password. The default is "Password: ".

xlogin.Login.promptFont
> The font used to display both prompts.

xlogin.Login.promptColor
> The color used to display both prompts.

xlogin.Login.fail
> A message which is displayed when the authentication fails. The default is "Login Failed".

xlogin.Login.failFont
> The font used to display the failure message.

xlogin.Login.failColor
> The color used to display the failure message.

xlogin.Login.failTimeout
> The time (in seconds) that the fail message is displayed. The

default is 30 seconds.

xlogin.Login.translations

This specifies the translations used for the login widget. Refer to the X Toolkit documentation for a complete discussion on translations. The default translation table is:

Ctrl<Key>H:	delete-previous-character() \n\
Ctrl<Key>D:	delete-character() \n\
Ctrl<Key>B:	move-backward-character() \n\
Ctrl<Key>F:	move-forward-character() \n\
Ctrl<Key>A:	move-to-begining() \n\
Ctrl<Key>E:	move-to-end() \n\
Ctrl<Key>K:	erase-to-end-of-line() \n\
Ctrl<Key>U:	erase-line() \n\
Ctrl<Key>X:	erase-line() \n\
Ctrl<Key>C:	restart-session() \n\
Ctrl<Key>\\:	abort-session() \n\
<Key>BackSpace:	delete-previous-character() \n\
<Key>Delete:	delete-previous-character() \n\
<Key>Return:	finish-field() \n\
<Key>:	insert-char() \

The actions which are supported by the widget are:

delete-previous-character
　　　Erases the character before the cursor.

delete-character
　　　Erases the character after the cursor.

move-backward-character
　　　Moves the cursor backward.

move-forward-character
　　　Moves the cursor forward.

move-to-begining
　　　Moves the cursor to the beginning of the editable text.

move-to-end
　　　Moves the cursor to the end of the editable text.

erase-to-end-of-line
　　　Erases all text after the cursor.

erase-line
　　　Erases the entire text.

finish-field
　　　If the cursor is in the name field, proceeds to the password field; if the cursor is in the password field, check the current name/password pair. If the name/password pair are valid, *xdm* starts the session. Otherwise the failure message is displayed and the user is prompted to try again.

abort-session
　　　Terminates and restarts the server.

abort-display
　　　Terminates the server, disabling it. This is a rash action and is not accessible in the default configuration. It can be used to stop *xdm* when shutting the system down, or when using xdmshell.

restart-session
>   Resets the X server and starts a new session. This can be used
>   when the resources have been changed and you want to test them,
>   or when the screen has been overwritten with system messages.

insert-char
>   Inserts the character typed.

set-session-argument
>   Specifies a single word argument which is passed to the session
>   at startup. See the sections on **Xsession** and **Typical usage**.

The Xstartup file
>   This file is typically a shell script. It is run as "root" and should be very
>   careful about security. This is the place to put commands which make
>   fake entries in /etc/utmp, mount users' home directories from file servers,
>   display the message of the day, or abort the session if logins are not
>   allowed. Various environment variables are set for the use of this script:

DISPLAY	is set to the associated display name
HOME	is set to the home directory of the user
USER	is set to the user name
PATH	is set to the value of **DisplayManager.DISPLAY.systemPath**
SHELL	is set to the value of **DisplayManager.DISPLAY.systemShell**

>   No arguments of any kind are passed to the script. *Xdm* waits until this
>   script exits before starting the user session. If the exit value of this script
>   is non-zero, *xdm* discontinues the session immediately and starts another
>   authentication cycle.

The Xsession program
>   This is the command which is run as the user's session. It is run with the
>   permissions of the authorized user, and has several environment variables
>   specified:

DISPLAY	is set to the associated display name
HOME	is set to the home directory of the user
USER	is set to the user name
PATH	is set to the value of **DisplayManager.DISPLAY.userPath**
SHELL	is set to the user's default shell (from /etc/passwd)

>   At most installations, *Xsession* should look in $HOME for a file *xsession*
>   which would contain commands that each user would like to use as a ses-
>   sion. This would replace the system default session. *Xsession* should also
>   implement the system default session if no user-specified session exists.
>   See the section **Typical Usage** below.

>   An argument may be passed to this program from the authentication
>   widget using the 'set-session-argument' action. This can be used to select
>   different styles of session. One very good use of this feature is to allow
>   the user to escape from the ordinary session when it fails. This would
>   allow users to repair their own *xsession* if it fails, without requiring
>   administrative intervention. The section on typical usage demonstrates
>   this feature.

The Xreset file

Symmetrical with *Xstartup*, this script is run after the user session has terminated. Run as root, it should probably contain commands that undo the effects of commands in *Xstartup*, removing fake entries from */etc/utmp* or unmounting directories from file servers. The collection of environment variables that were passed to *Xstartup* are also given to *Xreset*.

Typical Usage

Actually, *xdm* is designed to operate in such a wide variety of environments that "typical" is probably a misnomer. However, this section will focus on making *xdm* a superior solution to traditional means of starting X from /etc/ttys or manually.

First off, the *xdm* configuration file should be set up. A good thing to do is to make a directory (*/usr/lib/X11/xdm* comes immediately to mind) which will contain all of the relevant files. Here is a reasonable configuration file, which could be named *xdm-config* :

```
DisplayManager.servers:          /usr/lib/X11/xdm/Xservers
DisplayManager.errorLogFile:     /usr/lib/X11/xdm/xdm-errors
DisplayManager*resources:        /usr/lib/X11/xdm/Xresources
DisplayManager*startup:          /usr/lib/X11/xdm/Xstartup
DisplayManager*session:          /usr/lib/X11/xdm/Xsession
DisplayManager*reset:            /usr/lib/X11/xdm/Xreset
```

As you can see, this file simply contains references to other files. Note that some of the resources are specified with ''*'' separating the components. These resources can be made unique for each different display, by replacing the ''*'' with the display-name, but normally this is not very useful. See the **Reources** section for a complete discussion.

The first file */usr/lib/X11/xdm/Xservers* contains the list of displays to manage. Most workstations have only one display, numbered 0, so the file will look like this:

```
:0 local /usr/bin/X11/X :0
```

This will keep */usr/bin/X11/X* running on this display and manage a continuous cycle of sessions.

The file */usr/lib/X11/xdm/xdm-errors* will contain error messages from *xdm* and anything output to stderr by *Xstartup, Xsession or Xreset*. When you have trouble getting *xdm* working, check this file to see if *xdm* has any clues to the trouble.

The next configuration entry, */usr/lib/X11/xdm/Xresources*, is loaded onto the display as a resource database using *xrdb (1)*. As the authentication widget reads this database before starting up, it usually contains parameters for that widget:

```
xlogin*login.translations: #override\
        <Key>F1: set-session-argument(failsafe) finish-field()\n\
        <Key>Return: set-session-argument() finish-field()
xlogin*borderWidth: 3
#ifdef COLOR
xlogin*greetColor: #f63
xlogin*failColor: red
xlogin*Foreground: black
```

```
xlogin*Background: #fdc
#else
xlogin*Foreground: black
xlogin*Background: white
#endif
```

The various colors specified here look reasonable on several of the displays we have, but may look awful on other monitors. As X does not currently have any standard color naming scheme, you might need to tune these entries to avoid disgusting results. Please note the translations entry; it specifies a few new translations for the widget which allow users to escape from the default session (and avoid troubles that may occur in it). Note that if #override is not specified, the default translations are removed and replaced by the new value, not a very useful result as some of the default translations are quite useful (like "<Key>: insert-char ()" which responds to normal typing).

The *Xstartup* file used here simply prevents login while the file */etc/nologin* exists. As there is no provision for displaying any messages here (there isn't any core X client which displays files), the user will probably be baffled by this behavior. I don't offer this as a complete example, but simply a demonstration of the available functionality.

Here is a sample *Xstartup* script:

```
#!/bin/sh
#
# Xstartup
#
# This program is run as root after the user is verified
#
if [ -f /etc/nologin ]; then
        exit 1
fi
exit 0
```

The most interesting script is *Xsession*. This version recognizes the special "failsafe" mode, specified in the translations in the *Xresources* file above, to provide an escape from the ordinary session:

```
#!/bin/sh
#
# Xsession
#

#
# check to see if the failsafe option is desired
#

case $# in
1)
        case $1 in
        failsafe)
                #
                # this is about as failsafe as I can imagine,
                # unfortunately, xterm frequently fails; but
                # no other client will be as useful generally.
```

```
                              #
                              exec xterm -geometry 80x24+50+50
                              ;;
                esac
        esac

        startup=$HOME/.xsession
        resources=$HOME/.Xresources

        #
        # check for a user-specific session and execute it
        #
        # Note:        the -x flag to test is not supported in all versions of
        #        unix, check with local authorities before proceeding...
        #
        if [ -f $startup ]; then
                if [ -x $startup ]; then
                        exec $startup
                else
                        exec /bin/sh $startup
                fi
        else
                #
                # a simple default session.  Check to see
                # if the user has created a default resource file
                # and load it, start the ugly window manager and
                # use xterm as the session control process.
                #
                if [ -f $resources ]; then
                        xrdb -load $resources
                fi
                uwm &
                exec xterm -geometry 80x24+10+10 -ls
        fi
```

Finally, the *Xreset* script in this demonstration is particularly boring. It does nothing:

```
#!/bin/sh
#
# Xreset
#
# This program is run as root after the session terminates but
# before the display is closed
#
```

SOME OTHER POSSIBILITIES

You can also use *xdm* to run a single session at a time, using the 4.3 *init* options or other suitable daemon by specifying the server on the command line:

```
xdm -server ":0 localTransient /usr/bin/X :0"
```

Or, you might have a file server and a collection of X terminals. The configuration for this could look identical to the sample above, except the

Xservers file might look like:

    extol:0 foreign X terminal on Keith's desk
    exalt:0 foreign X terminal on Jim's desk
    explode:0 foreign X terminal on Bob's desk

This would direct *xdm* to manage sessions on all three of these terminals. See the section "Controlling Xdm" above for a description of using signals to enable and disable these terminals in a manner reminisent of init(8).

One thing that *xdm* isn't very good at doing is coexisting with other window systems. To use multiple window systems on the same hardware, you'll probably be more interested in *xinit* .

SEE ALSO

X(1), xinit(1) and the proposed protocol for X terminal management.

BUGS

COPYRIGHT

Copyright 1988, Massachusetts Institute of Technology.
See *X(1)* for a full statement of rights and permissions.

AUTHOR

Keith Packard, MIT X Consortium

NAME
>   xdpr – dump an X window directly to a printer

SYNOPSIS
>   **xdpr** [*filename*] [**–display** *host:display*] [**–P***printer*] [**–device**
>   *printer_device*] [option ...]

DESCRIPTION
>   *Xdpr* uses the commands *xwd*(1), *xpr*(1), and *lpr*(1) to dump an X win-
>   dow, process it for a particular printer type, and print it out on the printer
>   of your choice. This is the easiest way to get a printout of a window.
>   *Xdpr* by default will print the largest possible representation of the win-
>   dow on the output page.
>
>   The options for *xdpr* are the same as those for *xpr*, *xwd*, and *lpr*. The
>   most commonly-used options are described below; see the manual pages
>   for these commands for more detailed descriptions of the many options
>   available.

>   *filename*
>>   Specifies a file containing a window dump (created by *xwd*) to be
>>   printed instead of selecting an X window.

>   **-P***printer*
>>   Specifies a printer to send the output to. If a printer name is not
>>   specified here, *xdpr* (really, *lpr*) will send your output to the
>>   printer specified by the *PRINTER* environment variable. Be sure
>>   that type of the printer matches the type specified with the *–dev-*
>>   *ice* option.

>   **-display** *host:display*[*.screen*]
>>   Normally, *xdpr* gets the host and display number to use from the
>>   environment variable "DISPLAY". One can, however, specify
>>   them explicitly; see *X*(1).

>   **-device** *printer-device*
>>   Specifies the device type of the printer. Available printer devices
>>   are "ln03" for the DEC LN03, "pp" for the IBM 3812 Page-
>>   Printer, and "ps" for any postscript printer (e.g. DEC LN03R or
>>   LPS40). The default is "ln03".

>   **-help** This option displays the list of options known to xdpr.

>   Any other arguments will be passed to the *xwd*(1), *xpr*(1), and *lpr*(1)
>   commands as appropriate for each.

SEE ALSO
>   xwd(1), xpr(1), lpr(1), xwud(1), X(1)

ENVIRONMENT
>   DISPLAY - for which display to use by default.
>   PRINTER - for which printer to use by default.

COPYRIGHT
>   Copyright 1985, 1988, Massachusetts Institute of Technology.
>   See *X(1)* for a full statement of rights and permissions.

AUTHOR
>   Paul Boutin, MIT Project Athena
>   Michael R. Gretzinger, MIT Project Athena
>   Jim Gettys, MIT Project Athena

NAME
      xdpyinfo - display information utility for X

SYNOPSIS
      xdpyinfo [-display *displayname*]

DESCRIPTION
      Xdpyinfo is a utility for displaying information about an X server. It is
      used to examine the capabilities of a server, the predefined values for vari-
      ous parameters used in communicating between clients and the server, and
      the different types of screens and visuals that are available.

EXAMPLE
      The following shows a sample produced by *xdpyinfo* when connected to
      display that supports an 8 plane Pseudocolor screen as well as a 1 plane
      (monochrome) screen.

      name of display: empire:0.0
      version number: 11.0
      vendor string: MIT X Consortium
      vendor release number: 3
      maximum request size: 16384 longwords (65536 bytes)
      motion buffer size: 0
      bitmap unit, bit order, padding: 32, MSBFirst, 32
      image byte order: MSBFirst
      keycode range: minimum 8, maximum 129
      default screen number: 0
      number of screens: 2

      screen #0:
        dimensions: 1152x900 pixels (325x254 millimeters)
        resolution: 90x90 dots per inch
        root window id: 0x8006d
        depth of root window: 1 plane
        number of colormaps: minimum 1, maximum 1
        default colormap: 0x80065
        default number of colormap cells: 2
        preallocated pixels: black 1, white 0
        options: backing-store YES, save-unders YES
        current input event mask: 0x1b8003c
          ButtonPressMaskButtonReleaseMaskEnterWindowMask
          LeaveWindowMaskSubstructureNotifyMaskSubstructureRedirectMask
          FocusChangeMaskColormapChangeMaskOwnerGrabButtonMask
        number of visuals: 1
        default visual id: 0x80064
        visual:
          visual id: 0x80064
          class: StaticGray
          depth: 1 plane
          size of colormap: 2 entries
          red, green, blue masks: 0x0, 0x0, 0x0
          significant bits in color specification: 1 bits

      screen #1:
        dimensions: 1152x900 pixels (325x254 millimeters)
        resolution: 90x90 dots per inch
        root window id: 0x80070
        depth of root window: 8 planes

```
number of colormaps:    minimum 1, maximum 1
default colormap:    0x80067
default number of colormap cells:    256
preallocated pixels:    black 1, white 0
options:    backing-store YES, save-unders YES
current input event mask:    0x0
number of visuals:    1
default visual id:  0x80066
visual:
  visual id:    0x80066
  class:    PseudoColor
  depth:    8 planes
  size of colormap:    256 entries
  red, green, blue masks:    0x0, 0x0, 0x0
  significant bits in color specification:    8 bits
```

ENVIRONMENT
    DISPLAY
        To get the default host, display number, and screen.

SEE ALSO
    X(1), xwininfo(1), xprop(1), xrdb(1)

BUGS
    Due to a bug in the Xlib interface, there is currently no portable way to determine the depths of pixmap images that are supported by the server.

COPYRIGHT
    Copyright 1988, Massachusetts Institute of Technology.
    See *X(1)* for a full statement of rights and permissions.

AUTHOR
    Jim Fulton, MIT X Consortium

NAME

xedit - simple text editor for X

SYNTAX

xedit [*-toolkitoption* ...] [filename]

OPTIONS

Xedit accepts all of the standard X Toolkit command line options (see *X(1)*), plus:

filename Specifies the file that is to be loaded during start-up. This is the file which will be edited. If a file is not specified, *xedit* lets you load a file or create a new file after it has started up.

DESCRIPTION

Xedit provides a window consisting of the following three areas:

Commands Menu	Lists editing commands (for example, **Undo** or **Search**).
Message Window	Displays *xedit* messages. In addition, this window can be used as a scratch pad.
Edit Window	Displays the text of the file that you are editing or creating.

COMMANDS

Quit	Quits the current editing session. If any changes have not been saved, *xedit* displays a warning message and allows you to save the file.
Save	Stores a copy of the original, unedited file in *file*.BAK. Then, overwrites the original file with the edited contents.
Edit	Allows the text displayed in the Edit window to be edited.
Load	Loads the specified file and displays it in the Edit window.
Undo	Undoes the last edit only.
More	Undoes each edit previous to the last edit, which must first be undone with the **Undo** command.
Jump	Advances the cursor from the beginning of the file to the text line that corresponds to the selected line number.
<<	Searches from the cursor back to the beginning of the file for the string entered in the Search input box. If you do not enter a string in the Search input box, *xedit* automatically copies the last string that you selected from any X application into the Search input box and searches for that string.
Search >>	Searches from the cursor forward to the end of the file for the string entered in the search input box. If you do not enter a string in the Search input box, *xedit* automatically copies the last string that you

selected from any X application into the
Search input box and searches for that
string.

Replace   Replaces the last searched-for string with
the string specified in the Replace input
box. If no string has been previously
searched for, searches from the insert cursor
to the end of the file for the next occurrence
of the search string and highlights it.

All   Repositions the cursor at the beginning of
the file and replaces all occurrences of the
search string with the string specified in the
Replace input box.

X DEFAULTS

For *xedit*, the available class identifiers are:

ButtonBox
Command
Scrollbar
Text

For *xedit*, the available name identifiers are:

All
Edit
EditWindow
Jump
Load
MessageWindow
More
Quit
Replace
Save
Undo
xedit

For *xedit*, the available resources are:

EnableBackups   Specifies that, when edits made to an existing
file are saved, *xedit* is to copy the original version of that file to *file*.BAK before it saves the
changes. If the value of this option is specified
as off, a backup file is not created.

background   Specifies the background color to be displayed
in command buttons. The default is white.

border   Specifies the border color of the *xedit* window.

borderWidth   Specifies the border width, in pixels, of the
xedit window.

font   Specifies the font displayed in the *xedit* window.

foreground   Specifies the foreground color of the *xedit* window. The default is black.

geometry   Specifies the geometry (window size and screen
                            location) to be used as the default for the *xedit*
                            window. For information about the format of
                            the geometry specification, see *X(1)*.

internalHeight   Specifies the internal horizontal padding (spac-
                            ing between text and button border) for com-
                            mand buttons.

internalWidth   Specifies the internal vertical padding (spacing
                            between text and button border) for command
                            buttons.

KEY BINDINGS

Each specification included in the *XtActions* file modifies a key setting for
the editor that *xedit* uses. When defining key specifications, you must use
the following resource specification: text.EventBindings: .XtActions

Each key specification assigns an editor command to a named key and/or
mouse combination and has the format:

key: *function*

key   Specifies the key or mouse button that is used to invoke
                            the named function.

function   Specifies the function to be invoked when the named
                            key is pressed.

For more information about specifications in the *XtActions* file, see *X(1)*.

FILES

~/.XtActions
/usr/lib/X11/.XtActions

SEE ALSO

X(1), xrdb(1)

RESTRICTIONS

Large numbers of certain edit functions (for example, Undo or More) tend
to degrade performance over time. If there is a noticeable decrease in
response time, save and reload the file.

BUGS

It is not clear how to select a line number for the *Jump* command.

The string searches don't work properly.

COPYRIGHT

Copyright 1988, Digital Equipment Corporation.

NAME
>   xev - print contents of X events

SYNOPSIS
>   **xev** [–display *displayname*] [–geometry *geom*]

DESCRIPTION
>   *Xev* creates a window and then asks the X server to send it notices called
>   *events* whenever anything happens to the window (such as being moved,
>   resized, typed in, clicked in, etc.). It is useful for seeing what causes
>   events to occur and to display the information that they contain.

OPTIONS
>   **–display** *display*
>   This option specifies the X server to contact.
>
>   **–geometry** *geom*
>   This option specifies the size and/or location of the window.

SEE ALSO
>   X(1), xwininfo(1), xdpyinfo(1), Xlib Programmers Manual, X Protocol
>   Specification

COPYRIGHT
>   Copyright 1988, Massachusetts Institute of Technology.
>   See *X(1)* for a full statement of rights and permissions.

AUTHOR
>   Jim Fulton, MIT X Consortium

NAME
xeyes – watch over your shoulder

SYNOPSIS
xeyes [-option ...]

DESCRIPTION
Xeyes watches what you do and reports to the Boss.

OPTIONS
–fg *foreground color*
> choose a different color for the pupil of the eyes.

–bg *background color*
> choose a different color for the background.

–outline *outline color*
> choose a different color for the outline of the eyes.

–center *center color*
> choose a different color for the center of the eyes.

–backing { *WhenMapped Always NotUseful* }
> selects an appropriate level of backing store.

–geometry *geometry*
> define the initial window geometry; see *X(1)*.

–display *display*
> specify the display to use; see *X(1)*.

–bd *border color*
> choose a different color for the window border.

–bw *border width*
> choose a different width for the window border.

SEE ALSO
X(1), X Toolkit documentation

COPYRIGHT
Copyright 1988, Massachusetts Institute of Technology.
See *X(1)* for a full statement of rights and permissions.

AUTHOR
Keith Packard, MIT X Consortium

3

NAME
     xfd - font displayer for X

SYNOPSIS
     xfd [-options ...] -fn *fontname*

OPTIONS
     –display *display*
          Specifies the display to use.

     –geometry *geometry*
          Specifies an initial window geometry.

     –bw *number*
          Allows you to specify the width of the window border in pixels.

     –rv   The foreground and background colors will be switched. The
          default colors are black on white.

     –fw   Overrides a previous choice of reverse video. The foreground
          and background colors will not be switched.

     –fg *color*
          On color displays, determines the foreground color (the color of
          the text).

     –bg *color*
          On color displays, determines the background color.

     –bd *color*
          On color displays, determines the color of the border.

     –bf *fontname*
          Specifies the font to be used for the messages at the bottom of
          the window.

     –tl *title*   Specifies that the title of the displayed window should be *title*.

     –in *iconname*
          Specifies that the name of the icon should be *iconname*.

     –icon *filename*
          Specifies that the bitmap in file *filename* should be used for the
          icon.

     –verbose
          Specifies that extra information about the font should be
          displayed.

     –gray   Specifies that a gray background should be used.

     –start *charnum*
          Specifies that character number *charnum* should be the first char-
          acter displayed.

DESCRIPTION
     Xfd creates a window in which the characters in the named font are
     displayed. The characters are shown in increasing order from left to right,
     top to bottom. The first character displayed at the top left will be charac-
     ter number 0 unless the -start option has been supplied in which case the
     character with the number given in the -start option will be used.

     The characters are displayed in a grid of boxes, each large enough to hold
     any single character in the font. If the -gray option has been supplied, the
     characters will be displayed using XDrawImageString using the fore-
     ground and background colors on a gray background. This permits deter-
     mining exactly how XDrawImageString will draw any given character. If

-gray has not been supplied, the characters will simply be drawn using the foreground color on the background color.

All the characters in the font may not fit in the window at once. To see additional characters, click the right mouse button on the window. This will cause the next window full of characters to be displayed. Clicking the left mouse button on the window will cause the previous window full of characters to be displayed. *Xfd* will beep if an attempt is made to go back past the 0th character.

Note that if the font is a 8 bit font, the characters 256-511 (100-1ff in hexidecimal), 512-767 (200-2ff in hexidecimal), ... will display exactly the same as the characters 0-255 (00-ff in hexidecimal). *Xfd* by default creates a window big enough to display 16 rows of 16 columns (totally 256 characters).

Clicking the middle button on a character will cause that character's number to be displayed in both decimal and hexidecimal at the bottom of the window. If verbose mode is selected, additional information about that particular character will be displayed as well. The displayed information includes the width of the character, its left bearing, right bearing, ascent, and its descent. If verbose mode is selected, typing '<' or '>' into the window will display the minimum or maximum values respectively taken on by each of these fields over the entire font.

The font name is interpreted by the X server. To obtain a list of all the fonts available, use *xlsfonts(1)*.

The window stays around until the xfd process is killed or one of 'q', 'Q', ' ', or ctrl-c is typed into the *Xfd* window.

X DEFAULTS
Xfd uses the following X resources:

BorderWidth   Set the border width of the window.

BorderColor   Set the border color of the window.

ReverseVideo   If "on", reverse the definition of foreground and background color.

Foreground   Set the foreground color.

Background   Set the background color.

BodyFont   Set the font to be used in the body of the window. (I.e., for messages, etc.) This is not the font that *Xfd* displays, just the font it uses to display information about the font being displayed.

IconName   Set the name of the icon.

IconBitmap   Set the file we should look in to get the bitmap for the icon.

Title   Set the title to be used.

SEE ALSO
X(1), xlsfonts(1), xrdb(1)

BUGS
It should display the name of the font somewhere.

Character information displayed in verbose mode is sometimes clipped to the window boundary, hiding it from view.

It should be rewritten to use the X toolkit.

It should skip over pages full of non-existent characters.

COPYRIGHT
Copyright 1988, Massachusetts Institute of Technology.
See *X(1)* for a full statement of rights and permissions.

AUTHOR
Mark Lillibridge, MIT Project Athena

NAME
          xfed – font editor for X Version 11 bdf fontfiles

SYNOPSIS
          xfed [–options ...] *filename*

DESCRIPTION
          xfed lets you interactively edit existing bdf-fontfiles. When run, *xfed*
          opens a window showing a magnified character of the font. There are
          four buttons to interact with *xfed*, two stepping buttons to advance to the
          previous/next character in the font, a write-file button and an exit button.
          If you leave *xfed* without saving a modified font, a dialog window will
          appear, asking if you want save changes before quitting. The write option
          moves the original fontfile to a backup file (filename˜) and saves the
          edited font under the original name.

OPTIONS
          xfed accepts the following options:

          –display *host:dpy*
                    the server to be used. See *X(1)* for details.

          –geometry *geometry*
                    the placement and size of the bitmap window on the screen. See
                    X(1) for details.

          –psize *number*
                    the pixel magnification factor.

          –nogrid no grid in the edit window (not very useful).

          –bw *number*
                    border width in pixels.

          –fg *colorname*
                    foreground color.

          –bg *colorname*
                    background color.

          –bd *colorname*
                    border color. Note, that this color is also used for the grid.

          –font *fontname*
                    font used for text in the font editor.

          The window created by *xfed* has several subwindows. At the top, a win-
          dow displays the name of the file being edited. Below this window, two
          similar windows display information about the font and the character
          being displayed. Below this window is a direct access window through
          which any character in the font can be accessed.

          The direct access window has a vertical bar which represents the relative
          position of the displayed character in the font. The vertical bar can be
          "dragged" with any mouse button to access a character. Alternatively, you
          may type the desired character with the pointer in this window to access a
          character.

          Below the direct access window is the edit window which displays the
          character with pixels magnified by the factor **psize**. The command buttons
          to step through the font, save the font, or exit the editor are to the right of
          the edit window. Two windows below the command buttons display the

character in actual size using the foreground and background colors.

COMMANDS

Two arrows point into the edit window on the top and right sides. To change the bounding box for the current character they may be "dragged" with any mouse button.

Button 1 (usually the left button) turns on pixels.

Button 2 (usually th middle button) inverts pixels.

Button 3 (usually the right button) turns off pixels.

Four editing commands which are typed directly from the keyboard with the pointer within the bounding box of the characte are:r

i   Insert a horizontal line at the pointer position

d   Delete a horizontal line at the pointer position

I   Insert a vertical line at the pointer position

D   Delete a vertical line at the pointer position

The direct access window (above the edit window):

Any key pressed in this window will display that character in the edit window and move the vertical bar to the corresponding positon in the font.

Pushing a mouse button in this window will move the vertical bar to that position, and thus display the corresponding character in the edit window.

FILE FORMAT

see X-Doc 'Character Bitmap Distribution Format 2.1'

X DEFAULTS

xfed uses the routine *XGetDefault(3X)* to read defaults.

Geometry

The size and location of the bitmap window. The default depends on the font.

PixelSize

The initial pixel magnification factor. The default depends on the font.

NoGrid

No grid will be used in the edit window if true. The default is false.

BorderWidth

The border width. The default value is 2.

Foreground

The foreground color. Bits which are 1 in the bitmap are displayed in this color. This option is useful only on color displays. The default value is ''black''.

Background
> The window's background color. Bits which are 0 in the bitmap are displayed in this color. This option is useful only on color displays. The default value is "white".

BorderColor
> The border color. This option is useful only on color displays. The default value is "black".

BodyFont
> The text font. The default value is "fixed". If *xfed* is given variable width font it will not display the current character while the direct access bar is "dragged".

3

ENVIRONMENT
> DISPLAY - the default host and display number.
> XENVIRONMENT - the name of the defaults file to use.

SEE ALSO
> X(1), BITMAP(1), X-Doc 'Character Bitmap Distribution Format 2.1'

BUGS
> Limited edit features.
>
> No "undo" command.
>
> Unable to change font characteristics and character properties.
>
> If you move the pointer too fast while holding a pointer button down, some squares may be 'missed'. This is caused by limitations in how frequently the X server can sample the mouse location.
>
> There is no way to write to a file other than that specified on the command line.

COPYRIGHT
> Copyright 1988, Network Computing Devices, Inc.

AUTHOR
> Olaf Brandt
> Network Cumputing Devices, Inc.
> Palo Alto, CA
>
>
> Copyright (c) 1988 by Siemens
> Claus Gittinger
> Software Consultant
> Siemens Munich
> Dep. D-St-Sp-4
> Charles-de-Gaullestr. 2a
> 8000 Munich/Neuperlach
> West Germany
> Email: ..!decvax!unido!sinix!claus

NAME
    xfig – Facility for Interactive Generation of figures under X11
SYNOPSIS
    xfig [**-ri[ght]**] [**-le[ft]**] [**-L[andscape]**] [**-P[ortrait]**] [**-w[idth]**
    inches] [**-h[eight]** *inches*] [**-no[track]**] [**-tr[ack]**] [*file*]
DESCRIPTION
    Xfig is a menu-driven tool that allows the user to draw and manipulate
    objects interactively in an X window. It runs under X version 11 release
    2 and requires a three-button mouse. *File* specifies the name of a file to
    be edited. The description of objects in the file will be read at the start of
    xfig.

    The output from *xfig* can be printed in several ways

    troff - f2p (*xfig* to *pic*(1) translator, also known by its previous name
    ftop(1L)) is used to translate *xfig* files into *pic*(1) language. The resulting
    file may then be processed in the same maner as any other *pic* file.

    postscript - f2ps (*xfig* to *postscript* translator) is used to produce a
    postscript file from an *xfig* file. The *postscript* file can be sent directly to
    a postscript printer.

    LaTeX - fig2latex (*xfig* to *LaTeX* translator) produces a *LaTeX* file from
    an *xfig* file. This file contains *LaTeX* picture environment commands and
    can be processed along with other *LaTeX* commands.

    PiCTeX - fig2tex (*xfig* to *PiCTeX* translator) produces a *PiCTeX* file from
    an *xfig* file. This file contains macros that can be used with the *PiCTeX*
    environment under *TeX* or *LaTeX*.

OPTIONS
    –ri   Change the position of the panel window to the right of the can-
             vas window (default: left).

    –le   Change the position of the panel window to the left of the canvas
             window.

    –L   Make *xfig* come up in landscape mode (10" x 7.5").

    –P   Make *xfig* come up in portrait mode (7.5" x 10"). This is the
             default.

    -w *inches*
             Make *xfig* come up *inches* wide.

    -h *inches*
             Make *xfig* come up *inches* high.

    -tr   Turn on cursor (mouse) tracking arrows.

    -no   Turn off cursor (mouse) tracking arrows.

GRAPHICAL OBJECTS
    The objects in *xfig* are divided into **primitive objects** and **compound
    object**. The primitive objects are: *ARC, CIRCLE, CLOSED SPLINE,
    ELLIPSE, POLYLINE, POLYGON, SPLINE,* and *TEXT*. A primitive can
    be moved, rotated, flipped, copied or erased. A compound object is com-
    posed of primitive objects. The primitive objects that constitute a com-
    pound can not be individually modified, but they can be manipulated as an
    entity; a compound can be moved, rotated, flipped, copied or erased. An
    extra function that can be applied to a compound object is **scaling**, which
    is not available for primitive objects.

DISPLAY WINDOWS
    Five windows comprise the display area of *xfig*: the top ruler, the side

ruler, the panel window, the message window, and the canvas window. The message window always appears below the others; it is the area in which messages are sent and received. The panel window can be placed to the left or right of the the canvas window (default: left).

POP-UP MENU

The pop-up menu appears when the right mouse button is pressed with the cursor positioned within the canvas window. Positioning the cursor over the desired menu entry and releasing the button selects a menu entry.

There are a number of file accessing functions in the pop-up menu. Most of the time when one of these functions is selected, the user will be asked for a file name. If the specified file can be located and the access permission are granted, *xfig* will carry out the function. However in case things go wrong, *xfig* will abort the function and printed the causes on the message window.

Undo   Undo the last object creation or modification.

Redisplay
         Redraw the canvas.

Remove all
         Remove all objects on the canvas window (can be undone).

Edit file ...
         The current contents of the canvas are cleared and objects are read from the specified file. The user will be asked for a file name. This file will become the current file.

Save   Save the current contents of the canvas in the current file. If no file is being edited, the user will be asked for a file name as in the "Save in ..." function.

Read file ...
         Read objects from the specified file and merge them with objects already shown on the canvas. (The user will be asked for a file name.)

Save as ...
         Save objects on the screen into a file specified by the user. (The user will be asked for a file name.)

Status Show the name of the current file and directory.

Change Directory
         Change the working directory. Any file name without a full path name will employ the current working directory.

Save & Exit
         Save the objects in the current file and exit from *xfig*. If there is no current file, the user will be asked for a file name. No confirmation will be asked.

Quit   Exit from *xfig*, discarding all objects. The user will be asked to confirm the action, by clicking the left button.

Save as BITMAP ...
         Create a bitmap picture of the drawings for use with other tools (for example, for use as an icon). The smallest rectangular area of pixels that encompasses the figure is written to the named file (the user will be asked for a file name) from top row to bottom and left to right (in Sun raster format). Only *TEXT* objects that are parts of compound objects will be treated as parts of the picture; other texts are saved as objects in *xfig* format following the

bitmap data. The coordinates of these text objects can be used to identify locations on the bitmap.

PANEL WINDOW MANIPULATION FUNCTIONS

Icons in the panel window represent object manipulation functions, modes and other drawing or modification aids. Manipulation functions are selected by positioning the cursor over it and clicking the left mouse button. The selected icon is highlighted, and a message describing its function appears in the message window.

The left and middle buttons are used to creat and modify objects in the canvas window. Most actions start with clicking of the left button and end with clicking of the right button. There is no need to hold down a button while positioning the cursor.

PANEL WINDOW COMMAND DESCRIPTIONS

Entries in the panel window can be classified into two categories: object creation/modification/removal commands (only one of which may be active at any one time), and drawing aids (which act as toggle switches). There are two ways for drawing circles, two for ellipses, two for splines and two for closed splines. There are two basic splines. One is the interpolated spline in which the spline pass thorough the entered points (knots). The other is the normal spline in which on control points are passed by the spline (except for the two end points in the open spline).

OBJECT CREATION/MODIFICATION/REMOVAL

Multiple commands are grouped thematically in the following descriptions (which is listed alphabetically).

ADD/DELETE ARROWS

Add or delete arrow heads for *POLYLINE, POLYGON, SPLINE* or *CLOSED SPLINE* objects (points of a *BOX* can not be added or deleted).

ADD/DELETE POINTS

Add or delete points for *POLYLINE, POLYGON, SPLINE* or *CLOSED SPLINE* objects (points of a *BOX* can not be added or deleted).

ARC   Create an arc. Specify three points using the left button.

BOX   Create rectangular boxes. Start with the left button and terminate with the right button.

BREAK COMPOUND

Break a compound object to allow manipulation of its component parts. Click the left button on the bounding box of the compound object.

CIRCLE

Create circles by specifying their radii or diameters. Click the left button on the canvas window, move the cursor until the desired radius or diameter is reached, then click the middle button to terminate. The circle will be drawn after the pressing of the middle button.

CLOSED INTERPOLATED SPLINE

Create closed or periodic splines. The function is similar to *POLYGON* except that a closed interpolated spline is drawn. The spline will pass through the points (knots).

CLOSED SPLINE

Create closed or periodic spline objects. The function is similar to *POLYGON* except that a closed spline will be drawn instead of polygon. The entered points are just control points; i.e., the spline will not pass any of these points.

COPY   Copy object. Click the left button over part of the object to be copied (for *CIRCLE* and *ELLIPSE* objects, position on their circumferences). Drag the object to the desired position and click the middle button. This function as well as the following three functions (*MOVE, MOVE POINT, REMOVE*) will cause point markers (manipulation aids) to be shown on the canvas window. There are no markers for *CIRCLE* or *ELLIPSE* objects.

ELLIPSE
          Create ellipses using the same procedure as for the drawing of circles.

GLUE   Glue the objects within a bounding box into a compound object (the bounding box itself is not part of the figure; it is a visual aid for manipulating the compound).

INTERPOLATED SPLINE
          Create (cubic spline) spline objects. Enter control vectors in the same way as for creation of a *POLYLINE* object. At least three points (two control vectors) must be entered. The spline will pass through the entered points.

MOVE   Move objects in the same way as in *COPY*.

MOVE POINT
          Modify the position of points of *POLYLINE, BOX, POLYGON, ELLIPSE, ARC* and *SPLINE* objects. *Click the left button over the desired point, reposition the point, and click the middle button. Note that BOX and POLYGON objects are internally stored as POLYLINE objects, and therefore moving certain points may open these objects.*

POLYGON
          Same as *POLYLINE* except that a line segment is drawn connecting the first and last points entered.

POLYLINE
          Create polylines (line segments connecting a sequence of points). Enter points by clicking the left button at the desired positions on the canvas window. Click the middle button to terminate.

REMOVE
          Remove (or delete) objects.

SCALE COMPOUND
          Only compound objects can be scaled. Click the left button on a corner of the bounding box, stretch the bounding box to the desired size, and click the middle button. Or click the left button on a side of the bounding box, stretch that side to the desired size, and click the middle button.

SPLINE Create (quadratic spline) spline objects. Enter control vectors in the same way as for creation of a *POLYLINE* object. At least three points (two control vectors) must be entered. The spline will pass only the two end points.

TEXT   Create text strings. Click the left button at the desired position on the canvas window, then enter text from the keyboard. A DEL or ^H (backspace) will delete a character, while a ^U will kill the entire line. Terminate by clicking the middle button or typing the return key. To edit text, click on an existing text string with the left button. Insertion of characters will take place at that point.

TURN   Turn *POLYGON* into a *CLOSED INTERPOLATED SPLINE* object, or turn *POLYLINE* into a *INTERPOLATED SPLINE* object.

DRAWING AIDS

Drawing aids act as toggle switches. More than one can be selected at a time (except for *GRID* and the line drawing modes).

AUTO FORWARD/BACKWARD ARROW
> Automatically add forward/backward arrow heads to *POLYLINE*, *SPLINE* or *ARC* objects.

FLIP   Invert the object (middle button) or produce a mirror-image copy of an object (left button). Point to part of the object ("the handle"), click the appropriate button.

GRID   Display either the quarter- or half-inch grids (left button).

MAGNET
> Round points to the nearest 1/16 of an inch. This affects every function, and is provided as an alignment aid.

UNRESTRICTED
> Allow lines to be drawn with any slope.

MANHATTAN
> Enforce drawing of lines in the horizontal and vertical direction only. Both *MANHATTAN* and *MOUNTAIN* can be turned on simultaneously. The creations of *POLYGON*, *POLYLINE* and *SPLINE* objects are affected by these two modes.

MOUNTAIN
> Enforce drawing of only diagonal lines. Both *MANHATTAN* and *MOUNTAIN* can be turned on simultaneously. The creations of *POLYGON*, *POLYLINE* and *SPLINE* objects are affected by these two modes.

MANHATTAN MOUNTAIN
> Allow lines to be drawn at any slope allowed when in MOUNTIAIN or MANHATTAN modes.

LATEX LINE
> Allow lines to be drawn only at slopes which can be handled by LaTeX picture environment lines: slope = x/y, where x,y are integers in the range [-6,6].

LATEX VECTOR
> Allow lines to be drawn only at slopes which can be handled by LaTeX picture environment vectors: slope = x/y, where x,y are integers in the range [-4,4].

ROTATE
> Rotate the object (middle button) or copy (left button) +90 degrees.

SOLID/DASHED LINE STYLE
> Toggle between solid and dashed line styles. The dash length is fixed at 0.05 inch.

X DEFAULTS

The overall widget name(Class) is xfig.fig(Fig.TopLevelShell). This set of resources correspond to the command line arguments:

trackCursor	(boolean:on) -track and -notrack arguments
justify	(boolean:false) -right and -left arguments
landscape	(boolean:false) -Landscape and -Portrait arguments
debug	(boolean:off) -debug arguments
width	(integer:7.5 or 10 inches) -width argument
height	(integer:10 or 7.5 inches) -height argument
reverseVideo	(boolean:off) -inverse argument

These arguments correspond to the widgets which make up *xfig*.

overall window	form(Form)
side panel	form.panel(Form.Box)
icons	form.panel.button(Form.Box.Command)
top ruler	form.truler(Form.Label)
side ruler	form.sruler(Form.Label)
canvas	form.canvas(Form.Label)
message window	form.message(Form.Command)
menu	form.popup_menu.menu(Form.OverrideShell.Box)
menu title	form.popup_menu.menu.title (Form.OverrideShell.Box.Label)
menu items	form.popup_menu.menu.pane (Form.OverrideShell.Box.Command)

For example, to set the background of the panel to blue the resource would be:
xfig*form.panel.background: blue

NOTE: The font used in the canvas cannot be changed at this time.

BUGS

Text strings will appear differently on hard copy, because the display fonts are fixed-width fonts while the fonts used by the typesetter systems are variable-width fonts.

A double quote in a text string should be preceded by a back slash if the it is to be printed through *pic*(1).

Objects that extend beyond the canvas window may cause image shrinkage in hard copy printed by *pic*(1), since it will try to fit every object onto a single 8.5" x 11" page.

Ellipses which are too narrow may cause *xfig* to loop forever.

Objects which are created while one of the *grids* is on may appear ragged. This can be corrected by selecting *Redisplay* from the pop-up menu.

The X11 cursors are not the original ones but chosen from X11's cursor font.

SEE ALSO

Brian W. Kernighan *PIC - A Graphics Language for Typesetting User Manual*
ditroff(1), f2p(1), f2ps(1), fig2latex(1), fig2tex(1), pic(1), troff(1), tex(1), latex(1)

ACKNOWLEDGEMENT
Many thanks goes to Professor Donald E. Fussell who inspired the creation of this tool.

AUTHORS
Original author:
Supoj Sutanthavibul
University of Texas at Austin
(supoj@sally.utexas.edu)

Manual page modified by:
R. P. C. Rodgers
UCSF School of Pharmacy
San Francisco, CA 94118

The LaTeX line drawing modes were contributed by:
Frank Schmuck
Cornell University

X11 port by:
Ken Yap
Rochester
(ken@cs.rochester.edu)

Variable window sizes, cleanup of X11 port, right hand side panel under
X11, X11 manual page provided by:
Dana Chee
Bellcore
(dana@bellcore.com)

Cleanup of color port to X11 by:
John T. Kohl
MIT
(jtkohl@athena.mit.edu)

NAME

    xgranite – make a random background

SYNOPSIS

    xgranite [-display *display*] [-width *width*] [-height *height*] [-darkness *darkness*]

DESCRIPTION

    xgranite makes a random background that somewhat resembles granite.

OPTIONS

    The various options are as follows:

    -display *display*

        Specifies the server to connect to; see *X(1)*.

    -width *width*

        Specifies the width of the random bitmap. If no width is specified the width of the screen is used.

    -height *height*

        Specifies the height of the random bitmap. If no height is specified the height of the screen is used.

    -darknes *darknes*

        Specifies how dark to make the random pattern.

    For a completely random background don't use **-width** or **-height**.

SEE ALSO

    X(1), xsetroot(1), xset(1), xrdb(1)

AUTHOR

    Program: Rusty C. Wright
                    rusty@cartan.berkeley.edu
                    ucbvax!cartan!rusty

NAME
    xgsh – X based visual shell

SYNOPSIS
    xgsh [**-config config**]

DESCRIPTION
    Xgsh is a visual interface shell that runs on top of the MIT X Window
    system on bitmapped workstations. It uses a configuration file passed as
    an argument to define a set of selectable commands with controlling
    parameters and an associated single line shell command. For a login shell,
    xgsh must be linked to a name that is the same as the *config* ®name in the
    configuration library directory. When a command is selected (more on
    that later), name arguments may optionally be selected and then the com-
    mand is "Start"ed. When started, xgsh generates a terminal emulation (see
    vif) or associated icon window and runs the single line shell command
    with name arguments filled in. Some configurations allow multiple Jobs to
    be run.

    The visual interface consists of four panels and a few non-interactive win-
    dows. The Top Level panel allows selection of a current command group,
    as defined by the configuration. It consists of a title bar and a set of
    selectable items (either text strings or icons). Each title bar includes
    selection buttons for Cancel, Reset and Accept, which have loose interpre-
    tations in the various panels. In the Top Level panel Cancel logs you out,
    Reset clears any command selection in progress and Accept Starts an exe-
    cution. The Command Panel consists of a set of selectable commands
    specified by the current top level with associated parameters and a single
    line "csh" command. When a command is selected from the panel, its
    "csh" equivalent is displayed in the Cmdstr window and set as the current
    command. If the command requires name arguments (for files or...) a
    Name Panel will pop up for name input. The Name Panel consists of a
    set of selectable names and possibly a NEWNAME widget that allows a
    new name to be input via. keyboard to the Newname panel. If you select
    the NEWNAME widget, a Newname panel pops up so that you may enter
    a new name via. keyboard. Once entered, the "Accept" button must be
    selected to accept the name or the "Cancel" button to return to the Name
    panel. Once name selection is done, the name will be entered in the
    Cmdstr. This can be indicated by selecting Accept in the name panel or it
    may be implicit if only n names are required. After command selection is
    complete, you select the "Accept" button on the Cmd panel to start up the
    Job. The associated window (usually a tty emulation vif window) is
    created and the command string is run (per csh) with its "stdio" tied to the
    associated window. To control the Job, you may pop up a menu on the
    window by pressing mouse Button2 and selecting Kill will terminate the
    Job. This is often necessary for non-interactive Jobs, since the window
    will be configured to linger after completion so the output can be read.
    The Pause and Continue selections may be used to suspend/resume Job
    processing. You may bring up the Directory Browser (see dirb(1)) at any
    time by selecting the button in the Top Level panel title bar. The "Can-
    cel" button can be used to abort a command selection in process.

    Primary Selection is done by pressing the LEFT mouse button when the
    mouse is positioned over the item. Similarily, pop up menu items are
    selected as follows: press and hold the RIGHT mouse button then move
    the mouse to the item to be selected and release the button.

    A help window associated with each panel may be accessed by pressing
    the MIDDLE mouse button while the mouse is positioned in the panel and

zapped by pressing the MIDDLE mouse button inside the help window.

FILES

/usr/local/lib/xgsh/*.xgs
/usr/local/lib/xgsh/*xgs.hlp
/usr/lib/X11/vif
/usr/lib/X11/dirb

BUGS

If the command string is badly contructed the resultant Job will fail ungracefully. The current interface is easy to outgrow, but there is no capability for the user to extend their environment. Once in a while, processes (particularily script) get left dangling and cause problems for the pty's. Since a vhangup() is done on the pty's before use, I can't explain it.

3

NAME
    xhop – Displays "Real Plane Fractals"

SYNOPSIS
    xlock [**–display** *display*] [**–geometry** *geometry*] [**–color**] [**–time**
    timeout]

DESCRIPTION
    xhop displays the "real plane" iterative fractals from the September 1986
    issue of Scientific American in a window. The pattern changes after
    timeout seconds, or when the Return or Space key is pressed.

OPTIONS
    –display *display*
        xhop will be run on the X display called *display*.

    –geometry *geometry*
        The **xhop** window will be sized and positioned according to the
        specified *geometry*.

    –color
        The *color* option installs a hue ramp at full saturation and intensity,
        so that the pixels are drawn in successive colors.

    –time *timeout*
        The **time** option sets the number of seconds that each unique fractal
        will remain on the screen before being replaced by the next one to
        timeout.

SEE ALSO
    X(1), Xlib Documentation.

COPYRIGHT
    Copyright (c) 1988 by Patrick J. Naughton
    (naughton@wind.Sun.COM)

    Window Systems Group
    Sun Microsystems, Inc.
    Mountain View, CA 94043
    415/336-1080

    Permission to use, copy, modify, and distribute this software and its docu-
    mentation for any purpose and without fee is hereby granted, provided that
    the above copyright notice appear in all copies and that both that copy-
    right notice and this permission notice appear in supporting documenta-
    tion.

NAME
>   xhost - server access control program for X

SYNOPSIS
>   **xhost** [[+-]hostname ...]

DESCRIPTION
>   The *xhost* program is used to add and delete hosts to the list of machines
>   that are allowed to make connections to the X server. This provides a
>   rudimentary form of privacy control and security. It is only sufficient for
>   a workstation (single user) environment, although it does limit the worst
>   abuses. Environments which require more sophisticated measures should
>   use the hooks in the protocol for passing authentication data to the server.
>
>   The server initially allows network connections only from programs run-
>   ning on the same machine or from machines listed in the file */etc/X*.hosts*
>   (where * is the display number of the server). The *xhost* program is usu-
>   ally run either from a startup file or interactively to give access to other
>   users.
>
>   Hostnames that are followed by two colons (::) are used in checking DEC-
>   net connections; all other hostnames are used for TCP/IP connections.

OPTIONS
>   *Xhost* accepts the following command line options described below. For
>   security, the options that effect access control may only be run from the
>   same machine as the server.

>   **[+]***hostname*
>> The given *hostname* (the plus sign is optional) is added to the
>> list of machines that are allowed to connect to the X server.

>   **−***hostname*
>> The given *hostname* is removed from the list of machines that
>> are allowed to connect to the server. Existing connections are
>> not broken, but new connection attempts will be denied. Note
>> that the current machine is allowed to be removed; however,
>> further connections (including attempts to add it back) will not
>> be permitted. Resetting the server (thereby breaking all connec-
>> tions) is the only way to allow local connections again.

>   +   Access is granted to everyone, even if they aren't on the list of
>>   allowed hosts (i.e. access control is turned off).

>   −   Access is restricted to only those machines on the list of allowed
>>   hosts (i.e. access control is turned on).

>   *nothing* If no command line arguments are given, the list of hosts that
>>   are allowed to connect is printed on the standard output along
>>   with a message indicating whether or not access control is
>>   currently enabled. This is the only option that may be used
>>   from machines other than the one on which the server is run-
>>   ning.

FILES
>   /etc/X*.hosts

SEE ALSO
>   X(1), Xserver(1)

ENVIRONMENT
>   **DISPLAY**
>>   to get the default host and display to use.

BUGS

You can't specify a display on the command line because **–display** is a valid command line argument (indicating that you want to remove the machine named *"display"* from the access list).

COPYRIGHT

Copyright 1988, Massachusetts Institute of Technology.
See *X(1)* for a full statement of rights and permissions.

AUTHORS

Bob Scheifler, MIT Laboratory for Computer Science,
Jim Gettys, MIT Project Athena (DEC).

NAME
    xinit - X Window System initializer

SYNOPSIS
    xinit [[client] options] [-- [server] [display] options]

DESCRIPTION
    The *xinit* program is used to start the X Window System server and a first
    client program (usually a terminal emulator) on systems that cannot start
    X directly from */etc/init* or in environments that use multiple window sys-
    tems. When this first client exits, *xinit* will kill the X server and then ter-
    minate.

    If no specific client program is given on the command line, *xinit* will look
    for a file in the user's home directory called *.xinitrc* to run as a shell script
    to start up client programs. If no such file exists, *xinit* will use the follow-
    ing as a default:

        xterm -geometry +1+1 -n login -display :0

    If no specific server program is given on the command line, *xinit* will look
    for a file in the user's home directory called *.xserverrc* to run as a shell
    script to start up the server. If no such file exists, *xinit* will use the fol-
    lowing as a default:

        X :0

    Note that this assumes that there is a program named *X* in the current
    search path. However, servers are usually named *Xdisplaytype* where
    displaytype is the type of graphics display which is driven by this server.
    The site administrator should, therefore, make a link to the appropriate
    type of server on the machine, or create a shell script that runs *xinit* with
    the appropriate server.

    An important point is that programs which are run by *.xinitrc* and by
    .xserverrc should be run in the background if they do not exit right away,
    so that they don't prevent other programs from starting up. However, the
    last long-lived program started (usually a window manager or terminal
    emulator) should be left in the foreground so that the script won't exit
    (which indicates that the user is done and that *xinit* should exit).

    An alternate client and/or server may be specified on the command line.
    The desired client program and its arguments should be given as the first
    command line arguments to *xinit*. To specify a particular server command
    line, append a double dash (--) to the *xinit* command line (after any client
    and arguments) followed by the desired server comand.

    Both the client program name and the server program name must begin
    with a slash (/) or a period (.). Otherwise, they are treated as an argu-
    ments to be appended to their respective startup lines. This makes it pos-
    sible to add arguments (for example, foreground and background colors)
    without having to retype the whole command line.

    If an explicit server name is not given and the first argument following the
    double dash (--) is a colon followed by a digit, *xinit* will use that number
    as the display number instead of zero. All remaining arguments are
    appended to the server command line.

EXAMPLES
    Below are several examples of how command line arguments in *xinit* are
    used.

xinit   This will start up a server named *X* and run the user's *xinitrc*, if it exists, or else start an *xterm*.

xinit -- /usr/bin/X11/Xqdss :1
                   This is how one could start a specific type of server on an alternate display.

xinit -geometry =80x65+10+10 -fn 8x13 -j -fg white -bg navy
                   This will start up a server named *X*, and will append the given arguments to the default *xterm* command. It will ignore *xinitrc*.

xinit -e widgets -- ./Xsun -l -c
                   This will use the command *./Xsun -l -c* to start the server and will append the arguments *-e widgets* to the default *xterm* command.

xinit /usr/ucb/rsh fasthost cpupig -display ws:1 -- :1 -a 2 -t 5
                   This will start a server named *X* on display 1 with the arguments *-a 2 -t 5*. It will then start a remote shell on the machine **fasthost** in which it will run the command *cpupig*, telling it to display back on the local workstation.

Below is a sample *xinitrc* that starts a clock, several terminals, and leaves the window manager running as the "last" application. Assuming that the window manager has been configured properly, the user then chooses the "Exit" menu item to shut down X.

```
xrdb -load $HOME/.Xres
xsetroot -solid gray &
xclock -g 50x50-0+0 -bw 0 &
xload -g 50x50-50+0 -bw 0 &
xterm -g 80x24+0+0 &
xterm -g 80x24+0-0 &
uwm
```

Sites that want to create a common startup environment could simply create a default *xinitrc* that references a site-wide startup file:

```
#!/bin/sh
. /usr/local/lib/site.xinitrc
```

Another approach is to write a script that starts *xinit* with a specific shell script. Such scripts are usually named *x11*, *xstart*, or *startx* and are a convenient way to provide a simple interface for novice users:

```
#!/bin/sh
xinit /usr/local/bin/startx -- /usr/bin/X11/Xhp :1
```

ENVIRONMENT VARIABLES
DISPLAY
                   This variable gets set to the name of the display to which clients should connect.

XINITRC
                   This variable specifies an init file containing shell commands to start up the initial windows. By default, *xinitrc* in the home directory will be used.

SEE ALSO
          X(1), Xserver(1), xterm(1), xrdb(1)

COPYRIGHT
Copyright 1988, Massachusetts Institute of Technology.
See *X(1)* for a full statement of rights and permissions.

AUTHOR
Bob Scheifler, MIT Laboratory for Computer Science

NAME
      xipr – dump an X window directly to the printer
SYNOPSIS
      xipr [options for *xwdimp*] [–nobdrs] [host:display]
DESCRIPTION
      Xipr runs *xwd* and *xwdimp* to dump an X window, process it for the
      Imagen laser printer, and print it out.
OPTIONS
      The '–nobdrs' option (along with the display specification) is given to
      xwd, all other options are given to *xwdimp*
ENVIRONMENT
      DISPLAY – the default host and display number
SEE ALSO
      xwd(1), xdpr(1), xwud(1)
AUTHOR
      Marshall T. Rose, Northrop Research and Technology Center

NAME
>   xkill - kill a client by its X resource

SYNOPSIS
>   **xkill** [–display *displayname*] [–id *resource*] [–button number] [–all]

DESCRIPTION
>   *Xkill* is a utility for forcing the X server to close connections to clients.
>   This program is very dangerous, but is useful for aborting programs that
>   have displayed undesired windows on a user's screen. If no resource
>   identifier is given with *-id*, *xkill* will display a special cursor as a prompt
>   for the user to select a window to be killed. If a pointer button is pressed
>   over a non-root window, the server will close its connection to the client
>   that created the window.

OPTIONS
>   **–display** *displayname*
>>   This option specifies the name of the X server to contact.
>
>   **–id** *resource*
>>   This option specifies the X identifier for the resource whose
>>   creator is to be aborted. If no resource is specified, *xkill* will
>>   display a special cursor with which you should select a window
>>   to be kill.
>
>   **–button** *number*
>>   This option specifies the number of pointer button that should be
>>   used in selecting a window to kill. If the word "any" is specified,
>>   any button on the pointer may be used. By default, the first but-
>>   ton in the pointer map (which is usually the leftmost button) is
>>   used.
>
>   **–all**   This option indicates that all clients with top-level windows on
>>   the screen should be killed. *Xkill* will ask you to select the root
>>   window with each of the currently defined buttons to give you
>>   several chances to abort. Use of this option is highly
>>   discouraged.

XDEFAULTS
>   **Button**   Specifies a specific pointer button number or the word "any" to
>>   use when selecting windows.

SEE ALSO
>   X(1), xwininfo(1), XKillClient and XGetPointerMapping in the Xlib Pro-
>   grammers Manual, KillClient in the X Protocol Specification

COPYRIGHT
>   Copyright 1988, Massachusetts Institute of Technology.
>   See *X(1)* for a full statement of rights and permissions.

AUTHOR
>   Jim Fulton, MIT X Consortium
>   Dana Chee, Bellcore

NAME
     xload - load average display for X

SYNOPSIS
     xload [*-toolkitoption* ...] [-scale *integer*] [-update *seconds*]

DESCRIPTION
     The *xload* program displays a periodically updating histogram of the sys-
     tem load average. This program is nothing more than a wrapper around
     the Athena Load widget.

OPTIONS
     Xload accepts all of the standard X Toolkit command line options along
     with the following additional options:

     –scale *integer*
               This option specifies the minimum number of tick marks in the
               histogram, where one division represents one load average point.
               If the load goes above this number, *xload* will create more divi-
               sions, but it will never use fewer than this number. The default
               is 1.

     –update *seconds*
               This option specifies the frequency in seconds at which *xload*
               updates its display. If the load average window is uncovered
               (by moving windows with a window manager or by the *xrefresh*
               program), the graph will be also be updated. The minimum
               amount of time allowed between updates is 5 seconds (which is
               also the default).

     –hl *color*
               This option specifies the color of the label and scale lines.

     The following standard X Toolkit arguments are commonly used with
     xload:

     –bd *color*
               This option specifies the border color. The default is *black*.

     –bg *color*
               This option specifies the background color. The default is *white*.

     –bw *pixels*
               This option specifies the width in pixels of the border around the
               window. The default value is 2.

     –fg *color*
               This option specifies the graph color. The default color is *black*.

     –fn *fontname*
               This option specifies the font to be used in displaying the name
               of the host whose load is being monitored. The default is *6x10*.

     –rv   This option indicates that reverse video should be simulated by
               swapping the foreground and background colors.

     –geometry *geometry*
               This option specifies the prefered size and postion of the win-
               dow.

     –display *display*
               This option specifies the X server to contact.

     –xrm *resourcestring*
               This option specifies a resource string to be used. This is espe-
               cially useful for setting resources that do not have separate

command line options.

X DEFAULTS

This program uses the *Load* widget in the X Toolkit. It understands all of the core resource names and classes as well as:

width (class **Width**)

Specifies the width of the load average graph.

height (class **Height**)

Specifies the height of the load average graph.

update (class **Interval**)

Specifies the frequency in seconds at which the load should be redisplayed.

scale (class **Scale**)

Specifies the initial number of ticks on the graph. The default is 1.

minScale (class **Scale**)

Specifies the minimum number of ticks that will be displayed. The default is 1.

foreground (class **Foreground**)

Specifies the color for the graph. The default is *black* since the core default for background is *white*.

highlight (class **Foreground**)

Specifies the color for the text and scale lines. The default is the same as for the **foreground** resource.

label (class **Label**)

Specifies the label to use on the graph. The default is the hostname.

font (class **Font**)

Specifies the font to be used for the label. The default is *fixed*.

reverseVideo (class **ReverseVideo**)

Specifies that the foreground and background should be reversed.

SEE ALSO

X(1), xrdb(1), mem(4), Athena Load widget

DIAGNOSTICS

Unable to open display or create window. Unable to open /dev/kmem. Unable to query window for dimensions. Various X errors.

BUGS

This program requires the ability to open and read the special system file */dev/kmem*. Sites that do not allow general access to this file should make *xload* belong to the same group as */dev/kmem* and turn on the *set group id* permission flag.

Reading /dev/kmem is inherently non-portable. Therefore, the widget upon which this application is based must be ported to each new operating system.

Border color has to be explicitly specified when reverse video is used.

COPYRIGHT

Copyright 1988, Massachusetts Institute of Technology.
See *X(1)* for a full statement of rights and permissions.

AUTHORS

K. Shane Hartman (MIT-LCS) and Stuart A. Malone (MIT-LCS);
with features added by Jim Gettys (MIT-Athena), Bob Scheifler (MIT-LCS), and Tony Della Fera (MIT-Athena)

NAME
xlock – Locks the local X display till a password is entered.

SYNOPSIS
xlock [**–color**] [**–root**] [**–time** *timeout*]

DESCRIPTION
xlock locks the X server till the user enters their password at the key-board. While **xlock** is running, all new server connections are refused. The screen saver is disabled. The mouse cursor is turned off. The screen is blanked and the "real plane" iterative fractals from the September 1986 issue of Scientific American are put on the screen. The pattern changes after 10-20K iterations or when the Return key is pressed.

If the password of the user who started **xlock** is typed, then the screen is unlocked and the X server is restored. When typing the password, charac-ters are not echoed to the screen, but Control-U and Control-H are active as killline and erase respectively.

OPTIONS
–color
>The *color* option installs a hue ramp at full saturation and intensity, so that the pixels are drawn in successive colors.

–root
>The *root* option allows the root password to unlock the server as well as the user who started xlock.

–time timeout
>The *time* option sets the number of seconds that each unique fractal will remain on the screen before being replaced by the next one to *timeout*.

BUGS
"kill -KILL xlock " causes server to be unusable, since **xlock** has removed all hosts (including localhost) from the access control list to lock out all new X clients, and SIGKILL cannot be caught by any program, **xlock** will terminate before restoring the access control list. This will leave the X server in a state where
"you can no longer connect to that server, and this operation cannot be reversed short of resetting the server."   -From the X11R2 Xlib Documentation page 140.

SEE ALSO
X(1), Xlib Documentation.

COPYRIGHT
Copyright (c) 1988 by Patrick J. Naughton
(naughton@wind.Sun.COM)

Window Systems Group
Sun Microsystems, Inc.
Mountain View, CA 94043
415/336-1080

Permission to use, copy, modify, and distribute this software and its docu-mentation for any purpose and without fee is hereby granted, provided that the above copyright notice appear in all copies and that both that copy-right notice and this permission notice appear in supporting documenta-tion.

CONTRIBUTORS
milliken@heron.bbn.com   karlton@wsl.dec.com
dana@thumper.bellcore.com   vesper@3d.dec.com

3

NAME
   xlogo - X Window System logo
SYNOPSIS
   xlogo [-*toolkitoption* ...]
DESCRIPTION
   The *xlogo* program displays the X Window System logo. This program is
   nothing more than a wrapper around the Athena Logo widget.
OPTIONS
   Xlogo accepts all of the standard X Toolkit command line options, of
   which the following are used most frequently:

   –bg *color*
           This option specifies the color to use for the background of the
           window. The default is *white*. A correct color for the back-
           ground is something like *maroon*.

   –bd *color*
           This option specifies the color to use for the border of the win-
           dow. The default is *black*.

   –bw *number*
           This option specifies the width in pixels of the border surround-
           ing the window.

   –fg *color*
           This option specifies the color to use for displaying the logo.
           The default is *black*. A correct color for the background is
           something like *silver,* which you can approximate with a shade
           of gray, like #aa9.

   –rv   This option indicates that reverse video should be simulated by
           swapping the foreground and background colors.

   –geometry *geometry*
           This option specifies the prefered size and position of the logo
           window.

   –display *display*
           This option specifies the X server to contact.

   –xrm *resourcestring*
           This option specifies a resource string to be used. This is espe-
           cially useful for setting resources that do not have separate com-
           mand line options.

X DEFAULTS
   This program uses the *Logo* widget in the X Toolkit. It understands all of
   the core resource names and classes as well as:

   width (class **Width**)
           Specifies the width of the logo. The default width is 100 pixels.

   height (class **Height**)
           Specifies the height of the logo. The default height is 100 pix-
           els.

   foreground (class **Foreground**)
           Specifies the color for the logo. The default is *black* since the
           core default for background is *white*.

   reverseVideo (class **ReverseVideo**)
           Specifies that the foreground and background should be reversed.

ENVIRONMENT
> **DISPLAY**
>> to get the default host and display number.
>
> **XENVIRONMENT**
>> to get the name of a resource file that overrides the global resources stored in the RESOURCE_MANAGER property.

SEE ALSO
> X(1), xrdb(1), Athena Logo widget

COPYRIGHT
> Copyright 1988, Massachusetts Institute of Technology.
> See *X(1)* for a full statement of rights and permissions.

AUTHORS
> Ollie Jones of Apollo Computer wrote the logo graphics routine, based on a graphic design by Danny Chong and Ross Chapman of Apollo Computer.

3

NAME

xlsfonts - server font list displayer for X

SYNOPSIS

xlsfonts [-options ...] [-fn pattern]

DESCRIPTION

Xlsfonts lists the fonts that match the given *pattern*. The wildcard character "*" may be used to match any sequence of characters (including none), and "?" to match any single character. If no pattern is given, "*" is assumed.

The "*" and "?" characters must be quoted to prevent them from being expanded by the shell.

OPTIONS

–display *host:dpy*

This option specifies the X server to contact.

–l   This option indicates that a long listing should be generated for each font.

–m   This option indicates that long listings should also print the minimum and maximum bounds of each font.

–C   This option indicates that listings should use multiple columns. This is the same as **-n 0**.

–1   This option indicates that listings should use a single column. This is the same as **-n 1**.

-w *width*

This option specifies the width in characters that should be used in figuring out how many columns to print. The default is 79.

-n *columns*

This option specifies the number of columns to use in displaying the output. By default, it will attempt to fit as many columns of font names into the number of character specified by **-w** *width*.

SEE ALSO

X(1), Xserver(1), xset(1), xfd(1)

ENVIRONMENT

DISPLAY

to get the default host and display to use.

BUGS

Doing "xlsfonts -l" can tie up your server for a very long time. This is really a bug with single-threaded non-preemptible servers, not with this program.

COPYRIGHT

Copyright 1988, Massachusetts Institute of Technology.
See *X(1)* for a full statement of rights and permissions.

AUTHOR

Mark Lillibridge, MIT Project Athena

NAME
   xlswins - server window list displayer for X

SYNOPSIS
   xlswins [-options ...] [windowid ...]

DESCRIPTION
   Xlswins lists the window tree. By default, the root window is used as the starting point, although a specific window may be specified using the *-id* option. If no specific windows are given on the command line, the root window will be used.

OPTIONS
   –display *displayname*
   This option specifies the X server to contact.

   –l   This option indicates that a long listing should be generated for each window. This includes a number indicating the depth, the geometry relative to the parent as well as the location relative to the root window.

   –format *radix*
   This option specifies the radix to use when printing out window ids. Allowable values are: *hex, octal,* and *decimal.* The default is hex.

   –indent *number*
   This option specifies the number of spaces that should be indented for each level in the window tree. The default is 2.

SEE ALSO
   X(1), Xserver(1), xwininfo(1), xprop(1)

ENVIRONMENT
   DISPLAY
   to get the default host and display to use.

BUGS
   This should be integrated with xwininfo somehow.

COPYRIGHT
   Copyright 1988, Massachusetts Institute of Technology.
   See *X(1)* for a full statement of rights and permissions.

AUTHOR
   Jim Fulton, MIT X Consortium

NAME
       xmag - magnify parts of the screen
SYNOPSIS
       xmag [-option ...]
DESCRIPTION
       The *xmag* program allows you to magnify portions of the screen. If no
       explicit region is specified, a square centered around the pointer is
       displayed indicating the area to be enlarged. Once a region has been
       selected, a window is popped up showing a blown up version of the
       region in which each pixel in the source image is represented by a small
       square of the same color. Pressing Button1 on the pointer in the enlarge-
       ment window pops up a small window displaying the position, number,
       and RGB value of the pixel under the pointer until the button is released.
       Pressing the space bar or any other pointer button removes the enlarged
       image so that another region may be selected. Pressing "q", "Q", or
       "^C" in the enlargement window exits the program.

OPTIONS
       –display *display*
              This option specifies the X server to use for both reading the
              screen and displaying the enlarged version of the image.

       –geometry *geom*
              This option specifies the size and/or location of the enlargement
              window. By default, the size is computed from the size of the
              source region and the desired magnification. Therefore, only one
              of **–source** *size* and **–mag** *magfactor* options may be specified if
              a window size is given with this option.

       –source *geom*
              This option specifies the size and/or location of the source region
              on the screen. By default, a 64x64 square centered about the
              pointer is provided for the user to select an area of the screen.
              The size of the source is used with the desired magnification to
              compute the default enlargement window size. Therefore, only
              one of **–geometry** *size* and **–mag** *magfactor* options may be
              specified if a source size is given with this option.

       –mag *magfactor*
              This option specifies an integral factor by which the source
              region should be enlarged. The default magnification is 5. This
              is used with the size of the source to compute the default
              enlargement window size. Therefore, only one of **-geometry**
              size and **–source** *geom* options may be specified if a
              magnification factor is given with this option.

       –bw *pixels*
              This option specifies the width in pixels of the border surround-
              ing the enlargement window.

       –bd *color*
              This option specifies the color to use for the border surrounding
              the enlargement window.

       –bg *colororpixelvalue*
              This option specifies the name of the color to be used as the
              background of the enlargement window. If the name begins
              with a percent size (%), it is interpreted to be an absolute pixel
              value. This is useful when displaying large areas since pixels
              that are the same color as the background do not need to be

painted in the enlargement. The default is to use the BlackPixel of the screen.

−fn *fontname*
This option specifies the name of a font to use when displaying pixel values (used when Button1 is pressed in the enlargement window).

−z
This option indicates that the server should be grabbed during the dynamics and the call to XGetImage. This is useful for ensuring that clients don't change their state as a result of entering or leaving them with the pointer.

X DEFAULTS
The *xmag* program uses the following X resources:

geometry (class **Geometry**)
Specifies the size and/or location of the enlargement window.

source (class **Source**)
Specifies the size and/or location of the source region on the screen.

magnification (class **Magnification**)
Specifies the enlargement factor.

borderWidth (class **BorderWidth**)
Specifies the border width in pixels.

borderColor (class **BorderColor**)
Specifies the color of the border.

background (class **Background**)
Specifies the color or pixel value to be used for the background of the enlargement window.

font (class **Font**)
Specifies the name of the font to use when displaying pixel values when the user presses Button1 in the enlargement window.

SEE ALSO
X(1), xwd(1)

BUGS
This program will behave strangely on displays that support windows of different depths.

Because the window size equals the source size times the magnification, you only need to specify two of the three parameters. This can be confusing.

Being able to drag the pointer around and see a dynamic display would be very nice.

Another possible interface would be for the user to drag out the desired area to be enlarged.

COPYRIGHT
Copyright 1988, Massachusetts Institute of Technology.

AUTHOR
Jim Fulton, MIT X Consortium

NAME
       xman - display manual pages

SYNOPSIS
       xman [-options ...]

DESCRIPTION
       Xman is a manual page browser. The default size of the initial *xman* win-
       dow is small so that you can leave it running throughout your entire login
       session. In the initial window there are three options: *Help* will pop up a
       window with on-line help, *Quit* will exit, and *Manual Page* will pop up a
       window with a manual page browser in it. You may pop up more than
       one manual page browser window from a single execution of *xman*.

       For further information on using *xman* please read the on-line help infor-
       mation. The rest of this manual page will discuss customization of *xman*.

       Xman accomodates new manual sections by the use of the environment
       variable MANPATH and by directory description files named *mandesc*.
       Xman will search each directory specified in the environment variable
       MANPATH for the following subdirectories only: man0, man1, ..., man8,
       manl (local), and mann (new). (It usually ignores the information in man0
       unless there is a *mandesc* file that specifically tells it not to.) These sub-
       directories each represent a separate section of the manual. These sub-
       directories should contain man pages. Any manual section can be
       renamed by an optional *mandesc* file.

       As an example, if MANPATH was set to */usr/man:/usr/sipb/man* and there
       was no *mandesc* file in /usr/man, *xman* would put all of the files in the
       default section names (e.g. manl gets a section name of local). But if
       there were a *mandesc* file in /usr/sipb/man which contained the line *lSIPB
       Programs*, then *xman* would put all files in the manl subdirectory in a new
       section called "SIPB Programs". *Xman* will search the *mandesc* file until
       there are no more lines of information. This flexibility is ideal for courses
       that have their own manual pages.

       Xman creates temporary files in /tmp for all unformatted man pages and
       all apropos searches.

COMMAND LINE OPTIONS
       -helpfile *filename*
              Specifies a helpfile to use other than the default.

       -bothshown
              Allows both the manual page and manual directory to be on the
              screen at the same time.

       -notopbox
              Starts without the Top Menu with the three buttons in it.

       -geometry *WxH+X+Y*
              Sets the size and location of the Top Menu with the three buttons
              in it.

       -pagesize *WxH+X+Y*
              Sets the size and location of all the Manual Pages.

       -bw *pixels* or **-borderwidth** *pixels*
              Specifies the width of the border for all windows in *xman*.

       -bd *color* or **-bordercolor** *color*
              Specifies the color of the borders of all windows in *xman*.

       -fg *color* or **-foreground** *color*
              Specifies the foreground color to be used.

-**bg** *color* or -**background** *color*
> Specifies the background color to be used.

-**fn** *font* or -**font** *font*
> Specifies the font to use for all buttons and labels.

-**display** *host:display[.screen]*
> Specifies a display other than the default specified by the DISPLAY environment variable.

-**name** *name*
> Specifies the name to use when retrieving resources.

-**title** *title*
> Specifies the title of this application.

-**xrm** *resources*
> Allows a resource to be specified on the command line.

3

X DEFAULTS
> The *xman* program uses the following X resources: **foreground, background, width, height, borderWidth,** and **borderColor.**
>
> In order to change the default values for widget resources you need to know widget names. Below are the names of some of the most common widgets. You can also reference Widgets by class. The most common classes are **Label, Command,** and **Text.**

topBox	the top menu
help	the help window
manualBrowser	the manual page display window
xmanCommands	manual page command popup menu
xmanSections	manual page section popup menu
xmanSearch	manual page search popup menu

> In addition, *xman* has application-specific resources which allow unique *xman* customizations.

manualFontNormal	The font to use for normal text in the manual pages.
manualFontBold	The font to use for bold text in the manual pages.
manualFontItalic	The font to use for italic text in the manual pages.
directoryFontNormal	
	The font to use for the directory text.
bothShown	Either 'true' or 'false', specifies whether or not you want both the directory and the manual page shown at start up.
directoryHeight	The height in pixels of the directory, when the directory and the manual page are shown simultaneously.
topCursor	The cursor to use in the top box.
helpCursor	The cursor to use in the help window.
manpageCursor	The cursor to use in the manual page window.
searchEntryCursor	The cursor to use in the search entry text widget.
helpFile	Use this rather than the system default helpfile.
topBox	Either 'true' or 'false', determines whether the top box (containing the help, quit and manual page buttons) or a manual page is put on the screen at start-

up. The default is true.

verticalList   Either 'true' or 'false', determines whether the direc-
                            tory listing is vertically or horizontally organized.
                            The default is horizontal (false).

Here are a few examples of how to string all this information together into
a resource specification that can be used on the command line with the
-xrm flag, or added to your .Xresource or .Xdefaults file.

xman*Command.foreground: Blue   All command buttons will be
                                         blue.

xman*topBox*foreground: Blue   Everything in the top menu has
                                         a blue foreground.

xman*Text.border: Red   All text widgets have a red
                                         border.

xman*Label.font: 9x15   All label buttons have a 9x15
                                         font.

FILES

/usr/man/* or those specified in the MANPATH.
mandesc

SEE ALSO

X(1), X(8C), man(1), apropos(1)

ENVIRONMENT

DISPLAY - the default host and display to use.
MANPATH - the search path for manual pages. Directories are separated
by colons (e.g. /usr/man:/mit/kit/man:/foo/bar/man).

BUGS

The -fn and -font option only specify the fonts for the command button
and not the text of the manpages or directories.
Protocol error upon selecting "Remove This Manpage".
Specification of the *mandesc* file format is not given in the man page.

COPYRIGHT

Copyright 1988 by Massachusetts Institute of Technology.
See *X(1)* for a full statement of rights and permissions.

AUTHORS

Chris Peterson, MIT Project Athena from the V10 version written by
Barry Shein of Boston University.

NAME

    xmessage - X window system message display program.

SYNOPSIS

    xmessage [-options ...] -m <message>

DESCRIPTION

    Xmessage opens a window on the screen that will contain the text of a message from either the command line or stdin. This text may have a scroll bar along the left side to allow the user to browse through relatively long messages. Along the lower edge of the message is list of words with boxes around them, clicking the left mouse button on any of these "buttons" (words with boxes around them) will cause the message to go away. If there is more than one "button" then some state will be returned to the invoker of the xmessage process via a change of the exit status of the program.

    This program serves two functions, firstly it can be a method for shell scripts to present the user with information much as 'echo' allows in a tty environment, as well as allowing the user you answer simple questinos. Secondly it allows much of the functionality of 'cat' again in a windowing verses tty environment.

    It should be noted that this program is intended for short messages, and will be quite slow when asked to handle long files from stdin. Although xmessage can accept input from stdin, this input is not allowed to come from a tty, if this is attempted, and error message will be printed. If xmessage is executed with an incorrect argument then it will print a usage message to standard out, as well as to an xmessage window.

COMMAND LINE OPTIONS

    These are the command line options that xmessage understands. Please note that some of these are inherited from the XToolkit and as the list of default toolkit options changes xman will follow.

    -printlabel

        This will case the program to print the label of the button pressed to standard output (stdout), I envision this to be useful when popping up a message to a friend, as in: "ready to go to lunch". This allows you to know if he clicked the yes or the no button.

    -noscroll (-nsb)

        The scroll bar is active on the text window by default, this causes it to be removed.

    -buttons <button> <button> ...

        This option will cause xmessage to create one button for each arguement the follows it until something starts with a '-'. The string passed to the button is the name of the Command button widget created and will be the default text displayed to the user. Since this is the name of the widget it may be used to change any of the Xresources associated with that button.

    -message <word> <word> ...

        This must be the last argument in the command list, as every argument after this one is assumed to be part of the message. There is no limit to the length of this message.

-geometery (height)x(width)+(x_offset)+(y_offset)
>Sets the size and location of the window created by xmessage.

-bw <pixels>

-borderwidth <pixels>
>Specifies the width of the border for all windows in xmessage.

-bd <color>

-bordercolor <color>
>Specifies the color of the borders of all windows in xmessage.

-fg <color>

-foreground <color>
>Specifies the foreground color to be used.

-bg <color>

-background <color>
>Specifies the background color to be used.

-fn <font>

-font <font>
>Specifies the font to use for all buttons and text.

-display <host:display[.screen]>
>Specifies a display other than the default specified by the DISPLAY environment variable to use to use.

-name <name>
>Specifies the name to use when retrieving resources.

-title <title>
>Specifies the title of this application.

-xrm <resource>
>Allows a resource to be specified on the command line.

WIDGET AND RESOURCE NAMES

Resource management is an important part of X Toolkit applications, and xmessage is not exception, all objects in xmessage can have many of their distinguishing characteristics changed by changing the resources associated with them, below is a brief list of the resources and what they modify.

foreground	- foreground color
background	- background color
width & height	- size
borderWidth	- border width
borderColor	- border color

In order to change the default values for the widget resources you need to have the names, thus, below I have specified the names of some of the most common widgets.

xmessage - (argv[0])	- shell widget that contains everything displayed.
text	- the text window.

<button name>   - each of the buttons. "okay" is
                                 default.

You can also reference Widgets by class, The important classes for this
application are: Command and Text.

Here are a few example of how to string all this information together into
a resource specification, that can be used on the command line with the
-xrm flag, or added to your .Xresource file.

xmessage*Command.foreground: Blue All command buttons will be
                                        blue.

xmessage*foreground: Blue   Everything in the xmessage
                                        window has a blue foreground.

xmessage*Text.border: Red   The text widget has a red
                                        border.

In addition Xmessage has a few specific application resources, that allow
customizations that are specific to xmessage.

ScrollText
          A Boolean reasource that determines whether you are allowed to
          scroll the text widget the default value is TRUE.

printLabel
          A Boolean resource that determines whether or not the label of
          the buton pressed to exit the program is printed, default value is
          FALSE.

ERROR MESSAGES
          Xmessage errors may be printed into their owm xmessage window, this
          invocation of xmessage has a different name. This allows its resources to
          be specified seperatly, the name of xmessage error program is
          xmessage_error.

EXIT STATUS
          Xmessage will exit with status zero (0) when there is only one button in
          the list, and it is clicked to exit. If there is more than one button in the
          list then the exit status will corrospond the number of the button pressed,
          starting at one (1) for the first button, and counting up. Zero (0) is not
          used to because no button should have a prefered place over the others.

SEE ALSO
          X(1), X(8C), echo(1), cat(1)

BUGS
          There must be some, somewhere.

AUTHORS
          Copyright 1988 by Massachusetts Institute of Technology.
          Chris Peterson, MIT Project Athena

NAME
>   *xmh* – X window interface to the MH message handling system.

SYNOPSIS
>   **xmh** [-path *mailpath*] [-initial *foldername*] [-flag] [*-toolkitoption* ...]

DESCRIPTION
>   The *xmh* program provides a window-oriented front end to the MH message handling system. It is designed to take advantage of a large graphical display and pointer; it will not function on an ordinary terminal at all.
>
>   *Xmh* consists of user-interface code only. To actually do things with your mail, it makes calls to the *mh* package.
>
>   Please don't be misled by the size of this document. *Xmh* really is easy to use!

INSTALLATION
>   The current version of *xmh* requires that the user is already set up to use *mh*, version 6. To do so, see if there is a file called .mh_profile in your home directory. If you do, check to see if it contains a line that starts with "Current-Folder". If it does, then you've been using version 4 or earlier of *mh*; to convert to version 6, you must remove that line. (Failure to do so causes spurious output to stderr, which can hang *xmh* depending on your setup.)
>
>   If you do not already have a .mh_profile, you can create one (and everything else you need) by typing "inc" to the shell.
>
>   For more information, refer to the *mh (1)* documentation.

RUNNING XMH
>   Run *xmh* as you would any other X application (e.g., xterm). It will accept a command-line display (of the form "-display host:dpy"); the default display is specified in the environment variable DISPLAY.
>
>   The rest of this document will probably be rather hard to follow without actually running *xmh* and seeing the things being described.

BASIC SCREEN LAYOUT
>   *Xmh* starts out with a single screen. There will be 6 or 7 areas on the screen:
>
>   –   A list of your folders. (New users of mh will see only "inbox" here.)
>   –   A list of the global and folder-oriented commands.
>   –   A list of the messages in one of your folders (initially, this will show the messages in "inbox").
>   –   A list of the message-oriented commands.
>   –   A view of one of your messages. (Initially this is blank.)
>   –   A list of commands for the message being viewed.
>
>   And, there will possibly be:

– A list of message-sequences defined for this folder. This appears just below the list of messages in this folder. (Message-sequences are discussed below; if you don't know what they are, then you won't have any.)

XMH AND THE TOOLKIT

Xmh uses the X Toolkit. Many of the features described below (scrollbars, buttonboxes, etc.) are actually part of the Toolkit, and are described here only for completeness. For more information, see the Toolkit documentation.

SCROLLBARS

Some parts of the screen will have a vertical area on the left containing a grey bar. This area is a *scrollbar*. They are used whenever the data in a window takes up more space than can be displayed. The grey bar indicates what portion of your data is visible. Thus, if the entire length of the area is grey, then you are looking at all your data. If only the first half is grey, then you are looking at the top half of your data.

You can use the pointer in the scrollbar to change what part of the data is visible. If you click with the middle button, then the top of the grey area will move to where the pointer is, and the corresponding portion of data will be displayed. If you hold down the middle button, you can drag around the grey area. This makes it easy to get to the top of the data: just press with the middle, drag off the top of the scrollbar, and release.

If you click with button 1, then the data to the right of the pointer will scroll to the top of the window. If you click with pointer button 3, then the data at the top of the window will scroll down to where the pointer is.

BUTTONBOXES

Any area consisting of many words or short phrases, each enclosed in a box, is called a *buttonbox*. Each box is actually a button that you can press by moving the pointer onto it and pressing pointer button 1. If a given buttonbox has more buttons in it than can fit, it will be displayed with a scrollbar, so you can always scroll to the button you want.

ADJUSTING THE RELATIVE SIZES OF AREAS

If you're not satisfied with the size of the various areas on the screen, they can easily be changed. Near the right edge of the border between each region is a black box, called a *grip*. Simply point to that grip with the pointer, press a pointer button, drag up or down, and release. Exactly what happens depends on which pointer button you press.

If you drag with the middle button, then only that border will move. This mode is simplest to understand, but is probably the least useful.

If you drag with pointer button 1, then you are adjusting the size of the window above. *Xmh* will attempt to compensate by adjusting some window below it.

If you drag with pointer button 3, then you are adjusting the size of the window below. *Xmh* will attempt to compensate by adjusting some window above it.

All windows have a mininum and maximum size; you will never be allowed to move a border past the point where it would make a window have an invalid size.

SELECTED FOLDER

The selected folder is whichever foldername is highlighted in the top buttonbox. Note that this is not necessarily the same folder that is being viewed. To change the selected folder, just press on the desired folder button.

GENERAL COMMANDS AND FOLDER COMMANDS

The second buttonbox contains commands of a global nature:

Quit XMH

Exits *xmh*, after first checking that you won't lose any changes.

Compose Message

Composes a new message. A new window will be brought up; for a description of it, see COMPOSITION WINDOWS, below.

Open Folder

Display the data in the selected folder. Thus, the selected folder also becomes the viewed folder.

Open Folder in New Window

Creates a new screen, and displays the selected folder in that screen. Note, however, that you may not display the same folder in more than one screen at a time.

Create Folder

Create a new folder. You will be prompted for a name for the new folder; to enter the name, point the pointer at the blank box provided and type. Hit the Confirm button when finished, or hit Abort to cancel this operation.

Delete Folder

Destroy the selected folder. You will be asked to confirm this action (see CONFIRMATION WINDOWS).

HIGHLIGHTED MESSAGES, SELECTED MESSAGES AND THE CURRENT MESSAGE

It is possible to highlight a set of messages in the list of messages for the viewed folder. To highlight a message, just click on it with pointer button 1. To highlight a range of messages, click on the first one with pointer button 1 and on the last one with pointer button 3.

The selected messages are the same as the highlighted messages, if any. If no messages are highlighted, then the selected messages are considered the same as the current message.

The current message is indicated by a '+' next to the message number. It usually corresponds to the message currently being viewed.

MESSAGE COMMANDS

The third buttonbox (fourth if you have message-sequences displayed) contains commands to deal with messages:

Incorporate New Mail
Add any new mail received to your inbox folder, and set the
current message to be the first new message. (This button is
selectable only if "inbox" is the folder being viewed.)

View Next Message
View the first selected message. If no messages are highlighted,
view the current message. If current message is already being
viewed, view the first unmarked message after the current message.

View Previous Message
View the last selected message. If no messages are highlighted,
view the current message. If current message is already being
viewed, view the first unmarked message before the current message.

Mark Deleted
Mark the selected messages for deletion. If no messages are
highlighted, then this will automatically display the next
unmarked message.

Mark Move
Mark the selected messages to be moved into the current folder.
(If the current folder is the same as the viewed folder, this command will just beep.) If no messages are highlighted, then this
will automatically display the next unmarked message.

Mark Copy
Mark the selected messages to be copied into the current folder.
(If the current folder is the same as the viewed folder, this com-
mand will just beep.)

Unmark Remove any of the above three marks from the selected messages.

View in New Window
Create a new window containing only a view of the first selected
message.

Reply Create a composition window in reply to the first selected message.

Forward
Create a composition window whose body is initialized to be the
contents of the selected messages.

Use as Composition
Create a composition window whose body is initialized to be
this message. Note that any changes you make in the composition will also be saved in this message. This function is meant
to be used with the "drafts" folder (see COMPOSITION WIN-
DOWS).

Commit Changes
Execute any deletions, moves, and copies that have been marked
in this folder.

Print Print the selected messages. *Xmh* normally prints by invoking
the *enscript*(1) command, but you may change the command it
uses. (See CUSTOMIZING, below).

Pack folder
Renumber the messages in this folder so they start with 1 and

increment by 1.

Sort folder
Sort the messages in this folder in chronological order. As a side effect, this also packs the folder.

Force Rescan
Rebuild the list of messages. This can be used whenever you suspect *xmh*'s idea of what messages you have is wrong. (In particular, this is useful if you ever change things using straight mh commands without using *xmh*.)

Pick Messages
Define a new message-sequence. (See MESSAGE-SEQUENCES.)

The following buttons will appear but will be sensitive only if the current folder has any message-sequences defined (See MESSAGE-SEQUENCES).

Open Sequence
Change the viewed sequence to be the same as the selected sequence.

Add to Sequence
Add the selected messages to the selected sequence.

Remove from Sequence
Remove the selected messages from the selected sequence.

Delete Sequence
Remove the selected sequence entirely. Note the messages themselves are not affected; they simply are no longer grouped together as a message-sequence.

VIEW WINDOWS

The commands in these windows are the same as the message commands by the same name, except instead of affecting the selected messages, they affect the viewed message. In addition there is the "Edit View" button, which allows you to edit the message being viewed. While editing, the "Edit View" button will change to a "Save View" button, which should be pressed to save your edits.

COMPOSITION WINDOWS

Aside from the normal text editing functions, there are six command buttons associated with composition windows:

Close   Close this composition window. If changes have been made since the most recent Save or Send, you will be asked to confirm losing them.

Send   Send this composition.

Reset   Replace the current composition with an empty message. If changes have been made since the most recent Send or Save, you will be asked to confirm losing them.

Compose
Bring up another new composition window.

Save   Save this composition in your drafts folder. (If you do not have a folder named "drafts", one will be created.) Then you can safely close the composition. At some future date, you can continue working on the composition by opening your drafts folder, selecting the message, and using the "Use as Composition" command.

Insert   Insert a related message into the composition. If the composition window was created with a *Reply* button, the related message is the message being replied to, otherwise no related message is defined and this button is inactive. The message will be filtered before being inserted; see **ReplyInsertFilter** under CUSTOMIZING below.

TEXT EDITING COMMANDS

All of the text editing commands are actually defined by the Text widget in the X Toolkit. The commands may be bound to different keys than the defaults described below through the standard X Toolkit key re-binding mechanisms. See the X Toolkit and Athena Widgets documentation for more details.

Whenever you are asked to enter any text, you will be using a standard text editing interface. Various control and meta keystroke combinations are bound to a somewhat Emacs-like set of commands. In addition, the pointer buttons may be used to select a portion of text or to move the insertion point in the text. Pressing pointer button 1 causes the insertion point to move to the pointer. Double-clicking button 1 selects a word, triple-clicking selects a paragraph, and quadruple-clicking selects everything. Any selection may be extended in either direction by using pointer button 3.

In the following, a *line* refers to one displayed row of characters in the window. A *paragraph* refers to the text between carriage returns. Text within a paragraph is broken into lines based on the current width of the window.

The following keystroke combinations are defined:

Control-A
    Move to the beginning of the current line.

Control-B, Control-H, Backspace
    Move backward one character.

Control-D
    Delete the next character.

Control-E
    Move to the end of the current line.

Control-F
    Move forward one character.

Control-J, LineFeed
    Create a new paragraph with the same indentation as the previous one.

Control-K
    Kill the rest of this line.

Control-L
    Refresh. Repaint this window.

Control-M, Return
    New paragraph.

Control-N
>   Move down to the next line.

Control-O
>   Break this paragraph into two.

Control-P
>   Move up to the previous line.

Control-V
>   Move down to the next screen-full of text.

Control-W
>   Kill the selected text.

Control-Y
>   Insert the last killed text.

Control-Z
>   Scroll the text one line up.

Meta-<   Move to the beginning of the document.

Meta->   Move to the end of the document.

Meta-[Move backward one paragraph.

Meta-]   Move forward one paragraph.

Meta-B   Move backward one word.

Meta-D   Kill the next word.

Meta-F   Move forward one word.

Meta-H, Meta-Delete
>   Kill the previous word.

Meta-I   Insert a file. If any text is selected, use the selected text as the filename. Otherwise, a box will appear in which you can type the desired filename.

Meta-V   Move up to the previous screen-full of text.

Meta-Y   Stuff the last selected text here. Note that this can be text selected in some other text subwindow. Also, if you select some text in an xterm window, it may be inserted in an *xmh* window with this command. Pressing pointer button 2 is equivalent to this.

Meta-Z   Scroll the text one line down.

Delete   Delete the previous character.

CONFIRMATION WINDOWS

Whenever you press a button that may cause you to lose some work or is otherwise dangerous, a window will appear asking you to confirm the action. This window will contain an "Abort" or "No"button and a "Confirm" or "Yes" button. Pressing the "Abort" button cancels the operation, and pressing the "Confirm" will proceed with the operation. (A very handy shortcut exists: if you press the original, offending button again, it will be interpreted as a "Confirm". If you press any other command button, it will be interpreted as an "Abort".)

MESSAGE-SEQUENCES

A mh message sequence is just a set of messages associated with some name. They are local to a particular folder; two different folders can have sequences with the same name. In all folders, the sequence "all" is predefined; it consists of the set of all messages in that folder. (The sequence "cur" is also usually defined for every folder; it consists of only the current message. *Xmh* hides "cur" from the user, instead placing a "+" by the current message. Also, *xmh* does not support the "unseen" sequence, so that one is also hidden from the user.)

The message sequences for a folder are displayed as buttons containing the names of the sequences (including one for "all"). The table of contents (aka "toc") is at any one time displaying one message sequence. This is called the "viewed sequence"; if it's not "all", its name will be displayed in the title bar just after the folder name. Also, at any time one of the sequence buttons will be highlighted. This is called the "selected sequence". Note that the viewed sequence and the selected sequence are not necessarily the same. (This all pretty much corresponds to the way the folder buttons work.)

The **Open Sequence, Add to Sequence, Remove from Sequence**, and **Delete Sequence** buttons are active only if the viewed folder contains message-sequences.

Note that none of the above actually effect whether a message is in the folder. Remember that a sequence is a set of messages within the folder; the above operations just affect what messages are in that set.

To create a new sequence, press the "Pick" button. A new window will appear, with lots of places to enter text. Basically, you can describe the sequence's initial set of messages based on characteristics of the message. Thus, you can define a sequence to be all the messages that were from a particular person, or with a particular subject, and so on. You can also connect things up with boolean operators, so you can select all things from "weissman" with the subject "xmh".

Hopefully, the layout is fairly obvious. The simplest cases are the easiest: just point to the proper field and type. If you enter in more than one field, it will only select messages which match all non-empty fields.

The more complicated cases arise when you want things that match one field or another one, but not necessarily both. That's what all the "or" buttons are for. If you want all things with the subject "xmh" or "xterm", just press the "or" button next to the "Subject:" field. Another box will appear where you can enter another subject.

If you want all things either from "weissman" or with subject "xmh", but not necessarily both, select the "-Or-" button. This will essentially double the size of the form. You can then enter "weissman" in a from: box on the top half, and "xmh" in a subject: box on the lower part.

If you ever select the "Skip" button, then only those messages that *don't* match the fields on that row are included.

Finally, in the bottom part of the window will appear several more boxes. One is the name of the sequence you're defining. (It defaults to the name of the selected sequence when "Pick" was pressed, or to "temp" if "all" was the selected sequence.) Another box defines which sequence to look through for potential members of this sequence; it defaults to the viewed sequence when "Pick" was pressed.

Two more boxes define a date range; only messages within that date range will be considered. These dates must be entered in 822-style format: each date is of the form "dd mmm yy hh:mm:ss zzz", where dd is a one or two digit day of the month, mmm is the three-letter abbreviation for a month, and yy is a year. The remaining fields are optional: hh, mm, and ss specify a time of day, and zzz selects a time zone. Note that if the time is left out, it defaults to midnight; thus if you select a range of "7 nov 86" - "8 nov 86", you will only get messages from the 7th, as all messages on the 8th will have arrived after midnight.

"Date field" specifies which date field in the header to look at for this date range; it probably won't be useful to anyone. If the sequence you're defining already exists, you can optionally merge the old set with the new; that's what the "Yes" and "No" buttons are all about. Finally, you can "OK" the whole thing, or "Cancel" it.

In general, most people will rarely use these features. However, it's nice to occasionally use "Pick" to find some messages, look through them, and then hit "Delete Sequence" to put things back in their original state.

CUSTOMIZING XMH
As with all standard X applications, *xmh* may be customized through entries in the resource manager. The following resource manager entries are defined: [Note: the entry names must be entered in either all lower-case, or in the exact case shown below.]

BackGround
Background color. Currently, this will effect only buttons. (Default is white.)

ButtonFont
What font to use for button names. (Default is "timrom10".)

CheckNewMail
If True, *xmh* will check at regular intervals to see if new mail has arrived for any of the folders. A visual indication will be given if new mail is waiting to be retrieved. (Default is True.)

CompButtonLines
How many rows of buttons to display under a composition. (Default is 1.)

CompFont
What font to use when composing a message. (Default is "6x13".)

CompGeometry
Initial geometry for windows containing compositions.

CompLines
How many lines of a composition to display. (Default is 20.)

ConfirmFont
What font to use for confirmation windows. (Default is "timrom10b".)

FolderButtonLines
How many rows of folder command buttons to display. (Default is 1.)

FolderLines
How many rows of foldername buttons to display. (Default is

1.)

ForeGround

Foreground color. Currently, this will effect only title bars and buttons. (Default is black.)

Geometry

Default geometry to use. (Default is none.)

HideBoringHeaders

If "on", then *xmh* will attempt to skip uninteresting header lines within messages by scrolling them off. (Default is "on".)

InitialFolder

Which folder to display on startup. May also be set with the command-line option **-initial**. (Default is "inbox".)

InitialIncFile

The file name of your incoming mail drop. *xmh* tries to construct a filename for the "inc -file" command, but in some installations (e.g. those using the Post Office Protocol) no file is appropriate. In this case, **InitialIncFile** should be specified as the empty string, and *inc* will be invoked without a -file argument.

LabelFont

What font to use for the title bars. (Default is "timrom10i".)

MailPath

The full path prefix for locating your mail folders. May also be set with the command-line option, **-path**. (Default is the "Path" component in $HOME/.mh_profile, or "$HOME/Mail" if none.)

MailWaitingFlag

If True, *xmh* will attempt to set an indication in it's icon when new mail is waiting to be retrieved. If this option is True, then CheckNewMail is assumed to be True as well. The **-flag** command line option is a quick way to turn MailWaitingFlag on.

MhPath What directory in which to find the mh commands. If a command isn't found here, then the directories in the user's path are searched. (Default is "/usr/local/mh6".)

PickGeometry

Initial geometry for pick windows.

PickEntryFont

What font to use for user text fields in pick windows. (Default is "timrom10".)

PickTextFont

What font to use for static text fields in pick windows. (Default is "timrom10".)

PrintCommand

What sh command to execute to print a message. Note that stdout and stderr must be specifically redirected! If a message or range of messages is selected for printing, the full file paths of each message file is appended to the specified print command. (Default is "enscript >/dev/null 2>/dev/null").

ReplyInsertFilter

A shell command to be executed when the *Insert* button is activated in a composition window. The full path and filename of the source message is added to the end of the command before being passed to *sh*(1). The default filter is *echo*; i.e. it merely inserts the name of the file into the composition. Other interesting filters are *awk -e '{print "   " $0}'* or */usr/new/mh.6.5/lib/mhl -form mhl.body.*

TempDir
Directory for *xmh* to store temporary directories. For privacy, a user might want to change this to a private directory. (Default is "/tmp".)

TocButtonLines
How many rows of message command buttons to display. (Default is 1.)

TocFont What font to use for a folder's table of contents. (Default is "6x13".)

TocGeometry
Initial geometry for master *xmh* windows.

TocLines
How many messages to display in a folder's table of contents. (Default is 10.)

TocWidth
How many characters to generate for each message in a folder's table of contents. (Default is 100. Use 80 if you plan to use *mhl* a lot.)

ViewButtonLines
How many rows of buttons to display under a view of a message. (Default is 1.)

ViewFont
What font to use for a view of a message. (Default is "6x13".)

ViewGeometry
Initial geometry for windows showing only a view of a message.

ViewLines
How many lines of a message to display. (Default is 20.)

If TocGeometry, ViewGeometry, CompGeometry, or PickGeometry are not specified, then the value of Geometry is used instead. If the resulting height is not specified (e.g., "", "=500", "+0-0"), then the default height is calculated from the fonts and line counts specified above. If the width is not specified (e.g., "", "=x300", "-0+0"), then half of the display width is used. If unspecified, the height of a pick window defaults to half the height of the display.

Any of these options may also be specified on the command line by using the standard X Toolkit resource specification mechanism. Thus, to run *xmh* showing all message headers,

% xmh -xrm '*HideBoringHeaders:off'

The initial text displayed in a composition window is generated by executing the corresponding *mh* command; i.e. *comp*, *repl*, or *forw* and therefore message components may be customized as specified for those commands. *Comp* is executed only once per invocation of *xmh* and the message template is re-used for each successive new composition.

FILES
  ˜/Mail

  ˜/.mh_profile

SEE ALSO
  X(1), xrdb(1), X Toolkit, mh(1) - the mh Message Handler

BUGS
  Printing support is minimal.

  Keyboard shortcuts for commands would be nice.

  Should handle the "unseen" message-sequence.

  Should determine by itself if the user hasn't used *mh* before, and offer to set things up for him or her.

  Still a few commands missing (rename folder, remail message).

  Needs sub-folder support.

COPYRIGHT
  Copyright 1988, Digital Equipment Corporation.
  See *X(1)* for a full statement of rights and permissions.

AUTHOR
  Terry Weissman, Digital Western Research Laboratory

NAME
xmille – X window mille bourne game

SYNOPSIS
xmille [*restore-file*]

DESCRIPTION
Xmille brings up a window for a mille bourne game. When selecting one of your cards, the left button plays the card, the right button discards the card and the middle button chooses whichever is appropriate, first trying to play the card, and then discarding it.

AUTHOR
Keith Packard
Dave Lemke
Dana Chee

SEE ALSO

NAME
>   xmodmap - utility for modifying keymaps in X

SYNOPSIS
>   **xmodmap** [-options ...] [filename]

DESCRIPTION
>   The *xmodmap* program is used to edit and display the keyboard *modifier map* and *keymap table* that are used by client applications to convert event keycodes into keysyms. It is usually run from the user's session startup script to configure the keyboard according to personal tastes.

OPTIONS
>   The following options may be used with *xmodmap*:

>   **–display** *display*
>>   This option specifies the host and display to use.

>   **–help**   This option indicates that a brief description of the command line arguments should be printed on the standard error. This will be done whenever an unhandled argument is given to *xmodmap*.

>   **–grammar**
>>   This option indicates that a help message describing the expression grammar used in files and with -e expressions should be printed on the standard error.

>   **–verbose**
>>   This option indicates that *xmodmap* should print logging information as it parses its input.

>   **–quiet**   This option turns off the verbose logging. This is the default.

>   **–n**   This option indicates that *xmodmap* should not change the mappings, but should display what it would do, like *make(1)* does when given this option.

>   **–e** *expression*
>>   This option specifies an expression to be executed. Any number of expressions may be specified from the command line.

>   **–pm**   This option indicates that the current modifier map should be printed on the standard output.

>   **–pk**   This option indicates that the current keymap table should be printed on the standard output.

>   **–pp**   This option indicates that the current pointer map should be printed on the standard output.

>   **–**   A lone dash means that the standard input should be used as the input file.

>   The *filename* specifies a file containing *xmodmap* expressions to be executed. This file is usually kept in the user's home directory with a name like *xmodmaprc*.

EXPRESSION GRAMMAR
>   The *xmodmap* program reads a list of expressions and parses them all before attempting execute any of them. This makes it possible to refer to keysyms that are being redefined in a natural way without having to worry as much about name conflicts.

>   **keycode** *NUMBER = KEYSYMNAME* ...
>>   The list of keysyms is assigned to the indicated keycode (which may be specified in decimal, hex or octal and can be determined

by running the *xev* program in the examples directory). Usually only one keysym is assigned to a given code.

keysym *KEYSYMNAME = KEYSYMNAME ...*

The *KEYSYMNAME* on the left hand side is looked up to find its current keycode and the line is replaced with the appropriate **keycode** expression. Note that if you have the same keysym bound to multiple keys, this might not work.

clear *MODIFIERNAME*

This removes all entries in the modifier map for the given modifier, where valid name are: Shift, Lock, Control, Mod1, Mod2, Mod3, Mod4 and Mod5 (case does not matter in modifier names, although it does matter for all other names). For example, ''clear Lock'' will remove all any keys that were bound to the shift lock modifier.

add *MODIFIERNAME = KEYSYMNAME ...*

This adds the given keysyms to the indicated modifier map. The keysym names are evaluated after all input expressions are read to make it easy to write expressions to swap keys (see the EXAMPLES section).

remove *MODIFIERNAME = KEYSYMNAME ...*

This removes the given keysyms from the indicated modifier map. Unlike **add,** the keysym names are evaluated as the line is read in. This allows you to remove keys from a modifier without having to worry about whether or not they have been reassigned.

pointer = default

This sets the pointer map back to its default settings (button 1 generates a code of 1, button 2 generates a 2, etc.).

pointer = *NUMBER ...*

This sets to pointer map to contain the indicated button codes. The list always starts with the first physical button.

Lines that begin with an exclamation point (!) are taken as comments.

If you want to change the binding of a modifier key, you must also remove it from the appropriate modifier map.

EXAMPLES

Many pointers are designed such the first button is pressed using the index finger of the right hand. People who are left-handed frequently find that it is more comfortable to reverse the button codes that get generated so that the primary button is pressed using the index finger of the left hand. This could be done on a 3 button pointer as follows:

% xmodmap -e "pointer = 3 2 1"

Many editor applications support the notion of Meta keys (similar to Control keys except that Meta is held down instead of Control). However, some servers do not have a Meta keysym in the default keymap table, so one needs to be added by hand. The following command will attach Meta to the Multi-language key (sometimes label Compose Character). It also takes advantage of the fact that applications that need a Meta key simply need to get the keycode and don't require the keysym to be in the first column of the keymap table. This means that applications that are looking for a Multi_key (including the default modifier map) won't notice any change.

    % keysym Multi_key = Multi_key Meta_L

One of the more simple, yet convenient, uses of *xmodmap* is to set the keyboard's "rubout" key to generate an alternate keysym. This frequently involves exchanging Backspace with Delete to be more comfortable to the user. If the *ttyModes* resource in *xterm* is set as well, all terminal emulator windows will use the same key for erasing characters:

```
% xmodmap -e "keysym BackSpace = Delete"
% echo "XTerm*ttyModes: erase ^?" | xrdb -merge
```

Some keyboards do not automatically generate less than and greater than characters when the comma and period keys are shifted. This can be remedied with *xmodmap* by resetting the bindings for the comma and period with the following scripts:

```
!
! make shift-, be < and shift-. be >
!
keysym comma = comma less
keysym period = period greater
```

One of the more irritating differences between keyboards is the location of the Control and Shift Lock keys. A common use of *xmodmap* is to swap these two keys as follows:

```
!
! Swap Caps_Lock and Control_L
!
remove Lock = Caps_Lock
remove Control = Control_L
keysym Control_L = Caps_Lock
keysym Caps_Lock = Control_L
add Lock = Caps_Lock
add Control = Control_L
```

The *keycode* command is useful for assigning the same keysym to multiple keycodes. Although unportable, it also makes it possible to write scripts that can reset the keyboard to a known state. The following script sets the backspace key to generate Delete (as shown above), flushes all existing caps lock bindings, makes the CapsLock key be a control key, make F5 generate Escape, and makes Break/Reset be a shift lock.

```
!
! On the HP, the following keycodes have key caps as listed:
!
!    101  Backspace
!     55  Caps
!     14  Ctrl
!     15  Break/Reset
!     86  Stop
!     89  F5
!
keycode 101 = Delete
keycode 55 = Control_R
clear Lock
add Control = Control_R
```

```
keycode 89 = Escape
keycode 15 = Caps_Lock
add Lock = Caps_Lock
```

ENVIRONMENT
> **DISPLAY**
>> to get default host and display number.

SEE ALSO
> X(1)

BUGS

> Every time a **keycode** expression is evaluated, the server generates a *MappingNotify* event on every client. This can cause some thrashing. All of the changes should be batched together and done at once. Clients that receive keyboard input and ignore *MappingNotify* events will not notice any changes made to keyboard mappings.

> *Xmodmap* should generate "add" and "remove" expressions automatically whenever a keycode that is already bound to a modifier is changed.

> There should be a way to have the *remove* expression accept keycodes as well as keysyms for those times when you really mess up your mappings.

COPYRIGHT
> Copyright 1988, Massachusetts Institute of Technology.
> Copyright 1987 Sun Microsystems, Inc.
> See *X(1)* for a full statement of rights and permissions.

AUTHOR
> Jim Fulton, MIT X Consortium, rewritten from an original by David Rosenthal of Sun Microsystems.

NAME
>   xmore - File browsing program for the X Window System.

SYNOPSIS
>   **xmore** [-options ...] filename

DESCRIPTION
>   Xmore pops up a window on the display specified, containing the file specified on the command line. This file may easily be viewed using the scrollbar to the left of the window.
>
>   For further information on using xmore please read the online help information. The rest of this manual page will dicsuss customization of xmore to suit the needs of a particular user.

OPTIONS
>   Xmore is build upon the *XToolkit (Xtk)* and as such understands all default command line options of the Xtk.

WIDGET AND RESOURCE NAMES
>   In order to change the default values for the widget resources you need to have the names, the name of the help widget is 'help'. In addition to the standard widget resources Xmore has the following application resources:

>   **textFontNormal**
>   **textFontItalic**
>>   The fonts to use for the two types of text.

>   **topCursor**
>   **helpCursor**
>>   The cursors to use in the main window and the help window, repectively.

>   **helpFile** Use this rather than the system default helpfile.

SEE ALSO
>   X(1), X(8C), more(1)

BUGS
>   The probably are some.

AUTHOR
>   Copyright 1988 by Massachusetts Institute of Technology.
>   Chris Peterson, MIT Project Athena, from the V10 version written by Barry Shein of Boston University.

NAME
    xpalette – color palette display and color mixer

SYNOPSIS
    xpalette [-*toolkitoption* ...] [-option ...]

DESCRIPTION
    Xpalette displays the contents of the currently active colormap in a win-
    dow. The created window shows a square for every color currently defined
    in the servers active colormap. The number of squares is the number of
    colormap-cells the server supports.

    To leave *xpalette* press the quit button.

OPTIONS
    Xpalette accepts all of the standard X Toolkit command line options along
    with the additional options listed below:

    –mixer   If the server supports colors and there is at least one writable
              color cell, *xpalette* also creates 3 mixer-scrollbars, which allow
              mixing red, green and blue values. The resulting color is shown
              both in the general colormap and in an extra square within the
              window.

X DEFAULTS
    This program uses the *Palette* and *Scrollbar* widgets in the X Toolkit. It
    understands all of the core resource names and classes as well as:

    mixer (class **Boolean**)
              Specifies whether or not a color-mixer should be shown. The
              default is False.

SEE ALSO
    X(1), Palette widget, Scrollbar widget

BUGS
    There might be some - it has been tested with Siemens servers running
    both monochrome and color, and with uVax Color-Workstations running
    color.

    It has not been tested with servers supporting more than one colormap.

NOTE
    Xpalette is quite boring on monochrome displays :-) .

COPYRIGHT
    Copyright 1988, Siemens Munich.

AUTHOR
    Claus Gittinger (..!decvax!unido!sinix!claus)

NAME
        xperfmon - X window system performance monitor

SYNOPSIS
        xperfmon [option ...]

DESCRIPTION
        xperfmon continuously displays several system statistics as a set of parallel
        line graphs. The name of the host is displayed in the upper left hand
        corner. The information is scaled so that it fills up the entire window.
        While *xperfmon* is running, it is possible to perform certain tasks by press-
        ing keys over the window:

        Q/q: Quit
        R: Reset graph and timer
        s: Decrease update interval (slower) by a small amount
        S: Decrease update interval (slower) by a large amount
        f: Increase update interval (faster) by a small amount
        F: Increase update interval (faster) by a large amount
        ?: Help

        xperfmon understands the following options:

        =*geometry*
                The xperfmon window is created with the specified size and
                location determined by the supplied geometry specification. See
                X(1) for a full explanation.

        host:display
                Run *xperfmon* on a specified display. Default is unix:0.

        –rv | -reverse
                Reverses black and white.

        –fw | -forward
                Forces colors to be as specified (rather than reversed).

        –bw | -border *pixels*
                Specify the border width in pixels. Default is 3.

        –fn | -font *fontname*
                The hostname and labels will be displayed in the specified font.
                The default is *6X10*.

        –u | -update *seconds*
                Specify the update interval for the graph in seconds. Default is
                1.

        –st | -stepsize *pixels*
                Specify the stepsize of the graph. Default is one pixel.

        –n | -not *stat stat stat...*
                A list of statistics not to be displayed. Specifying -n or -not on
                the commandline supercedes any statistics specified up to that
                time. All subsequent words on the command line that are statis-
                tics will be omited from the display. See immediately below.

        stat stat stat...
                A list of statistics to be displayed. If none are listed, all are
                displayed. If any are listed, only those listed are displayed
                unless -n or -not has been specified. Possible statistics are **user,
                system, idle, free, disk, interrupts, input, output,** and **colli-
                sion.** These refer to **User CPU percentage, System CPU per-
                centage, Free memory, Disk transfers, Interrupts, Input
                packets, Output packets,** and **Collision packets.**

ENVIRONMENT
>   DISPLAY - to get the default host and display number.

SEE ALSO
>   X(1), uwm(1), X(8C), mem(4), select(2)

AUTHORS
>   The X11 version of *xperfmon* was written by Emanuel Jay Berkenbilt, Project Athena on 1/21/1988. There is no record of previous authors.

BUGS

>   *xperfmon* requires the ability to open and read */dev/kmem*. On most systems, this requires the suid bit set with root ownership or the sgid bit set and membership in the same group as */dev/kmem*.

>   Occasionally, the *xperfon* window will not be updated correctly if its size changed too many times in rapid succession. This is a consequence of the way that exposure events are handled.

NAME
xphoon – set the X root window to display the PHase of the mOON

SYNOPSIS
xphoon   [-b]   [-t <interval>]   [-display <display>]

DESCRIPTION
Xphoon sets the X root window to display a picture of the moon in its current phase, including the partial lighting of the dark side by reflected earthlight.

The *-b* flag defeats the earthlight feature, forcing the dark side to be black. The *-t* flag can be used to have *xphoon* keep running and update the picture every *<interval>* minutes. (Normally, *xphoon* just sets the root picture and exits.)

NOTES
The original motivation for this program was that xsetroot was **too slow.** Loading a full-screen bitmap took about 15 seconds. We made a trivial program that had fullmoon.bitmap compiled in, and it ran in less than a second. (And incidentally, the executable was smaller than fullmoon.bitmap.) Then later we came up with the cheapmoons, the phase hacking, and finally the earthlight.

SEE ALSO
phoon(1), xsetroot(1)

AUTHORS
Copyright (C) 1988 by Jef Poskanzer and Craig Leres.

Permission to use, copy, modify, and distribute this software and its documentation for any purpose and without fee is hereby granted, provided that the above copyright notice appear in all copies and that both that copyright notice and this permission notice appear in supporting documentation. This software is provided "as is" without express or implied warranty.

The moon-phase computation is from "moontool.c" by John Walker.

NAME
    xpic - draw and edit diagrams, figures, pictures in X Windows

SYNOPSIS
    xpic [X Toolkit options] ... [xpic options] ...   file

DESCRIPTION
    Xpic is a program for drawing figures in X Windows. It has facilities for
    creating various graphic elements like lines, splines, circles, ellipses, and
    text with a number of different attributes (line thickness, line style, text
    font, text point size). It also has various facilities for editing the diagrams,
    either on an individual *element* basis, or by grouping elements into *blocks*.
    These editing facilities include copy, move, delete, paste, adjust, change
    attributes, get from disk, and put to disk. It also permits the saving and
    loading of pictures, and the adjustment of the grid to which picture ele-
    ments are aligned.

    While xpic runs under both Version 10 and 11 of the X Windows System,
    the version for X10 is completely unsupported, not distributed (it relies on
    too many local fixes to the Xsun server, some of which are derived from
    proprietary code) and generally not meant to be used any more. It is likely
    to vanish completely in the near future.

    The program is meant to be easy enough to use without a manual. (This is
    called a weak cop-out!)

SEE ALSO
    For a more complete description of the functions, and some advanced
    features, see
            DOCDIR/xpic.doc.
    For examples, see
            DOCDIR/*.x.

    x2ps(L), and *x2pic*(L) are supporting programs that convert from xpic's
    internal saved format to PostScript(tm) and pic format respectively.

AUTHOR
    Mark Moraes, CSRI, University of Toronto.
    <moraes@csri.toronto.edu>

BUGS
    (Bugs! In my program?!) Rubber banding boxes seem to leave debris
    when the box is being drawn (or adjusted) right to left or bottom to top.
    This might be an X server bug.
    Splines leave debris after rubberbanding or adjusting. This may be con-
    sidered a feature since I'm not sure how to fix it.
    Splines/lines leave old arrows around after an adjust of end segments.

TRADEMARKS
    PostScript is a registered trademark of Adobe Systems, Inc.

NAME

xplaces - take snapshot of personal X window configuration and print
command lines for all X applications

SYNOPSIS

xplaces

DESCRIPTION

xplaces prints on standard output the command lines used to startup the X
applications presently running and their geometry. The output, after a little editing, can be used in an initialization file.

EXAMPLE

Here is a configuration example:

xterm -sb -geometry 80x9+1+19 -title console -name console -C \
        -display unix:0 -e /e/moraes/.x11startup.bw2   &
xclock -geometry 100x100+1048+0   &
rcmd neat.ai /ai/bin/X11/xterm -display gerrard.csri:0 \
        -geometry 80x57+291+26 -ls   &
xterm -geometry 80x56+310+53 -e rlogin bay.csri   &
xterm -geometry 80x51+410+128 -title gerrard.csri   &

This will start up a console terminal window (which receives redirected
console output, preventing it from messing up the display), a clock and
three terminal windows, one of which is started up by the shell script
rcmd which starts up a command on a remote machine, putting it in the
background. *Rcmd* is useful only if the application on the remote machine
has no use for standard output and error because they get redirected to
/dev/null.

On Suns, the recommended way of running *X11* is by "x11". In that
case, the console xterm is automatically started up by the *x11* script, so
that command must be removed from the xplaces output, and the remaining xterms (and other applications can be added to the *x11startup.** file.

SEE ALSO

x11(x)

BUGS

xplaces can only print the command line if the application is well behaved
and sets the appropriate properties.

AUTHOR

Ken Yap (ken@cs.rochester.edu)
Mark Moraes (moraes@csri.toronto.edu)

NAME
        xpr – print an X window dump

SYNOPSIS
        xpr [–scale *scale*] [–density *dpi*] [–height *inches*] [–width
        inches] [–left *inches*] [–top *inches*] [–header *string*] [–trailer
        string] [–landscape] [–portrait] [–rv] [–compact] [–output
        filename] [–append *filename*] [–noff] [–split *n*] [–device *dev*
        ] [–cutoff *level*] [–noposition] *filename*

DESCRIPTION
        Xpr takes as input a window dump file produced by *xwd(1)* and formats it
        for output on the HP LaserJet (or other PCL printers), HP PaintJet, LN03,
        LA100, PostScript printers, or IBM PP3812 page printer. If no *filename*
        argument is given, the standard input is used. By default, *xpr* prints the
        largest possible representation of the window on the output page. Options
        allow the user to add headers and trailers, specify margins, adjust the scale
        and orientation, and append multiple window dumps to a single output
        file. Output is to standard output unless –output is specified.

        Command Options

        –scale *scale*
                Affects the size of the window on the page. The HP, LN03 and
                PostScript printers are able to translate each bit in a window pixel
                map into a grid of a specified size. For example each bit might
                translate into a 3x3 grid. This would be specified by –scale *3*.
                By default a window is printed with the largest scale that will fit
                onto the page for the specified orientation.

        –density *dpi*
                Indicates what dot-per-inch density should be used by the printer.

        –height *inches*
                Specifies the maximum height of the window on the page.

        –width *inches*
                Specifies the maximum width of the window.

        –left *inches*
                Specifies the left margin in inches. Fractions are allowed. By
                default the window is centered in the page.

        –top *inches*
                Specifies the top margin for the picture in inches. Fractions are
                allowed.

        –header *string*
                Specifies a header string to be printed above the window.

        –trailer *string*
                Specifies a trailer string to be printed below the window.

        –landscape
                Forces the window to printed in landscape mode. By default a
                window is printed such that its longest side follows the long side
                of the paper.

        –portrait
                Forces the window to be printed in portrait mode. By default a
                window is printed such that its longest side follows the long side
                of the paper.

−rv   Forces the window to be printed in reverse video.

−compact
         Uses simple run-length encoding for compact representation of
         windows with lots of white pixels.

−output *filename*
         Specifies an output file name. If this option is not specified, stan-
         dard output is used.

−append *filename*
         Specifies a filename previously produced by *xpr* to which the
         window is to be appended.

−noff   When specified in conjunction with **−append**, the window will
         appear on the same page as the previous window.

−split *n* This option allows the user to split a window onto several pages.
         This might be necessary for very large windows that would other-
         wise cause the printer to overload and print the page in an
         obscure manner.

−device *dev*
         Specifies the device on which the file will be printed. Currently
         xpr understands the following *devs*:

ljet	HP LaserJet series and other monochrome PCL devices such as ThinkJet, QuietJet, RuggedWriter, HP2560 series, and HP2930 series printers
pjet	HP PaintJet (color mode)
ln03	DEC LN03
la100	DEC LA100
ps	PostScript printers
pp	IBM PP3812

         The default device is *ljet*. **-device lw** (LaserWriter) is equivalent
         to -device ps and is provided only for backwards compatibility.

−cutoff *level*
         Changes the intensity level where colors are mapped to either
         black or white for monochrome output on a LaserJet printer. The
         level is expressed as percentage of full brightness. Fractions are
         allowed.

−noposition
         This option causes header, trailer, and image positioning com-
         mand generation to be bypassed for LaserJet and PaintJet printers.

SEE ALSO
         xwd(1), xdpr(1), xwud(1), X(1)

LIMITATIONS
         The current version of *xpr* can generally print out on the LN03 most X
         windows that are not   larger than two-thirds   of the screen. For exam-
         ple, it will be able to print out a large Emacs window, but it will usu-
         ally fail when trying to print out the   entire screen. The LN03 has
         memory limitations that can cause it to incorrectly print very large or
         complex   windows.   The two   most common   errors encountered
         are "band too complex" and "page memory exceeded." In the first
         case, a window may have a particular six pixel row that contains too
         many changes (from black to white to black). This will cause the printer
         to drop part of the line and possibly parts of the rest of the page. The
         printer will flash the number '1' on its front panel when this problem
         occurs. A possible solution to this problem is to increase the scale of

the picture, or to split the picture onto two or more pages. The second problem, "page memory exceeded," will occur if the picture contains too much black, or if the picture contains complex half-tones such as the background color of a display. When this problem occurs the printer will automatically split the picture into two or more pages. It may flash the number '5' on its from panel. There is no easy solution to this problem. It will probably be necessary to either cut and paste, or rework to application to produce a less complex picture.

Xpr provides some support for the LA100. However, there are several limitations on its use: The picture will always be printed in portrait mode, there is no scaling and the aspect ratio will be slightly off.

Support for PostScript output currently cannot handle the **-append, -noff** or **-split** options.

The **-compact** option is *only* supported for PostScript output. It compresses white space but not black space, so it is not useful for reverse-video windows.

HP PRINTERS

If no **–density** is specified on the command line 300 dots per inch will be assumed for *ljet* and 90 dots per inch for *pjet*. Allowable *density* values for a LaserJet printer are 300, 150, 100, and 75 dots per inch. Consult the operator's manual to determine densities supported by other printers.

If no **–scale** is specified the image will be expanded to fit the printable page area.

The default printable page area is 8x10.5 inches. Other paper sizes can be accomodated using the **–height** and **–width** options.

Note that a 1024x768 image fits the default printable area when processed at 100 dpi with scale=1, the same image can also be printed using 300 dpi with scale=3 but will require considerably more data be transfered to the printer.

Xpr may be tailored for use with monochrome PCL printers other than the LaserJet. To print on a ThinkJet (HP2225A) *xpr* could be invoked as:

    xpr -density 96 -width 6.667 *filename*

or for black-and-white output to a PaintJet:

    xpr -density 180 *filename*

The monochrome intensity of a pixel is computed as 0.30*R + 0.59*G + 0.11*B. If a pixel's computed intensity is less than the **–cutoff** level it will print as white. This maps light-on-dark display images to black-on-white hardcopy. The default cutoff intensity is 50% of full brightness. Example: specifying **–cutoff 87.5** moves the white/black intensity point to 87.5% of full brightness.

A LaserJet printer must be configured with sufficient memory to handle the image. For a full page at 300 dots per inch approximately 2MB of printer memory is required.

Color images are produced on the PaintJet at 90 dots per inch. The PaintJet is limited to sixteen colors from its 330 color palette on each horizontal print line. *Xpr* will issue a warning message if more than sixteen colors are encountered on a line.

Specifying the **–rv**, reverse video, option for the PaintJet will cause black and white to be interchanged on the output image. No other colors are changed.

Multiplane images must be recorded by *xwd* in *ZPixmap* format. Single plane (monochrome) images may be in either *XYPixmap* or *ZPixmap* format.

Some PCL printers do not recognize image positioning commands. Output for these printers will not be centered on the page and header and trailer strings may not appear where expected.

The **–split** option is not supported for HP printers.

COPYRIGHT

Copyright 1988, Hewlett Packard Company.
Copyright 1988, Massachusetts Institute of Technology.
Copyright 1986, Marvin Solomon and the University of Wisconsin.
See *X(1)* for a full statement of rights and permissions.

AUTHORS

Michael R. Gretzinger, MIT Project Athena, Jose Capo, MIT Project Athena (PP3812 support), Marvin Solomon (University of Wisconsin), Larry Rupp (Hewlett Packard Company).

NAME
>   xpref – a preference setting tool

SYNOPSIS
>   xpref [normal Xaw options]

DESCRIPTION
>   *xpref* is sort of an Xaw version of *xset*. You can set your preferences via
>   buttons, scroll bars, or type-in text windows. Things that toggle (keyboard
>   auto repeat, screen blanking, and screen exposures) can be set with on/off
>   buttons and take effect immediately. Things that take values (keyboard
>   click, bell volume, pitch, and duration, mouse acceleration numerator,
>   acceleration denomintor, and threshold, and screen time-out and cycle) can
>   be set with a scroll bar or type-in text window and don't take effect until
>   you press the (label) button directly above the type-in window. Things
>   that toggle display the the current setting by dimming it (for example, if
>   keyboard repeat is off then the off button is dimmed). Things that take a
>   value display the current value in the type-in window and position the
>   scroll bar at that position.

OPTIONS
>   *xpref* takes all of the standard toolkit options.

X DEFAULTS
>   The available names (classes) for the widgets used are:

topForm	(Form)
keyForm	(Form)
keyLabel	(Label)
bellForm	(Form)
bellLabel	(Label)
mouseForm	(Form)
mouseLabel	(Label)
screenForm	(Form)
screenLabel	(Label)
thumbForm	(Form)
thumbButton	(Command)
thumbText	(Text)
thumbScroll	(Scrollbar)
toggleForm	(Form)
toggleLabel	(Label)
toggleOn	(Command)
toggleOff	(Command)
quitForm	(Form)
quitButton	(Command)

>   These can be used to set fonts, colors, etc. tailored to the user's needs. As
>   a color example:

xpref*keyForm.Background:	yellow
xpref*bellForm.Background:	orange
xpref*mouseForm.Background:	pink
xpref*screenForm.Background:	cyan
xpref*screenForm*Label.Background:	yellow

                    xpref*Label.Font: 9x15
                    xpref*thumbForm.Command.Font: helvetica10
                    xpref*toggleForm.Label.Font: helvetica12b

AUTHORS
        Program: Rusty C. Wright
                        rusty@cartan.berkeley.edu
                        ucbvax!cartan!rusty

        Man page: Dana Chee
                        dana@bellcore.com
                        {standard gateways}!bellcore!dana

NAME
> xprop - property displayer for X

SYNOPSIS
> **xprop** [-help] [-grammar] [-id *id*] [-root] [-name *name*] [-font *font*] [-display *display*] [-len *n*] [-notype] [-fs *file*] [-f *atom format* [*dformat*]]* [*format* [*dformat*] *atom*]*

SUMMARY
> The *prop* utility is for displaying window and font properties in an X server. One window or font is selected using the command line arguments or possibly in the case of a window, by clicking on the desired window. A list of properties is then given, possibly with formatting information.

OPTIONS
> **-help**   Print out a summary of command line options.
>
> **-grammar**
> > Print out a detailed grammar for all command line options.
>
> **-id** *id*   This argument allows the user to select window *id* on the command line rather than using the pointer to select the target window. This is very useful in debugging X applications where the target window is not mapped to the screen or where the use of the pointer might be impossible or interfere with the application.
>
> **-name** *name*
> > This argument allows the user to specify that the window named *name* is the target window on the command line rather than using the pointer to select the target window.
>
> **-font** *font*
> > This argument allows the user to specify that the properties of font *font* should be displayed.
>
> **-root**   This argument specifies that X's root window is the target window. This is useful in situations where the root window is completely obscured.
>
> **-display** *display*
> > This argument allows you to specify the server to connect to; see *X(1)*.
>
> **-len** *n*   Specifies that at most *n* bytes of any property should be read or displayed.
>
> **-notype**   Specifies that the type of each property should not be displayed.
>
> **-fs** *file*   Specifies that file *file* should be used as a source of more formats for properties.
>
> **-remove** *property-name*
> > Specifies the name of a property to be removed from the indicated window.
>
> **-f** *name format* [*dformat*]
> > Specifies that the *format* for *name* should be *format* and that the *dformat* for *name* should be *dformat*. If *dformat* is missing, " = $0+\n" is assumed.

DESCRIPTION
> For each of these properties, its value on the selected window or font is printed using the supplied formatting information if any. If no formatting information is supplied, internal defaults are used. If a property is not

defined on the selected window or font, "not defined" is printed as the value for that property. If no property list is given, all the properties possessed by the selected window or font are printed.

A window may be selected in one of four ways. First, if the desired window is the root window, the -root argument may be used. If the desired window is not the root window, it may be selected in two ways on the command line, either by id number such as might be obtained from *xwininfo*, or by name if the window possesses a name. The -id argument selects a window by id number in either decimal or hex (must start with 0x) while the -name argument selects a window by name.

The last way to select a window does not involve the command line at all. If none of -font, -id, -name, and -root are specified, a crosshairs cursor is displayed and the user is allowed to choose any visible window by pressing any pointer button in the desired window. If it is desired to display properties of a font as opposed to a window, the -font argument must be used.

Other than the above four arguments and the -help argument for obtaining help, and the -grammar argument for listing the full grammar for the command line, all the other command line arguments are used in specifing both the format of the properties to be displayed and how to display them. The -len *n* argument specifies that at most *n* bytes of any given property will be read and displayed. This is useful for example when displaying the cut buffer on the root window which could run to several pages if displayed in full.

Normally each property name is displayed by printing first the property name then its type (if it has one) in parentheses followed by its value. The -notype argument specifies that property types should not be displayed. The -fs argument is used to specify a file containing a list of formats for properties while the -f argument is used to specify the format for one property.

The formatting information for a property actually consists of two parts, a *format* and a *dformat*. The *format* specifies the actual formatting of the property (i.e., is it made up of words, bytes, or longs?, etc.) while the *dformat* specifies how the property should be displayed.

The following paragraphs describe how to construct *formats* and *dformats*. However, for the vast majority of users and uses, this should not be necessary as the built in defaults contain the *formats* and *dformats* necessary to display all the standard properties. It should only be necessary to specify *formats* and *dformats* if a new property is being dealt with or the user dislikes the standard display format. New users especially are encouraged to skip this part.

A *format* consists of one of 0, 8, 16, or 32 followed by a sequence of one or more format characters. The 0, 8, 16, or 32 specifies how many bits per field there are in the property. Zero is a special case meaning use the field size information associated with the property itself. (This is only needed for special cases like type INTEGER which is actually three different types depending on the size of the fields of the property)

A value of 8 means that the property is a sequence of bytes while a value of 16 would mean that the property is a sequence of words. The difference between these two lies in the fact that the sequence of words will be byte swapped while the sequence of bytes will not be when read by a machine of the opposite byte order of the machine that orginally wrote the property. For more information on how properties are formatted and stored, consult the Xlib manual.

Once the size of the fields has been specified, it is necessary to specify the type of each field (i.e., is it an integer, a string, an atom, or what?) This is done using one format character per field. If there are more fields in the property than format characters supplied, the last character will be repeated as many times as necessary for the extra fields. The format characters and their meaning are as follows:

a   The field holds an atom number. A field of this type should be of size 32.

b   The field is an boolean. A 0 means false while anything else means true.

c   The field is an unsigned number, a cardinal.

i   The field is a signed integer.

m   The field is a set of bit flags, 1 meaning on.

s   This field and the next ones until either a 0 or the end of the property represent a sequence of bytes. This format character is only usable with a field size of 8 and is most often used to represent a string.

x   The field is a hex number (like 'c' but displayed in hex - most useful for displaying window ids and the like)

An example *format* is 32ica which is the format for a property of three fields of 32 bits each, the first holding a signed integer, the second an unsigned integer, and the third an atom.

The format of a *dformat* unlike that of a *format* is not so rigid. The only limitations on a *dformat* is that one may not start with a letter or a dash. This is so that it can be distinguished from a property name or an argument. A *dformat* is a text string containing special characters instructing that various fields be printed at various points in a manner similar to the formatting string used by printf. For example, the *dformat* " is ($0, $1 \)\n" would render the POINT 3, -4 which has a *format* of 32ii as " is (3, -4)\n".

Any character other than a $, ?, \, or a (in a *dformat* prints as itself. To print out one of $, ?, \, or (preceed it by a \. For example, to print out a $, use \$. Several special backslash sequences are provided as shortcuts. \n will cause a newline to be displayed while \t will cause a tab to be displayed. \o where o is an octal number will display character number o.

A $ followed by a number *n* causes field number *n* to be displayed. The format of the displayed field depends on the formatting character used to describe it in the corresponding *format*. I.e., if a cardinal is described by 'c' it will print in decimal while if it is described by a 'x' it is displayed in hex.

If the field is not present in the property (this is possible with some properties), <field not available> is displayed instead. $n+ will display field number *n* then a comma then field number *n*+1 then another comma then ... until the last field defined. If field *n* is not defined, nothing is displayed. This is useful for a property that is a list of values.

A ? is used to start a conditional expression, a kind of if-then statement. ?*exp*(*text*) will display *text* if and only if *exp* evaluates to non-zero. This is useful for two things. First, it allows fields to be displayed if and only if a flag is set. And second, it allows a value such as a state number to be displayed as a name rather than as just a number. The syntax of *exp* is as follows:

exp   ::= *term* | *term=exp* | !*exp*

term   ::= *n* | $*n* | m*n*

The ! operator is a logical "not", changing 0 to 1 and any non-zero value to 0. = is an equality operator. Note that internally all expressions are evaluated as 32 bit numbers so -1 is not equal to 65535. = returns 1 if the two values are equal and 0 if not. *n* represents the constant value *n* while $*n* represents the value of field number *n*. m*n* is 1 if flag number *n* in the first field having format character 'm' in the corrsponding *format* is 1, 0 otherwise.

Examples: ?m3(count: $3\n) displays field 3 with a label of count if and only if flag number 3 (count starts at 0!) is on. ?$2=0(True)?!$2=0(False) displays the inverted value of field 2 as a boolean.

In order to display a property, *xprop* needs both a *format* and a *dformat*. Before *xprop* uses its default values of a *format* of 32x and a *dformat* of " = { $0+ }\n", it searches several places in an attempt to find more specific formats. First, a search is made using the name of the property. If this fails, a search is made using the type of the property. This allows type STRING to be defined with one set of formats while allowing property WM_NAME which is of type STRING to be defined with a different format. In this way, the display formats for a given type can be overridden for specific properties.

The locations searched are in order: the format if any specified with the property name (as in 8x WM_NAME), the formats defined by -f options in last to first order, the contents of the file specified by the -fs option if any, the contents of the file specified by the environmental variable XPROPFORMATS if any, and finally *xprop*'s built in file of formats.

The format of the files refered to by the -fs argument and the XPROP-FORMATS variable is one or more lines of the following form:

name format [*dformat*]

Where *name* is either the name of a property or the name of a type, *format* is the *format* to be used with *name* and *dformat* is the *dformat* to be used with *name*. If *dformat* is not present, " = $0+\n" is assumed.

EXAMPLES

To display the name of the root window: *xprop* -root WM_NAME

To display the window manager hints for the clock: *xprop* -name xclock WM_HINTS

To display the start of the cut buffer: *xprop* -root -len 100 CUT_BUFFER0

To display the point size of the fixed font: *xprop* -font fixed POINT_SIZE

To display all the properties of window # 0x200007: *xprop* -id 0x200007

ENVIRONMENT

DISPLAY

        To get default display.

XPROPFORMATS

        Specifies the name of a file from which additional formats are to be obtained.

SEE ALSO

        X(1), xwininfo(1)

COPYRIGHT
    Copyright 1988, Massachusetts Institute of Technology.
    See *X(1)* for a full statement of rights and permissions.

AUTHOR
    Mark Lillibridge, MIT Project Athena

NAME
>   xpseudoroot - create a pseudo root window

SYNOPSIS
>   **xpseudoroot** [-options ...] *property_name*

DESCRIPTION
>   The *xpseudoroot* program allows you to create pseudo root windows as
>   outlined in the Inter-Client Communications Conventions Manual. By
>   default it just makes a copy of the normal root window, but command line
>   options may be used to alter much of the screen-related information.
>
>   The command line argument *property_name* specifies the name of a pro-
>   perty on the screen's real root window in which to store the pseudo root
>   information. Applications can be run within the pseudo root window by
>   appending *.property_name* to the *displaynumber.screennumber* part of the
>   display name; for example: expo:0.0.*property_name*
>
>   **WARNING**: This is experimental code for implementing pseudo root win-
>   dows as specified by the Inter-Client Communications Conventions
>   Manual. The interfaces that it provides should be considered private to
>   the MIT implementation of Xlib and WILL CHANGE IN THE NEXT
>   RELEASE. The interfaces that it provides should not be incorporated into
>   any toolkits or applications. No effort will be made to provide backward
>   compatibility.

OPTIONS
>   **-display** *displayname*
>   >   This option specifies the name of the X server to contact.
>
>   **-geometry** *geom*
>   >   This option specifies size and location of the pseudo root win-
>   >   dow.
>
>   **-visuals** *visualid ...*
>   >   This option specifies a list of visuals to support on the pseudo
>   >   root window. Any number of numeric visual identifiers (in hex,
>   >   octal, or decimal) may be given per -*visuals*.
>
>   **-colormap** *colormapid*
>   >   This option specifies the numeric colormap identifier to be asso-
>   >   ciated with the pseudo root window.
>
>   **-Colormap** *visualid*
>   >   This option specifies a numeric visual identifier to be used in
>   >   creating a new colormap for the pseudo root window. If this
>   >   option is given, *xpseudoroot* will create a new colormap from
>   >   the given visual and set the black and white pixel fields to the
>   >   desired colors.
>
>   **-white** *pixel*
>   >   This option specifies the numeric pixel value to use for Whi-
>   >   tePixel when creating a new colormap with –*Colormap*. The
>   >   default is to copy the real screen's WhitePixel.
>
>   **-White** *colorname*
>   >   This option specifies the color to use when setting WhitePixel in
>   >   newly created colormaps. It may be used with –*white* to create
>   >   arbitrary WhitePixels.
>
>   **-black** *pixel*
>   >   This option specifies the numeric pixel value to use for Black-
>   >   Pixel when creating a new colormap with –*Colormap*. The

default is to copy the real screen's BlackPixel.

-**Black** *colorname*
This option specifies the color to use when setting BlackPixel in newly created colormaps. It may be used with *–black* to create arbitrary BlackPixels.

-**empty** This option indicates that any colormaps created with *–Colormap* should not have BlackPixel and WhitePixel preallocated (although the values may still be set with *–black* and *–white*). This leaves as much room as possible for running applications that would otherwise not find enough colors. This is not for general use as it guarantees that an application will be displayed in incorrect colors.

-**max** *number*
This option specifies the maximum number of installed colormaps that will be allowed on this screen. The default is to use the real screen's value.

-**min** *number*
This option specifies the minimum number of installed colormaps that will be allowed on this screen. The default is to use the real screen's value.

-**backingstore** *when*
This option specifies when backing store window attributes will be honored and takes one of the following arguments: **NotUseful**, **WhenMapped**, or **Always**. The default is to use the real screen's value.

-**saveunders** *boolean*
This option specifies whether or not this screen supports saveunders and takes one of the following arguments: *yes* or *no*.

-**name** *string*
This option specifies the name to be used for the pseudo root window.

SEE ALSO
X(1), xdpyinfo(1), xwininfo(1), xprop(1), Inter-Client Communications Conventions Manual

BUGS
This is a sample program that is primarily intended as a testbed for ICCCM pseudo roots. It should not be incorporated into any toolkit or application. Both the command line arguments and internal interfaces are **guaranteed** to change in the next release.

COPYRIGHT
Copyright 1988, Massachusetts Institute of Technology.
See *X(1)* for a full statement of rights and permissions.

AUTHOR
Jim Fulton, MIT X Consortium

NAME
>   xrdb - X server resource database utility

SYNOPSIS
>   **xrdb** [-option ...] [*filename*]

DESCRIPTION
>   *Xrdb* is used to get or set the contents of the RESOURCE_MANAGER property on the root window of screen 0. You would normally run this program from your X startup file.

>   The resource manager (used by the Xlib routine *XGetDefault(3X)* and the X Toolkit) uses the RESOURCE_MANAGER property to get user preferences about color, fonts, and so on for applications. Having this information in the server (where it is available to all clients) instead of on disk, solves the problem in previous versions of X that required you to maintain *defaults* files on every machine that you might use. It also allows for dynamic changing of defaults without editing files.

>   For compatibility, if there is no RESOURCE_MANAGER property defined (either because xrdb was not run or if the property was removed), the resource manager will look for a file called *Xdefaults* in your home directory.

>   The *filename* (or the standard input if - or no input file is given) is optionally passed through the C preprocessor with the following symbols defined, based on the capabilities of the server being used:

>   **HOST=hostname**
>   >   the hostname portion of the display to which you are connected.

>   **WIDTH=num**
>   >   the width of the screen in pixels.

>   **HEIGHT=num**
>   >   the height of the screen in pixels.

>   **X_RESOLUTION=num**
>   >   the x resolution of the screen in pixels per meter.

>   **Y_RESOLUTION=num**
>   >   the y resolution of the screen in pixels per meter.

>   **PLANES=num**
>   >   the number of bit planes for the default visual.

>   **BITS_PER_RGB=num**
>   >   the number of significant bits in an RGB color specification. This is the log base 2 of the number of distinct shades of each primary that the hardware can generate. Note that it is not related to the number of planes, which the log base 2 of the size of the colormap.

>   **CLASS=visualclass**
>   >   one of StaticGray, GrayScale, StaticColor, PseudoColor, TrueColor, DirectColor.

>   **COLOR** only defined if the default visual's type is one of the color options.

>   Lines that begin with an exclamation mark (!) are ignored and may be used as comments.

OPTIONS
>   *xrdb* program accepts the following options:

3

–help   This option (or any unsupported option) will cause a brief description of the allowable options and parameters to be printed.

–display *display*
          This option specifies the X server to be used; see *X(1)*.

-cpp *filename*
          This option specifies the pathname of the C preprocessor program to be used. Although *xrdb* was designed to use CPP, any program that acts as a filter and accepts the -D, -I, and -U options may be used.

-nocpp   This option indicates that *xrdb* should not run the input file through a preprocessor before loading it into the RESOURCE_MANAGER property.

–symbols
          This option indicates that the symbols that are defined for the preprocessor should be printed onto the standard output. It can be used in conjunction with **–query,** but not with the options that change the RESOURCE_MANAGER property.

–query   This option indicates that the current contents of the RESOURCE_MANAGER property should be printed onto the standard output. Note that since preprocessor commands in the input resource file are part of the input file, not part of the property, they won't appear in the output from this option. The **–edit** option can be used to merge the contents of the property back into the input resource file without damaging preprocessor commands.

–load   This option indicates that the input should be loaded as the new value of the RESOURCE_MANAGER property, replacing whatever what there (i.e. the old contents are removed). This is the default action.

–merge   This option indicates that the input should be merged with, instead of replacing, the current contents of the RESOURCE_MANAGER property. Since *xrdb* can read the standard input, this option can be used to the change the contents of the RESOURCE_MANAGER property directly from a terminal or from a shell script.

–remove This option indicates that the RESOURCE_MANAGER property should be removed from its window.

–edit *filename*
          This option indicates that the contents of the RESOURCE_MANAGER property should be edited into the given file, replacing any values already listed there. This allows you to put changes that you have made to your defaults back into your resource file, preserving any comments or preprocessor lines.

–backup *string*
          This option specifies a suffix to be appended to the filename used with **–edit** to generate a backup file.

–D*name[=value]*
          This option is passed through to the preprocessor and is used to define symbols for use with conditionals such as #*ifdef.*

    −Uname This option is passed through to the preprocessor and is used to remove any definitions of this symbol.

    −Idirectory
        This option is passed through to the preprocessor and is used to specify a directory to search for files that are referenced with *#include*.

FILES
Generalizes ˜/*Xdefaults* files.

SEE ALSO
X(1), XGetDefault(3X), Xlib Resource Manager documentation

ENVIRONMENT
    DISPLAY
        to figure out which display to use.

BUGS
The default for no arguments should be to query, not to overwrite, so that it is consistent with other programs.

COPYRIGHT
Copyright 1988, Digital Equipment Corporation.

AUTHORS
Phil Karlton, rewritten from the original by Jim Gettys

NAME
     xrefresh - refresh all or part of an X screen

SYNOPSIS
     xrefresh [-option ...]

DESCRIPTION
     Xrefresh is a simple X program that causes all or part of your screen to be
     repainted. This is useful when system messages have messed up your
     screen. *Xrefresh* maps a window on top of the desired area of the screen
     and then immediately unmaps it, causing refresh events to be sent to all
     applications. By default, a window with no background is used, causing
     all applications to repaint "smoothly." However, the various options can
     be used to indicate that a solid background (of any color) or the root win-
     dow background should be used instead.

ARGUMENTS
     –white   Use a white background. The screen just appears to flash
                 quickly, and then repaint.

     –black   Use a black background (in effect, turning off all of the elec-
                 tron guns to the tube). This can be somewhat disorienting as
                 everything goes black for a moment.

     –solid *color*
                 Use a solid background of the specified color. Try green.

     –root   Use the root window background.

     –none   This is the default. All of the windows simply repaint.

     –geometry *WxH+X+Y*
                 Specifies the portion of the screen to be repainted; see *X(1)*.

     –display *display*
                 This argument allows you to specify the server and screen
                 to refresh; see *X(1)*.

X DEFAULTS
     The *xrefresh* program uses the routine *XGetDefault(3X)* to read defaults,
     so its resource names are all capitalized.

     Black, White, Solid, None, Root
                 Determines what sort of window background to use.

     Geometry
                 Determines the area to refresh. Not very useful.

ENVIRONMENT
     DISPLAY - To get default host and display number.

SEE ALSO
     X(1)

BUGS
     It should have just one default type for the background.

COPYRIGHT
     Copyright 1988, Massachusetts Institute of Technology.
     See *X(1)* for a full statement of rights and permissions.

AUTHORS
     Jim Gettys, Digital Equipment Corp., MIT Project Athena

NAME
>   xrotmap – rotate an HSB colormap

SYNOPSIS
>   **xrotmap** [**–display** *connection*]

DESCRIPTION
>   *xrotmap* installs an HSB ramp colormap and then rotates it as fast as it
>   can. It will reinstall its colormap if any other application uninstalls it.
>   NB: This is highly anti-social.

OPTIONS
>   **–display** *connection*
>   >   Connect to X server display, *connection.*

SEE ALSO
>   X(1)

BUGS
>   The executable is useful only for vandalism, though the source may be
>   educational.

COPYRIGHT
>   Copyright (c) 1988 by Sun Microsystems, Inc.
>   David Lemke (lemke@wirehead.sun.com)
>
>   Permission to use, copy, modify, and distribute this software and its
>   documentation for any purpose and without fee is hereby granted, pro-
>   vided that the above copyright notice appear in all copies and that both
>   that copyright notice and this permission notice appear in supporting docu-
>   mentation.

3

NAME
      xset - user preference utility for X

SYNOPSIS
      xset [-display *display*] [-b] [b on/off] [b [*volume* [*pitch* [*duration*]]] [-
      c] [c on/off] [c [*volume*]] [[-+]fp[-+=] *path*[,*path*[,...]]] [fp default] [fp
      rehash] [[-]led [*integer*]] [led on/off] [m[ouse] [*acceleration* [*thres-
      hold*]]] [m[ouse] default] [p *pixel color*] [[-]r] [r on/off] [s [*length*
      [*period*]]] [s blank/noblank] [s expose/noexpose] [s on/off] [s default]
      [q]

DESCRIPTION
      This program is used to set various user preference options of the display.

OPTIONS
      –display *display*
            This option specifies the server to use; see *X(1)*.

      b   the **b** option controls bell volume, pitch and duration. This
             option accepts up to three numerical parameters, a preceding
             dash(-), or a 'on/off' flag. If no parameters are given, the
             'on' flag is used, the system defaults will be used. If the dash or
             'off' are given, the bell will be turned off. If only one numeri-
             cal parameter is given, the bell volume will be set to that value,
             as a percentage of its maximum. Likewise, the second numeri-
             cal parameter specifies the bell pitch, in hertz, and the third
             numerical parameter specifies the duration in milliseconds. Note
             that not all hardware can vary the bell characteristics. The X
             server will set the characteristics of the bell as closely as it can
             to the user's specifications.

      c   The **c** option controls key click. This option can take an
             optional value, a preceding dash(-), or an 'on/off' flag. If no
             parameter or the 'on' flag is given, the system defaults will be
             used. If the dash or 'off' flag is used, keyclick will be disabled.
             If a value from 0 to 100 is given, it is used to indicate volume,
             as a percentage of the maximum. The X server will set the
             volume to the nearest value that the hardware can support.

      fp= *path,...*
             The **fp=** sets the font path to the directories given in the path
             argument. The directories are interpreted by the server, not by
             the client, and are server-dependent. Directories that do not con-
             tain font databases created by *mkfontdir* will be ignored by the
             server.

      fp *default*
             The *default* argument causes the font path to be reset to the
             server's default.

      fp *rehash*
             The *rehash* argument causes the server to reread the font data-
             bases in the current font path. This is generally only used when
             adding new fonts to a font directory (after running *mkfontdir* to
             recreate the font database).

      –fp or **fp–**
             The **–fp** and **fp–** options remove elements from the current font
             path. They must be followed by a comma-separated list of
             directories.

+fp or **fp+**

This **+fp** and **fp+** options prepend and append elements to the current font path, respectively. They must be followed by a comma-separated list of directories.

led

The **led** option controls the keyboard LEDs. This controls the turning on or off of one or all of the LEDs. It accepts an optional integer, a preceding dash(-) or an 'on/off' flag. If no parameter or the 'on' flag is given, all LEDs are turned on. If a preceding dash or the flag 'off' is given, all LEDs are turned off. If a value between 1 and 32 is given, that LED will be turned on or off depending on the existance of a preceding dash. A common LED which can be controlled is the ''Caps Lock'' LED. ''xset led 3'' would turn led #3 on. ''xset -led 3'' would turn it off. The particular LED values may refer to different LEDs on different hardware.

m

The **m** option controls the mouse parameters. The parameters for the mouse are 'acceleration' and 'threshold'. The mouse, or whatever pointer the machine is connected to, will go 'acceleration' times as fast when it travels more than 'threshold' pixels in a short time. This way, the mouse can be used for precise alignment when it is moved slowly, yet it can be set to travel across the screen in a flick of the wrist when desired. One or both parameters for the **m** option can be omitted, but if only one is given, it will be interpreted as the acceleration. If no parameters or the flag 'default' is used, the system defaults will be set.

p

The **p** option controls pixel color values. The parameters are the color map entry number in decimal, and a color specification. The root background colors may be changed on some servers by altering the entries for BlackPixel and WhitePixel. Although these are often 0 and 1, they need not be. Also, a server may choose to allocate those colors privately, in which case an error will be generated. The map entry must not be a read-only color, or an error will result.

r

The **r** option controls the autorepeat. If a preceding dash or the 'off' flag is used, autorepeat will be disabled. If no parameters or the 'on' flag is used, autorepeat will be enabled.

s

The **s** option lets you set the screen saver parameters. This option accepts up to two numerical parameters, a 'blank/noblank' flag, an 'expose/noexpose' flag, an 'on/off' flag, or the 'default' flag. If no parameters or the 'default' flag is used, the system will be set to its default screen saver characteristics. The 'on/off' flags simply turn the screen saver functions on or off. The 'blank' flag sets the preference to blank the video (if the hardware can do so) rather than display a background pattern, while 'noblank' sets the preference to display a pattern rather than blank the video. The 'expose' flag sets the preference to allow window exposures (the server can freely discard window contents), while 'noexpose' sets the preference to disable screen saver unless the server can regenerate the screens without causing exposure events. The length and period parameters for the screen saver function determines how long the server must be inactive for screen saving to activate, and the period to change the background pattern to avoid burn in. The arguments are specified in seconds. If only one numerical parameter is given, it will be used for the length.

q   The **q** option gives you information on the current settings.

These settings will be reset to default values when you log out.

Note that not all X implementations are guaranteed to honor all of these options.

SEE ALSO

X(1), Xserver(1), xmodmap(1), xrdb(1), xsetroot(1)

COPYRIGHT

Copyright 1988, Massachusetts Institute of Technology.
See *X(1)* for a full statement of rights and permissions.

AUTHOR

Bob Scheifler, MIT Laboratory for Computer Science
David Krikorian, MIT Project Athena (X11 version)

NAME
>   xsetroot – root window parameter setting utility for X

SYNOPSIS
>   **xsetroot** [-help] [-def] [-display *display*] [-cursor *cursorfile maskfile*]
>   [-bitmap *filename*] [-mod *x y*] [-gray] [-grey] [-fg *color*] [-bg *color*]
>   [-rv] [-solid *color*] [-name *string*]

DESCRIPTION
>   The *setroot* program allows you to tailor the appearance of the background
>   ("root") window on a workstation display running X. Normally, you
>   experiment with *xsetroot* until you find a personalized look that you like,
>   then put the *xsetroot* command that produces it into your X startup file. If
>   no options are specified, or if *-def* is specified, the window is reset to its
>   default state. The *-def* option can be specified along with other options
>   and only the non-specified characteristics will be reset to the default state.

>   Only one of the background color/tiling changing options (-solid, -gray,
>   -grey, -bitmap, and -mod) may be specified at a time.

OPTIONS
>   The various options are as follows:

>   **-help**   Print a usage message and exit.

>   **-def**   Reset unspecified attributes to the default values. (Restores the
>   background to the familiar gray mesh and the cursor to the hol-
>   low x shape.)

>   **-cursor** *cursorfile maskfile*
>   This lets you change the pointer cursor to whatever you want
>   when the pointer cursor is outside of any window. Cursor and
>   mask files are bitmaps (little pictures), and can be made with the
>   *bitmap(1)* program. You probably want the mask file to be all
>   black until you get used to the way masks work.

>   **-bitmap** *filename*
>   Use the bitmap specified in the file to set the window pattern.
>   You can make your own bitmap files (little pictures) using the
>   *bitmap(1)* program. The entire background will be made up of
>   repeated "tiles" of the bitmap.

>   **-mod** *x y*
>   This is used if you want a plaid-like grid pattern on your screen.
>   x and y are integers ranging from 1 to 16. Try the different com-
>   binations. Zero and negative numbers are taken as 1.

>   **-gray**   Make the entire background gray. (Easier on the eyes.)

>   **-grey**   Make the entire background grey.

>   **-fg** *color*
>   Use ''color'' as the foreground color. Foreground and back-
>   ground colors are meaningful only in combination with -cursor,
>   -bitmap, or -mod.

>   **-bg** *color*
>   Use ''color'' as the background color.

>   **-rv**   This exchanges the foreground and background colors. Normally
>   the foreground color is black and the background color is white.

>   **-solid** *color*
>   Set the window color to ''color''.

-name *string*

Set the name of the root window to "string". There is no default value. Usually a name is assigned to a window so that the window manager can use a text representation when the window is iconified. This option is unused since you can't iconify the background.

-display *display*

Specifies the server to connect to; see *X(1)*.

SEE ALSO

X(1), xset(1), xrdb(1)

COPYRIGHT

Copyright 1988, Massachusetts Institute of Technology.
See *X(1)* for a full statement of rights and permissions.

AUTHOR

Mark Lillibridge, MIT Project Athena

NAME
:   *xsetsize* - allows you to move, resize, and iconify an windows from the command line.

SYNOPSIS
:   **xsetsize [-options ...]**

DESCRIPTION
:   *Xsetsize* allows you to move, resize and iconify a window from the command line. It is useful for placing window exactly, changing border widths, and testing robustness of programs.

    If you are executing this file on login, make sure that you give your window manager enough time to get set before trying to iconify the window.

OPTIONS
:   **–display** *display*
    :   This option specifies the name of the X server to contact.

    –geometry *geom*
    :   This option specifies the geometry string to be used when moving or resizing windows or icons. Note that icon sizing is not supported.

    –relative This option indicates that the geometry specification should be interpreted as a relative amount rather than an absolute amount. This allows you push windows around on the screen.

    –bw *pixels*
    :   This option specifies the width of the window border in pixels.

    –iconic This option indicates that the geometry, if given, should be used in moving the icon. It also causes the window to be iconified. Thus, "xsetsize -iconic" can be used to iconify a window without changing its size or location.

SEE ALSO
:   X(1), xwininfo(1), uwm(1), wm(1), xterm(1)

ENVIRONMENT
:   **WINDOWID**
    :   to determine the window to use when the **–env** option is given.

BUGS
:   There is a bug in uwm that does not allow the icon to be moved by anyone else once it has been created, so the geometry specification for the icon is ignored if it has previosly been iconified.

    Negative locations for the icons do not work.

COPYRIGHT
:   Copyright 1988, Massachusetts Institute of Technology.

AUTHOR
:   John E. Elsbree, Christopher J. VanHaren, Chris Peterson, MIT Project Athena; Jim Fulton, MIT X Consortium.

NAME
     xshell - X Window System, key/button command exec
SYNOPSIS
     xshell [*options*] [*host:display*] ...
DESCRIPTION
     Xshell is a program for starting up X applications with a single key or but-
     ton stroke. It displays a scallop shell icon in which button and key
     presses stand for different commands. The user can bind a command
     string to any key or button by inserting a line like the following in his or
     her

          xshell.action.keyname: command to be exec'ed

     Keynames are simply letters, numbers, and symbols as they appear on the
     keyboard (e.g. a, $, 9), or one of the following special names:

BackSpace	Clear	Formfeed
Space	Linefeed	Enter
Tab	Newline	Escape
R1	L1	F1
R2	L2	F2
R3	L3	F3
R4	L4	F4
R5	L5	F5
R6	L6	F6
R7	L7	F7
R8	L8	F8
R9	L9	F9
R10	L10	Prior
R11	Home	Next
R12	LeftArrow	Begin
R13	UpArrow	End
R14	RightArrow	Pause
R15	DownArrow	Delete
Select	Print	Execute
Insert	Undo	Redo
Menu	Find	Cancel
KeypadSpace	Keypad-	Keypad4
KeypadTab	Keypad.	Keypad5
KeypadEnter	Keypad/	Keypad6
Keypad=	Keypad0	Keypad7
Keypad*	Keypad1	Keypad8
Keypad+	Keypad2	Keypad9
Keypad,	Keypad3	Pf1
Pf2	Pf3	Pf4
Help	Break	ScriptSwitch
NumLock	LeftButton	MiddleButton
RightButton	Button4	Button5
Colon		

     Thus, the following '.Xdefaults' definitions specify that the Left Button
     will spawn a terminal window, the Middle Button an editor, the Right
     Button a calculator, $ a Bourne shell, and # a superuser shell:

          xshell.action.LeftButton: xterm =80x65-0+0 -fn 6x10
          xshell.action.MiddleButton: gnuemacs -w =80x65+0-0
          xshell.action.RightButton: xterm =20x20-0-0 -fn 6x10 -e dc

| xshell.action.$: | xterm =80x65+0+0 -fn 6x10 -e sh |
| xshell.action.#: | xterm =80x65+0+0 -fn 6x10 -e su |

Xshell breaks the command string up into words by removing all white space (i.e. tabs and spaces) and uses the vfork() and execvp() system calls to spawn off the command. A more complicated parsing algorithm could easily be added, but the current method is adequate (and fast and memory efficient).

One thing to keep in mind is that *xshell* is NOT a window manager. It was written to make popping up frequently used utilities as painless as possible (how many times have you found that you need just 1 more window....). It might make a nice addition to some of the more verbose window managers, but it runs quite nicely as a separate program.

ARGUMENTS

Xshell is designed to be somewhat compatible with *xclock* in the arguments that it takes. However, *xshell* will allow you to abbreviate its longer flags to any length you chose. Thus, the –reverse flag can be spelled out, given as –rev, or even just –r:

–fg *color* On color displays, determines the color of the foreground.

–bg *color* On color displays, determines the color of the background.

–bd *color* On color displays, determines the color of the border.

–bw *pixels* Specify the width in pixels of the border around the *xshell* window.

–v[olume] *n*
  Volume for calls to *XBeep*, used when errors (such as unbound key) are found.

–f[lash] *n* Number of times to flash the shell window to acknowledge a button or key press.

–d[elay] *n* One-hundredths of a second to wait between flashs (default is 5).

–r[everse] Reverse video (swap foreground and background).

+r[everse] Normal video (good for over-ridding values in the .Xdefaults).

–q[uiet] Do not 'beep' on errors (see volume).

+q[uiet] Do 'beep' on errors (see volume).

–s[mall] Use a smaller (48x48) version of the shell icon. The default icon is 96x96.

+s[mall] Use the larger (96x96) version of the shell icon.

=geometry By default *xshell* will create a window the size of whatever icon you select; the standard X window geometry argument will override this. See *X(1)* for details.

host:display
  specifies the display on which to put the *xshell* window. This overrides the DISPLAY environment variable.

X DEFAULTS

To make invoking *xshell* easier, each of the flags listed above may be specified in the user's

Foreground
> gives the foreground color.

Background
> gives the background color.

Border   gives the border color.

BorderWidth
> gives the border width.

ReverseVideo
> if "on", the shell icon should be white on black instead of black on white.

Volume   gives the volume to use in calls to XBeep().

Flash   gives the number of times to flash the shell window to acknowledge key or button presses.

Delay   gives hundredths of a second to wait in between flashes.

Quiet   prevents *xshell* from beeping at you when you mistype.

IconSize if "small", a halfsize (48x48) version of the scallopshell is used.

WindowGeometry
> gives the shell window size using standard X =WxH+X+Y notation.

ENVIRONMENT
> **DISPLAY** To get the default host and display number.

SEE ALSO
> wm(1), uwm(1), X(1), execl(3), vfork(2)

DIAGNOSTICS
> If **–quiet** is not given on the command line or ''xshell.Quiet: on'' does not appear in the user's *Xdefaults*, *xshell* will 'beep' if a key or button is pressed for which there is no definition in the *Xdefaults* file.

AUTHOR
> Mark D. Baushke
>
> This work is based upon Jim Fulton's X.V10R4 version of xshell.

BUGS
> *Xshell* uses the XGetDefault call to fetch the command string for a given key. Thus, in order to bind the colon ('':'') character to a command you must use the Colon keyword.
>
> A more 'user-friendly' interface could include dialog boxes that the user could pop up to type in a command directly so that a full shell doesn't have to be started. Then again, it is nice and compact now and if you really need to do that more than once you should use a real shell.
>
> This program along with has mostly been superceded by *uwm(1)*. However, it is still very handy to use.

NAME
   xshowcmap – show colormap

SYNOPSIS
   xshowcmap [**options**]

DESCRIPTION
   Xshowcmap displays the contents of the currently active colormap in a
   window. The created window shows a square for every color currently
   defined in the servers active colormap. The number of squares is the
   number of colormap-cells the server supports.

   Xshowcmap has been specially written to aid server debugging/verification.

   To leave *xshowcmap* type 'q' while the cursor is in its window.

   The following options are valid:

   -bd color
       as usual - change border color

   -bw number
       as usual - change border width

   host:display
       Name of the display.

BUGS
   There might be some - it has been tested with Siemens servers running
   both monochrome and color, and with uVax Color-Workstations running
   color.

AUTHORS
   Claus Gittinger (..!decvax!unido!sinix!claus)

NAME
     xsol – play solitaire

SYNOPSIS
     xsol [**–display** *connection*] [**–nodrag**]

DESCRIPTION
     xsol plays a solitaire game simliar to Klondike. The playing field is made
     up of seven slots, where stacks are built in descending value with alternat-
     ing suits. Aces are built on at the top, and ascending order in the same
     suit. Kings can be moved to any empty space in the playing field. The
     deck is gone through only once, card by card.
     The cards are moved using the Left mouse button (Button1). Pressing the
     button selects the card, and it (and any cards on it) can then by dragged to
     its destination, where releasing will place them. The deck cards are
     selected by clicking on them.

OPTIONS
     –display *connection*
          Connect to X server display, *connection.*

     –nodrag
          A button press selects the card, and a second press places it. *geom-*
          spec.

SEE ALSO
          X(1)

COPYRIGHT
          Copyright (c) 1988 by Sun Microsystems, Inc.
          David Lemke (lemke@wirehead.sun.com)

     Permission to use, copy, modify, and distribute this software and its
     documentation for any purpose and without fee is hereby granted, pro-
     vided that the above copyright notice appear in all copies and that both
     that copyright notice and this permission notice appear in supporting docu-
     mentation.

NAME
       xstring - prints a string in a window - X equivalent of echo (1)

SYNTAX
       xstring [*-toolkitoption* ...] string ...

OPTIONS
       Xstring accepts all of the standard X Toolkit command line options, plus:

       string   is printed in a window. If more than one string is given, they are
                   concatenated, separated by blanks.

DESCRIPTION
       Xstring provides a window with the command string printed in it, and
       wiats around till the mouse is clicked in it to send it away.

X DEFAULTS
       For *xstring* the available class identifiers are:

       XString
       Command

       For *xstring,* the available name identifiers are:

       xstring

       For *xstring,* the available resources are:

       background
                   Specifies the background color to be displayed. The default is
                   white.

       border   Specifies the border color of the *xstring* window.

       borderWidth
                   Specifies the border width, in pixels, of the *xstring* window.

       font   Specifies the font displayed in the *xstring* window.

       foreground
                   Specifies the foreground color of the *xstring* window. The default
                   is black.

       geometry
                   Specifies the geometry (window size and screen location) to be
                   used as the default for the *xstring* window. For information about
                   the format of the geometry specification, see ARGUMENTS.

SEE ALSO
       X(1), xrdb(1), echo(1)

NAME
        xterm – terminal emulator for X

SYNOPSIS
        xterm [-*toolkitoption* ...] [-option ...]

DESCRIPTION
        The *xterm* program is a terminal emulator for the X Window System. It
        provides DEC VT102 and Tektronix 4014 compatible terminals for pro-
        grams that can't use the window system directly. If the underlying operat-
        ing system supports terminal resizing capabilities (for example, the
        SIGWINCH signal in systems derived from 4.3bsd), *xterm* will use the
        facilities to notify programs running in the window whenever it is resized.

        The VT102 and Tektronix 4014 terminals each have their own window so
        that you can edit text in one and look at graphics in the other at the same
        time. To maintain the correct aspect ratio (height/width), Tektronix graph-
        ics will be restricted to the largest box with a 4014's aspect ratio that will
        fit in the window. This box is located in the upper left area of the win-
        dow.

        Although both windows may be displayed at the same time, one of them
        is considered the "active" window for receiving keyboard input and ter-
        minal output. This is the window that contains the text cursor and whose
        border highlights whenever the pointer is in either window. The active
        window can be choosen through escape sequences, the "Modes" menu in
        the VT102 window, and the "Tektronix" menu in the 4014 window.

OPTIONS
        The *xterm* terminal emulator accepts all of the standard X Toolkit com-
        mand line options along with the additional options listed below (if the
        option begins with a '+' instead of a '–', the option is restored to its
        default value):

        –help   This causes *xterm* to print out a verbose message describing its
                options.

        –132   Normally, the VT102 DECCOLM escape sequence that switches
                between 80 and 132 column mode is ignored. This option
                causes the DECCOLM escape sequence to be recognized, and
                the *xterm* window will resize appropriately.

        –ah   This option indicates that *xterm* should always highlight the text
                cursor and borders. By default, *xterm* will display a hollow text
                cursor whenever the focus is lost or the pointer leaves the win-
                dow.

        +ah   This option indicates that *xterm* should do text cursor highlight-
                ing.

        –b *number*
                This option specifies the size of the inner border (the distance
                between the outer edge of the characters and the window border)
                in pixels. The default is 2.

        –cc *characterclassrange:value[,...]*
                This sets classes indicated by the given ranges for using in
                selecting by words. See the section specifying character classes.

        –cr *color*
                This option specifies the color to use for text cursor. The
                default is to use the same foreground color that is used for text.

-cu   This option indicates that *xterm* should work around a bug in the *curses*(3x) cursor motion package that causes the *more*(1) program to display lines that are exactly the width of the window and are followed by a line beginning with a tab to be displayed incorrectly (the leading tabs are not displayed).

+cu   This option indicates that that *xterm* should not work around the *curses*(3x) bug mentioned above.

-e *program [arguments ...]*
        This option specifies the program (and its command line arguments) to be run in the *xterm* window. It also sets the window title and icon name to be the basename of the program being executed if neither *-T* nor *-n* are given on the command line. **This must be the last option on the command line.**

-fb *font*   This option specifies a font to be used when displaying bold text. This font must be the same height and width as the normal font. If only one of the normal or bold fonts is specified, it will be used as the normal font and the bold font will be produced by overstriking this font. The default bold font is "vtbold."

-j   This option indicates that *xterm* should do jump scrolling. Normally, text is scrolled one line at a time; this option allows *xterm* to move multiple lines at a time so that it doesn't fall as far behind. Its use is strongly recommended since it make *xterm* much faster when scanning through large amounts of text. The VT100 escape sequences for enabling and disabling smooth scroll as well as the "Modes" menu can be used to turn this feature on or off.

+j   This option indicates that *xterm* should not do jump scrolling.

-l   This option indicates that *xterm* should send all terminal output to a log file as well as to the screen. This option can be enabled or disabled using the "xterm X11" menu.

+l   This option indicates that *xterm* should not do logging.

-lf *filename*
        This option specifies the name of the file to which the output log described above is written. If *file* begins with a pipe symbol (|), the rest of the string is assumed to be a command to be used as the endpoint of a pipe. The default filename is "**XtermLog.***XXXXX*" (where *XXXXX* is the process id of *xterm*) and is created in the directory from which *xterm* was started (or the user's home directory in the case of a login window).

-ls   This option indicates that the shell that is started in the *xterm* window be a login shell (i.e. the first character of argv[0] will be a dash, indicating to the shell that it should read the user's .login or .profile).

+ls   This option indicates that the shell that is started should not be a login shell (i.e. it will be a normal "subshell").

-mb   This option indicates that *xterm* should ring a margin bell when the user types near the right end of a line. This option can be turned on and off from the "Modes" menu.

+mb   This option indicates that margin bell should not be rung.

-ms *color*
        This option specifies the color to be used for the pointer cursor.

The default is to use the foreground color.

–nb *number*
> This option specifies the number of characters from the right end of a line at which the margin bell, if enabled, will ring. The default is 10.

–rw
> This option indicates that reverse-wraparound should be allowed. This allows the cursor to back up from the leftmost column of one line to the rightmost column of the previous line. This is very useful for editing long shell command lines and is encouraged. This option can be turned on and off from the "Modes" menu.

+rw
> This option indicates that reverse-wraparound should not be allowed.

–s
> This option indicates that *xterm* may scroll asynchronously, meaning that the screen does not have to be kept completely up to date while scrolling. This allows *xterm* to run faster when network latencies are very high and is typically useful when running across a very large internet or many gateways.

+s
> This option indicates that *xterm* should scroll synchronously.

–sb
> This option indicates that some number of lines that are scrolled off the top of the window should be saved and that a scrollbar should be displayed so that those lines can be viewed. This option may be turned on and off from the "Modes" menu.

+sb
> This option indicates that a scrollbar should not be displayed.

–sf
> This option indicates that Sun Function Key escape codes should be generated for function keys.

+sf
> This option indicates that the standard escape codes should be generated for function keys.

–si
> This option indicates that output to a window should not automatically reposition the screen to the bottom of the scrolling region. This option can be turned on and off from the "Modes" menu.

+si
> This option indicates that output to a window should cause it to scroll to the bottom.

–sk
> This option indicates that pressing a key while using the scrollbar to review previous lines of text should cause the window to be repositioned automatically in the normal postion at the bottom of the scroll region.

+sk
> This option indicates that pressing a key while using the scrollbar should not cause the window to be repositioned.

–sl *number*
> This option specifies the number of lines to save that have been scrolled off the top of the screen. The default is 64.

–t
> This option indicates that *xterm* should start in Tektronix mode, rather than in VT102 mode. Switching between the two windows is done using the "Modes" menus.

+t
> This option indicates that *xterm* should start in VT102 mode.

–tm *string*
> This option specifies a series of terminal setting keywords followed by the characters that should be bound to those functions,

similar to the *stty* program. This is ignored when **–L** is given since *getty* resets the terminal. Allowable keywords include: intr, quit, erase, kill, eof, eol, swtch, start, stop, brk, susp, dsusp, rprnt, flush, weras, and lnext. Control characters may be specified as ˆchar (e.g. ˆc or ˆu) and ˆ? may be used to indicate delete.

–tn *name*
> This option specifies the name of the terminal type to be set in the TERM environment variable. This terminal type must exist in the *termcap(5)* database and should have *li#* and *co#* entries.

–ut
> This option indicates that *xterm* shouldn't write a record into the the system log file */etc/utmp*.

+ut
> This option indicates that *xterm* should write a record into the system log file */etc/utmp*.

–vb
> This option indicates that a visual bell is prefered over an audible one. Instead of ringing the terminal bell whenever a Control-G is received, the window will be flashed.

+vb
> This option indicates that a visual bell should not be used.

–C
> This option indicates that this window should receive console output. This is not supported on all systems.

–S*ccn*
> This option specifies the last two letters of the name of a pseudoterminal to use in slave mode. This allows *xterm* to be used as an input and output channel for an existing program and is sometimes used in specialized applications.

The following command line arguments are provided for compatibility with older versions. They may not be supported in the next release as the X Toolkit provides standard options that accomplish the same task.

%geom
> This option specifies the prefered size and position of the Tektronix window. It is shorthand for specifying the "**tekGeometry*" resource.

#geom
> This option specifies the prefered position of the icon window. It is shorthand for specifying the "**iconGeometry*" resource.

–T *string*
> This option specifies the title for *xterm*'s windows. It is equivalent to **-title**.

–n *string* This option specifies the icon name for *xterm*'s windows. It is shorthand for specifying the "**iconName*" resource. Note that this is not the same as the toolkit option **-name** (see below). The default icon name is the application name.

–r
> This option indicates that reverse video should be simulated by swapping the foreground and background colors. It is equivalent to **-reversevideo** or **-rv**.

–w *number*
> This option specifies the width in pixels of the border surrounding the window. It is equivalent to **-borderwidth** or **-bw**.

–L
> This option indicates that *xterm* was started by *init*. In this mode, *xterm* does not try to allocate a new pseudoterminal as *init* has already done so. In addition, the system program *getty* is run instead of the user's shell. **This option has been superceeded by the new *xdm* program; furthermore, this option**

should **never** be used by users when starting terminal windows.

The following standard X Toolkit command line arguments are commonly used with *xterm*:

–bg *color*
> This option specifies the color to use for the background of the window. The default is "white."

–bd *color*
> This option specifies the color to use for the border of the window. The default is "black."

–bw *number*
> This option specifies the width in pixels of the border surrounding the window.

–fg *color*
> This option specifies the color to use for displaying text. The default is "black".

–fn *font*   This option specifies the font to be used for displaying normal text. The default is "vtsingle."

–name *name*
> This option specifies the application name under which resources are to be obtained, rather than the default executable file name. *Name* should not contain "." or "*" characters.

–title *string*
> This option specifies the window title string, which may be displayed by window managers if the user so chooses. The default title is the command line specified after the -e option, if any, otherwise the application name.

–rv   This option indicates that reverse video should be simulated by swapping the foreground and background colors.

–geometry *geometry*
> This option specifies the prefered size and position of the VT102 window; see *X(1)*.

–display *display*
> This option specifies the X server to contact; see *X(1)*.

–xrm *resourcestring*
> This option specifies a resource string to be used. This is especially useful for setting resources that do not have separate command line options.

–iconic   This option indicates that *xterm* should ask the window manager to start it as an icon rather than as the normal window.

X DEFAULTS
> The program understands all of the core X Toolkit resource names and classes as well as:

iconGeometry (class **IconGeometry**)
> Specifies the prefered size and position of the application when iconified. It is not necessarily obeyed by all window managers.

termName (class **TermName**)
> Specifies the terminal type name to be set in the TERM environment variable.

title (class **Title**)
> Specifies a string that may be used by the window manager when displaying this application.

ttyModes (class **TtyModes**)
> Specifies a string containing terminal setting keywords and the characters to which they may be bound. This option is ignored when **−L** is given since *getty* resets the terminal. Allowable keywords include: intr, quit, erase, kill, eof, eol, swtch, start, stop, brk, susp, dsusp, rprnt, flush, weras, and lnext. Control characters may be specified as ˆchar (e.g. ˆc or ˆu) and ˆ? may be used to indicate delete. This is very useful for overriding the default terminal settings without having to do an *stty* every time an *xterm* is started.

utmpInhibit (class **UtmpInhibit**)
> Specifies whether or not *xterm* should try to record the user's terminal in */etc/utmp*.

sunFunctionKeys (class **SunFunctionKeys**)
> Specifies whether or not Sun Function Key escape codes should be generated for function keys instead of standard escape sequences.

The following resources are specified as part of the "vt100" widget (class "VT100"):

alwaysHighlight (class **AlwaysHighlight**)
> Specifies whether or not *xterm* should always display a highlighted text cursor. By default, a hollow text cursor is displayed whenever the pointer moves out of the window or the window loses the input focus.

font (class **Font**)
> Specifies the name of the normal font. The default is "vtsingle."

boldFont (class **Font**)
> Specifies the name of the bold font. The default is "vtbold."

c132 (class **C132**)
> Specifies whether or not the VT102 DECCOLM escape sequence should be honored. The default is "false."

charClass (class **CharClass**)
> Specifies comma-separated lists of character class bindings of the form [*low-*]*high:value*. These are used in determining which sets of characters should be treated the same when doing cut and paste. See the section on specifying character classes.

curses (class **Curses**)
> Specifies whether or not the last column bug in *curses*(3x) should be worked around. The default is "false."

background (class **Background**)
> Specifies the color to use for the background of the window. The default is "white."

foreground (class **Foreground**)
> Specifies the color to use for displaying text in the window. Setting the class name instead of the instance name is an easy way to have everything that would normally appear in the "text"

color change color. The default is "black."

cursorColor (class **Foreground**)
Specifies the color to use for the text cursor. The default is "black."

geometry (class **Geometry**)
Specifies the prefered size and position of the VT102 window.

tekGeometry (class **Geometry**)
Specifies the prefered size and position of the Tektronix window.

internalBorder (class **BorderWidth**)
Specifies the number of pixels between the characters and the window border. The default is 2.

jumpScroll (class **JumpScroll**)
Specifies whether or not jump scroll should be used. The default is "false".

logFile (class **Logfile**)
Specifies the name of the file to which a terminal session is logged. The default is "**XtermLog.***XXXXX*" (where *XXXXX* is the process id of *xterm*).

logging (class **Logging**)
Specifies whether or not a terminal session should be logged. The default is "false."

logInhibit (class **LogInhibit**)
Specifies whether or not terminal session logging should be inhibited. The default is "false."

loginShell (class **LoginShell**)
Specifies whether or not the shell to be run in the window should be started as a login shell. The default is "false."

marginBell (class **MarginBell**)
Specifies whether or not the bell should be run when the user types near the right margin. The default is "false."

multiScroll (class **MultiScroll**)
Specifies whether or not asynchronous scrolling is allowed. The default is "false."

nMarginBell (class **Column**)
Specifies the number of characters from the right margin at which the margin bell should be run, when enabled.

pointerColor (class **Foreground**)
Specifies the color of the pointer. The default is "black."

pointerShape (class **Cursor**)
Specifies the name of the shape of the pointer. The default is "xterm."

reverseVideo (class **ReverseVideo**)
Specifies whether or not reverse video should be simulated. The default is "false."

reverseWrap (class **ReverseWrap**)
Specifies whether or not reverse-wraparound should be enabled. The default is "false."

saveLines (class **SaveLines**)
Specifies the number of lines to save beyond the top of the screen when a scrollbar is turned on. The default is 64.

scrollBar (class **ScrollBar**)
>Specifies whether or not the scrollbar should be displayed. The default is "false."

scrollInput (class **ScrollCond**)
>Specifies whether or not output to the terminal should automatically cause the scrollbar to go to the bottom of the scrolling region. The default is "true."

scrollKey (class **ScrollCond**)
>Specifies whether or not pressing a key should automatically cause the scrollbar to go to the bottom of the scrolling region. The default is "false."

signalInhibit (class **SignalInhibit**)
>Specifies whether or not the entries in the "xterm X11" menu for sending signals to *xterm* should be disallowed. The default is "false."

3

tekInhibit (class **TekInhibit**)
>Specifies whether or not Tektronix mode should be disallowed. The default is "false."

tekStartup (class **TekStartup**)
>Specifies whether or not *xterm* should start up in Tektronix mode. The default is "false."

titeInhibit (class **TiteInhibit**)
>Specifies whether or not *xterm* should remove remove *ti* or *te* termcap entries (used to switch between alternate screens on startup of many screen-oriented programs) from the TERMCAP string.

translations (class **Translations**)
>Specifies the key and button bindings for menus, selections, "programmed strings", etc. See **KEY/BUTTON BINDINGS** below.

visualBell (class **VisualBell**)
>Specifies whether or not a visible bell (i.e. flashing) should be used instead of an audible bell when Control-G is received. The default is "false."

The following resources are specified as part of the "tek4014" widget (class "Tek4014"):

width (class **Width**)
>Specifies the width of the Tektronix window in pixels.

height (class **Height**)
>Specifies the height of the Tektronix window in pixels.

The following resources are specified as part of the "menu" widget:

menuBorder (class **MenuBorder**)
>Specifies the size in pixels of the border surrounding menus. The default is 2.

menuFont (class **Font**)
>Specifies the name of the font to use for displaying menu items.

menuPad (class **MenuPad**)
>Specifies the number of pixels between menu items and the

menu border. The default is 3.

The following resources are useful when specified for the Athena Scrollbar widget:

thickness (class **Thickness**)
Specifies the width in pixels of the scrollbar.

background (class **Background**)
Specifies the color to use for the background of the scrollbar.

foreground (class **Foreground**)
Specifies the color to use for the foreground of the scrollbar. The "thumb" of the scrollbar is a simple checkerboard pattern alternating pixels for foreground and background color.

EMULATIONS

The VT102 emulation is fairly complete, but does not support the blinking character attribute nor the double-wide and double-size character sets. *Termcap*(5) entries that work with *xterm* include "xterm", "vt102", "vt100" and "ansi", and *xterm* automatically searches the termcap file in this order for these entries and then sets the "TERM" and the "TERMCAP" environment variables.

Many of the special *xterm* features (like logging) may be modified under program control through a set of escape sequences different from the standard VT102 escape sequences. (See the *"Xterm Control Sequences"* document.)

The Tektronix 4014 emulation is also fairly good. Four different font sizes and five different lines types are supported. The Tektronix text and graphics commands are recorded internally by *xterm* and may be written to a file by sending the COPY escape sequence (or through the **Tektronix** menu; see below). The name of the file will be "**COPY**yy–MM–dd.hh:mm:ss", where yy, MM, dd, hh, mm and ss are the year, month, day, hour, minute and second when the COPY was performed (the file is created in the directory *xterm* is started in, or the home directory for a login *xterm*).

POINTER USAGE

Once the VT102 window is created, *xterm* allows you to select text and copy it within the same or other windows.

The selection functions are invoked when the pointer buttons are used with no modifiers, and when they are used with the "shift" key. The assignment of the functions described below to keys and buttons may be changed through the resource database; see **KEY/BUTTON BINDINGS** below.

Pointer button one (usually left) is used to save text into the cut buffer. Move the cursor to beginning of the text, and then hold the button down while moving the cursor to the end of the region and releasing the button. The selected text is highlighted and is saved in the global cut buffer and made the PRIMARY selection when the button is released. Double-clicking selects by words. Triple-clicking selects by lines. Quadruple-clicking goes back to characters, etc. Multiple-click is determined by the time from button up to button down, so you can change the selection unit in the middle of a selection. If the key/button bindings specify that an X selection is to be made, *xterm* will leave the selected text highlighted for as long as it is the selection owner.

Pointer button two (usually middle) 'types' (pastes) the text from the PRI-MARY selection, if any, otherwise from the cut buffer, inserting it as keyboard input.

Pointer button three (usually right) extends the current selection. (Without loss of generality, that is you can swap "right" and "left" everywhere in the rest of this paragraph...) If pressed while closer to the right edge of the selection than the left, it extends/contracts the right edge of the selection. If you contract the selection past the left edge of the selection, *xterm* assumes you really meant the left edge, restores the original selection, then extends/contracts the left edge of the selection. Extension starts in the selection unit mode that the last selection or extension was performed in; you can multiple-click to cycle through them.

By cutting and pasting pieces of text without trailing new lines, you can take text from several places in different windows and form a command to the shell, for example, or take output from a program and insert it into your favorite editor. Since the cut buffer is globally shared among different applications, you should regard it as a 'file' whose contents you know. The terminal emulator and other text programs should be treating it as if it were a text file, i.e. the text is delimited by new lines.

The scroll region displays the position and amount of text currently showing in the window (highlighted) relative to the amount of text actually saved. As more text is saved (up to the maximum), the size of the highlighted area decreases.

Clicking button one with the pointer in the scroll region moves the adjacent line to the top of the display window.

Clicking button three moves the top line of the display window down to the pointer position.

Clicking button two moves the display to a position in the saved text that corresponds to the pointer's position in the scrollbar.

Unlike the VT102 window, the Tektronix window dows not allow the copying of text. It does allow Tektronix GIN mode, and in this mode the cursor will change from an arrow to a cross. Pressing any key will send that key and the current coordinate of the cross cursor. Pressing button one, two, or three will return the letters 'l', 'm', and 'r', respectively. If the 'shift' key is pressed when a pointer buton is pressed, the corresponding upper case letter is sent. To distinquish a pointer button from a key, the high bit of the character is set (but this is bit is normally stripped unless the terminal mode is RAW; see *tty*(4) for details).

MENUS

Xterm has three different menus, named **xterm**, **Modes**, and **Tektronix**. Each menu pops up under the correct combinations of key and button presses. Most menus are divided into two section, separated by a horizontal line. The top portion contains various modes that can be altered. A check mark appears next to a mode that is currently active. Selecting one of these modes toggles its state. The bottom portion of the menu are command entries; selecting one of these performs the indicated function.

The **xterm** menu pops up when the "control" key and pointer button one are pressed in a window. The modes section contains items that apply to both the VT102 and Tektronix windows. Notable entries in the command section of the menu are the **Continue, Suspend, Interrupt, Hangup, Terminate** and **Kill** which sends the SIGCONT, SIGTSTP, SIGINT, SIGHUP, SIGTERM and SIGKILL signals, respectively, to the process group of the process running under *xterm* (usually the shell). The

Continue function is especially useful if the user has accidentally typed CTRL-Z, suspending the process.

The **Modes** menu sets various modes in the VT102 emulation, and is popped up when the "control" key and pointer button two are pressed in the VT102 window. In the command section of this menu, the soft reset entry will reset scroll regions. This can be convenient when some program has left the scroll regions set incorrectly (often a problem when using VMS or TOPS-20). The full reset entry will clear the screen, reset tabs to every eight columns, and reset the terminal modes (such as wrap and smooth scroll) to their initial states just after *xterm* has finished processing the command line options. The **Tektronix** menu sets various modes in the Tektronix emulation, and is popped up when the "control" key and pointer button two are pressed in the Tektronix window. The current font size is checked in the modes section of the menu. The **PAGE** entry in the command section clears the Tektronix window.

CHARACTER CLASSES

Clicking the middle mouse button twice in rapid succession will cause all characters of the same class (e.g. letters, white space, punctuation) to be selected. Since different people have different preferences for what should be selected (for example, should filenames be selected as a whole or only the separate subnames), the default mapping can be overridden through the use of the *charClass* (class *CharClass*) resource.

This resource is simply a list of *range:value* pairs where the range is either a single number or *low-high* in the range of 0 to 127, corresponding to the ASCII code for the character or characters to be set. The *value* is arbitrary, although the default table uses the character number of the first character occurring in the set.

The default table is:

```
static int charClass[128] = {
/* NUL  SOH  STX  ETX  EOT  ENQ  ACK  BEL */
    32,  1,   1,   1,   1,   1,   1,   1,
/* BS   HT   NL   VT   NP   CR   SO   SI */
    1,   32,  1,   1,   1,   1,   1,   1,
/* DLE  DC1  DC2  DC3  DC4  NAK  SYN  ETB */
    1,   1,   1,   1,   1,   1,   1,   1,
/* CAN  EM   SUB  ESC  FS   GS   RS   US */
    1,   1,   1,   1,   1,   1,   1,   1,
/* SP   !    "    #    $    %    &    ' */
    32,  33,  34,  35,  36,  37,  38,  39,
/* (    )    *    +    ,    -    .    / */
    40,  41,  42,  43,  44,  45,  46,  47,
/* 0    1    2    3    4    5    6    7 */
    48,  48,  48,  48,  48,  48,  48,  48,
/* 8    9    :    ;    <    =    >    ? */
    48,  48,  58,  59,  60,  61,  62,  63,
/* @    A    B    C    D    E    F    G */
    64,  48,  48,  48,  48,  48,  48,  48,
/* H    I    J    K    L    M    N    O */
    48,  48,  48,  48,  48,  48,  48,  48,
/* P    Q    R    S    T    U    V    W */
    48,  48,  48,  48,  48,  48,  48,  48,
/* X    Y    Z    [    \    ]    ^    _ */
    48,  48,  48,  91,  92,  93,  94,  48,
```

```
/*  '   a   b   c   d   e   f   g */
   96, 48, 48, 48, 48, 48, 48, 48,
/*  h   i   j   k   l   m   n   o */
   48, 48, 48, 48, 48, 48, 48, 48,
/*  p   q   r   s   t   u   v   w */
   48, 48, 48, 48, 48, 48, 48, 48,
/*  x   y   z   {   |   }   ~  DEL */
   48, 48, 48, 123, 124, 125, 126,  1};
```

For example, the string "33:48,37:48,45-47:48,64:48" indicates that the exclamation mark, percent sign, dash, period, slash, and ampersand characters should be treated the same way as characters and numbers. This is very useful for cutting and pasting electronic mailing addresses and Unix filenames.

KEY TRANSLATIONS

It is possible to rebind keys (or sequences of keys) to arbitrary strings for input, by changing the translations for the vt100 or tek4014 widgets. Changing the translations for events other than key and button events is not expected, and will cause unpredictable behavior.

The actions available for key translations are:

insert()   Processes the key in the normal way; i.e. inserts the ASCII character code corresponding to the keysym found in the keyboard mapping table into the input stream.

string(*string*)   Rebinds the key or key sequence to the string value; that is, inserts the string argument into the input stream. Quotation is necessary if the string contains whitespace or non-alphanumeric characters. If the string argument begins with the characters "0x", it is interpreted as a hex character constant and the corresponding character is sent in the normal way.

keymap(*name*)   The **keymap** action takes a single string argument naming a resource to be used to dynamically define a new translation table; the name of the resource is obtained by appending the string "Keymap" to *name*. The keymap name **None** restores the original translation table (the very first one; a stack is not maintained). Upper/lower case is significant.

insert-selection(*name*[,*name*]...)
                       Retrieves the value of the first (left-most) named selection that exists or cut buffer that is non-empty and inserts the value into the input stream. *Name* is the name of any selection, for example, **PRIMARY** or **SECONDARY**, or the name of a cut buffer: **CUT_BUFFER0**, ..., **CUT_BUFFER7**. Upper/lower case is significant.

For example, a debugging session might benefit from the following bindings:

```
*VT100.Translations: #override <Key>F13: keymap(dbx)
*VT100.dbxKeymap.translations: \
    <Key>F14: keymap(None) \n\
    <Key>F17: string("next") string(0x0d) \n\
```

                <Key>F18: string("step") string(0x0d) \n\
                <Key>F19: string("continue") string(0x0d) \n\
                <Key>F20: string("print ")
                        insert-selection(PRIMARY, CUT_BUFFER0)

KEY/BUTTON BINDINGS

Within the VT100 widget the key and button bindings for selecting text,
pasting text, and activating the menus are controlled by the translation
bindings. In addition to the actions listed above under **KEY TRANSLA-
TIONS**, the following actions are available:

mode-menu()   Posts one of the two mode menus, depending on which
                       button is pressed.

select-start()   Unselects any previously selected text and begins select-
                       ing new text.

select-extend()   Continues selecting text from the previous starting posi-
                       tion.

start-extend()   Begins extending the selection from the farthest (left or
                       right) edge.

select-end(*name*[,*name*]...)
                       Ends the text selection. *Name* is the name of a selec-
                       tion, or the name of a cut buffer into which the text is
                       to be copied. *Xterm* will assert ownership of all the
                       selections named and will copy the text into each of the
                       cut buffers. Upper/lower case is significant.

ignore()   Quietly discards the key or button event.

bell([*volume*])   Rings the bell at the specified volume increment
                       above/below the base volume.

The default bindings are:

                    <KeyPress>: insert() \n\
        Ctrl ~Meta <Btn1Down>: mode-menu() \n\
              ~Meta <Btn1Down>: select-start() \n\
              ~Meta <Btn1Motion>:select-extend() \n\
        Ctrl ~Meta <Btn2Down>: mode-menu() \n\
       ~Ctrl ~Meta <Btn2Down>: ignore() \n\
              ~Meta <Btn2Up>:   insert-selection
                                 (PRIMARY, CUT_BUFFER0) \n\
       ~Ctrl ~Meta <Btn3Down>: start-extend() \n\
              ~Meta <Btn3Motion>:select-extend() \n\
              ~Meta <BtnUp>:   select-end
                                 (PRIMARY, CUT_BUFFER0) \n\
                    <BtnDown>:   bell(0)

STARTING XTERM FROM INIT

**Warning, this feature is now obsolete and may not be supported in
future releases. Sites using this method should switch to *xdm* instead.**

On operating systems such as 4.3bsd and Ultrix, the server and initial
login window are normally started automatically by *init(8)*.

By convention, the pseudoterminal with the highest minor device number
(e.g. */dev/ttyqf* and */dev/ptyqf*) is renamed for the lowest display number
(e.g. */dev/ttyv0* and */dev/ptyv0*). Machines that have more than one display

can repeat this process using *ttyqe* for *ttyv1*, and so on.

Once the pseudoterminals are in place, a line similar to the following may be added to */etc/ttys* (replacing *Xqvss* with the appropriate server and putting it all on one line):

ttyv0 "/usr/bin/X11/xterm -L -geom 80x24+1+1 -display :0"
xterm on secure window="/usr/bin/X11/Xqvss :0"

Sites that used to run X10 should note that the colon in the server display number is required.

Although the release will install both the X server and *xterm* in /usr/bin/X11 by default, many sites choose to make a copy of both of these programs on the root partition (usually in /etc) so that they may still be used even if the partition containing /usr/bin/X11 isn't mounted.

Some versions of *init* have relatively small program name buffer sizes and treat all sharp signs as comment delimiters. Sites that wish to list large numbers of options on the xterm line will need to write a small shell script to exec the long xterm line. The best solution, of course, is to use *xdm*.

OTHER FEATURES

Xterm automatically highlights the window border and text cursor when the pointer enters the window (selected) and unhighlights them when the pointer leaves the window (unselected). If the window is the focus window, then the window is highlighted no matter where the pointer is.

In VT102 mode, there are escape sequences to activate and deactivate an alternate screen buffer, which is the same size as the display area of the window. When activated, the current screen is saved and replace with the alternate screen. Saving of lines scrolled off the top of the window is disabled until the normal screen is restored. The *termcap*(5) entry for *xterm* allows the visual editor *vi*(1) to switch to the alternate screen for editing, and restore the screen on exit.

In either VT102 or Tektronix mode, there are escape sequences to change the name of the windows and to specify a new log file name.

ENVIRONMENT

Xterm sets the environment variables "TERM" and "TERMCAP" properly for the size window you have created. It also uses and sets the environment variable "DISPLAY" to specify which bit map display terminal to use. The environment variable "WINDOWID" is set to the X window id number of the *xterm* window.

SEE ALSO

resize(1), X(1), pty(4), tty(4)
"Xterm Control Sequences"

BUGS

The **-L** option is no longer needed as the new *xdm* display manager system handles logging in in a much cleaner way. No more messing around with trying to match colors in */etc/ttys* or worrying about an unwanted login window. **This option may be removed in future releases.**

Xterm will hang forever if you try to paste too much text at one time. It is both producer and consumer for the pty and can deadlock.

Variable-width fonts are not handled reasonably.

This program still needs to be rewritten. It should be split into very modular sections, with the various emulators being completely separate

widgets that don't know about each other. Ideally, you'd like to be able
to pick and choose emulator widgets and stick them into a single control
widget.

The focus is considered lost if some other client (e.g., the window
manager) grabs the pointer; it is difficult to do better without an addition
to the protocol.

There needs to be a dialog box to allow entry of log file name and the
COPY file name.

Many of the options are not resettable after *xterm* starts.

The Tek widget does not support key/button re-binding.

This manual page is too long. There should be a separate users manual
defining all of the non-standard escape sequences.

All programs should be written to use X directly; then we could eliminate
this program.

COPYRIGHT
Copyright 1988, Massachusetts Institute of Technology.
See *X(1)* for a full statement of rights and permissions.

AUTHORS
Far too many people, including:

Loretta Guarino Reid (DEC-UEG-WSL), Joel McCormack (DEC-UEG-
WSL), Terry Weissman (DEC-UEG-WSL), Edward Moy (Berkeley),
Ralph R. Swick (MIT-Athena), Mark Vandevoorde (MIT-Athena), Bob
McNamara (DEC-MAD), Jim Gettys (MIT-Athena), Bob Scheifler (MIT X
Consortium), Doug Mink (SAO), Steve Pitschke (Stellar), Ron Newman
(MIT-Athena), Jim Fulton (MIT X Consortium), Dave Serisky (HP)

NAME

    xtools – easy way to start X programs

SYNOPSIS

    xinit xtools [-display hostname:dpy] [normal Xaw options]

DESCRIPTION

    xtools is a convenient way to start up your X applications when your system doesn't support starting up the X window system from the getty process.

    The applications that *xtools* starts up are specified in a .xtools file. You can have different *.xtools* files, one for each host. *xtools* first tries to open the file .xtools-fully.qualified.domain.name where "fully.qualified.domain.name" is the fully qualified domain name of your workstation (as returned by the gethostname() system call). If that file doesn't exist then, starting at the right, it trims off portions of the domain name and retries. Using the above example domain name, the following files would be tried in order:

    .xtools-fully.qualified.domain.name
    .xtools-fully.qualified.domain
    .xtools-fully.qualified
    .xtools-fully
    .xtools

    If none of the .xtools files with a machine or domain name exist then it uses just ".xtools".

CONFIGURATION FILE FORMAT

    The format of the .xtools file is similar to typing the commands to the shell. Notable differences are that csh-style tilde expansion is not implemented, quotes don't work, input and output redirection doesn't work; in other words, no shell metacharacters are recognized. In particular, it is important to note that the command lines in the expected to run in the background (for example, xterm). A bug in *xtools* requires you to put all of those commands that don't run in the background first. Here is a sample .xtools file

```
xrdb            .xrdb
xsetroot -grey
xhost           yuban ovaltine bosco
xset            m 8 8 r off c 100
twm &
xterm           -i #0x0-85+100 &
xterm           -i #0x0-85+240 -e cartan -e  &
xterm           -i -C -r #0x0-85+380 &
xperfmon        =175x290-115+0 &
xclock &
xbiff &
```

STARTING AND QUITING

    Since *xtools* is started by *xinit* the DISPLAY environment variable isn't set, so you must either set it prior to starting xinit, or you can use the -display option with *xtools* and *xtools* will propogate it down to the programs that it starts. Here's an example csh alias for starting the X Window System using *xtools* on a SUN workstation:

```
alias x 'xinit xtools -iconic -geo -1-100 -display ${hostname}":"0 ; \
setkeys reset ; \
clear'
```

where the hostname variable was set earlier with

```
set hostname = ' hostname | sed -e 's/..*//' '
```

Since *xtools* was started by *xinit* you must quit *xtools* in order to quit the
X Window System. *xtools* has a small window with two buttons labeled
"quit" and "help". The help button isn't implemented yet so it is
dimmed. When you click on the quit button a confirmation box pops up;
if you click on the "yep" button then *xtools* will send a kill signal to all
of the programs that it started.

OPTIONS

xtools takes all of the standard toolkit options. In addition, you may
specifiy an alternate configuration file by using the -file option following it
with the name of the configuration file.

X DEFAULTS

The available names and classes for the widgets used are:

NAME	CLASS
top	Shell
top.home	Shell.Form
top.home.home	Shell.Form.Label
top.home.quit	Shell.Form.Command
top.home.help	Shell.Form.Command
top.confirm	Shell.Shell
top.confirm.confirm	Shell.Shell.Form
top.confirm.confirm.confirm	Shell.Shell.Form.Label
top.confirm.confirm.yep	Shell.Shell.Form.Command
top.confirm.confirm.nope	Shell.Shell.Form.Command

These can be used to set fonts, colors, etc. tailored to the user's needs. As
a color example:

xtools*quit.Background:	mauve
xtools*confirm.yep.Background:	peach
xtools*confirm.nope.Background:	plum
xtools*geometry:	-1-100
xtools*icon:	on
xtools*home.font:	vbee-36
xtools*confirm.font:	vbee-36

AUTHOR

Rusty C. Wright

rusty@cartan.berkeley.edu
ucbvax!cartan!rusty

NAME

xtrek – X based multi-player space shoot 'em up game

SYNOPSIS

xtrek [**–display** *host:display*] [**–geometry** *WxH+X+Y*] [**–s** *ship-name*] [**–S**]

DESCRIPTION

Xtrek is a game based on shared memory and the X window environment. It is thoroughly described in xtrek.doc which probably lives in /usr/games/lib/xtrek/xtrek.me. Custom ship configuration is described by the xtrek_ship(6) man page.

OPTIONS

Xtrek will get the display from your **DISPLAY** environment variable unless it is specified on the command line. The –s option is used to specify a ship configuration. The –S option disables ship configuration if specified by the first person to start *Xtrek* (the one who starts the daemon).

AUTHOR

Chris Guthrie (chris@ic.berkeley.edu)

X11 version by Jeff Weinstein (jeff@polyslo.calpoly.edu)

Ship Configuration by Darin McGrew, Bill Webb, Jeff Weinstein and others at IBM ACIS Development.

SEE ALSO

xtrek_ship(6)

NAME

   xtrek.ship - Ship customization for xtrek(6)

SYNOPSIS

   xtrek.ship: [acdefgimprstvwxACDEFGIMPRSTVWX] ...

DESCRIPTION

   Xtrek(6) is a multi-player game of galactic warfare based on the Star Trek universe.

   The following describes the customization of ships allowed by specifying the **ship** default in your *Xdefaults* file. Customization is done by decreasing your ship's abilities in one area, in order to increase them in another area. The effect of one Unit of Customization (UoC) is described below for each ability.

   The **ship** default specifies your ship customization as a list of upper- and lower-case letters. Upper-case letters add one UoC to the associated abilities, while lower-case letters subtract one UoC from the associated abilities.

   Starting *xtrek*(6) with a "-s name" option will force it to use the *name* default instead of the **ship** default. This can be useful for keeping several ship descriptions available, selecting the desired ship when starting *xtrek*.

   Reasonable limits are made on the modifications allowed. One general limitation is that the number of upper-case letters cannot exceed the number of lower-case letters. Each ability will also have limitations listed.

ABILITIES

   Here are the abilities, and their associated letters. The effect of subtracting a UoC is listed in parenthesis.

   Army Transport **a/A**

   The default ship can carry a maximum of 10 armies. Each UoC increases (decreases) the maximum capacity of the ship by 4 armies. The maximum capacity must be at least 2 armies.

   Cloaking Cost **C**

   Cloaking normally costs 30 fuel units. Each UoC lowers (raises) the cost for your ship by 10 fuel units, within an allowable range of 0-30 fuel units. NOTE: There is no 'c' option.

   Heat Dissipation **d/D**

   Engines normally dissipate 5 heat units (allowing indefinite travel at warp 5). Each UoC raises (lowers) your ship's heat dissipation by 1 heat unit (allowing indefinite travel at 1 warp factor higher/lower than normal), with a minimum heat dissipation of 0 heat units. Weapons dissipate heat units at half the rate of engines, rounded down.

   Engine Efficiency **e/E**

   Normal engines travel indefinitely at warp 5 with standard fuel regeneration. Each UoC raises (lowers) this "breakeven speed" by 1 warp factor, with a minimum "breakeven speed" of warp 1. This translates into the following fuel costs:

Breakeven Speed	Fuel Cost/ Warp Factor	UoC Allocation Required
1	20/1 = 20	-4
2	20/2 = 10	-3

3	20/3 = 6	-2
4	20/4 = 5	-1
5	20/5 = 4	0
6	20/6 = 3	+1
7	20/7 = 2	+2
8-10	20/xx = 2	+3-5
11	20/11 = 1	+6
12-20	20/xx = 1	+7-15
21	20/21 = 0	+16

Fuel Capacity **f/F**

A normal ship has capacity of 10,000 fuel units. Each UoC raises (lowers) your ship's capacity by 2,500 fuel units, with a minimum capacity of 2,500 fuel units and a maximum of 32,500.

Fuel Generation **g/G**

A normal ship generates fuel at a rate of 20 fuel units (allowing indefinite travel at warp 5). Each UoC raises (lowers) the fuel generation rate by 4 (allowing indefinite travel at one warp factor higher/lower than normal), with a minimum rate of 0 fuel units.

Invisibility While Cloaked **i/I**

On the average, a normal ship is seen by other ships once every 2 seconds on short range scanners. Each UoC increases (decreases) this interval by 1 second. Appearance on long range scanners occurs half as often as on short range scanners.

Maneuverability **m/M**

This affects how quickly your ship can change directions while moving. Each UoC allows your ship to maneuver as well as a normal ship traveling one warp factor slower (faster). At the minimum setting (-5 UoC), warp 1 behaves like warp 6 normally does and navagation requires nearly stopping before turning.

Phaser Size **p/P**

Normal phasers have 10000 size units, and each UoC increases (decreases) this by 2500 size units. The damage inflicted by phasers is the square root of the Phaser Size. The minimum damage is 0 (you've scuttled your phasers). Phaser range, fuel required, and weapons heating are proportional to the damage inflicted by the phasers. The following chart correlates damage to the number of UoC allocated to Phaser Size:

Point Blank Phaser Damage	UoC Allocation Required
0	-4
50	-3
70	-2
86	-1
100	0
111	1
122	2
132	3
141	4
158	6
173	8
200	12

Repair Rate **r/R**

Ships normally have a base repair rate of 100 damage units. Each UoC increases (decreases) this by 50 damage units, with a minimum repair rate of 0 damage units.

Shield Strength **s/S**

Shields of normal ships can withstand 100 damage units. Each UoC increases (decreases) this by 25 damage units, with a minimum strength of 0 (no shields at all--not recommended).

Torpedo Size **t/T**

Normal photon torpedoes have 900 size units, and each UoC increases (decreases) this by 450 size units. The damage inflicted by torpedoes is the square root of the Torpedo Size. The minimum damage is 0 (you've scuttled your torpedoes). The fuel required and weapons heating are proportional to Torpedo Size. The following chart correlates damage to the number of UoC allocated to Torpedo Size:

Point Blank Torpedo Damage	UoC Allocation Required
0	-2
21	-1
30	0
36	1
42	2
47	3
51	4
60	6
67	8
79	12
90	16

Torpedo Velocity **v/V**

Normal photon torpedoes travel at warp 12. Each UoC increases (decreases) the torpedo velocity by 6 warp factors, with a minimum torpedo velocity of warp 0 (your torpedo launchers simply drop them in space as mines). The range of torpedoes increases linearly with velocity, and the fuel required to fire and the heat generated by firing photon torpedoes increases linearly with (torpedo velocity + 8)

Warp Engines **w/W**

Normal ships travel at a maximum of warp 9. Each UoC increases (decreases) this by two warp factors, with a minimum limit of warp 1. Acceleration increases linearly with (maximum warp speed + 1)

Ship Size **x/X**

The default ship can withstand 100 damage units. Each UoC increases (decreases) the strength of the ship by 15 damage units, with a minimum Ship Size withstanding 25 damage units.

NOTE

It may be helpful to some to think of ship customization in the following manner. You are given a ship hull, and are allocated 49 UoC with which to convert this hull into a viable starship. The default ship configuration allocates these UoC to create a general purpose ship. Obviously, some systems (eg, Heat Dissipation, Fuel Generation) must have some UoC allocated to them, while others are less essential (eg, Invisibility While Cloaked, Army Transport).

EXAMPLES

xtrek.ship: mmmPPP

This ship has -3 UoC for Maneuverability, and +3 UoC Phaser Size.

xtrek.ship: agwCCC

This ship has -1 UoC each for Army Transport, Fuel Generation, and Warp Engines, but with +3 UoC Cloaking Cost, he is not an easy target.

xtrek.torper: appppiiwDDGGGVTT

This ship has -1 UoC Army Transport, -4 UoC Phaser Size, -2 UoC Invisibility While Cloaked, and -1 UoC Warp Speed. But with +2 UoC Heat Dissipation, +3 UoC Fuel Generation, +1 UoC Torpedo Velocity and +2 UoC Torpedo Size, he'll keep you dodging photon torpedoes.

xtrek.ship: aattvviiEEMMPPPP

This ship has -2 UoC for Army Transport, -2 UoC Torpedo Size, and -2 UoC Torpedo Velocity and -2 UoC Invisibility While Cloaked. However, this ship has +2 UoC Engine Efficiency, +2 UoC Maneuverability, and +4 UoC for Phaser Size. It's a vicious fighter.

SEE ALSO

xtrek(6)

DIAGNOSTICS

If a specified ship customization is invalid, xtrek will exit with a warning message explaining the problem.

BUGS

The customization parameters may to be unbalanced.

Letters other than those understood are silently ignored.

NAME
    xtroff - Device Independent Troff Previewer for X Windows version 11.
SYNOPSIS
    xtroff [**Toolkit options**] [**-scrollbars**] [**-command Troff Command Pipe**]

    xtroff [**Toolkit Arguments**] [**-scrollbars**] [**troff output file**]
DESCRIPTION
    Xtroff reads (device independent) *troff*(L) output files and displays an approximation of the typeset output in a window. (In this document, wherever we refer to *troff*, we mean **ditroff**, not the Sun supplied *troff* which drives a CAT typesetter directly. **Ditroff** is part of the Documenter's WorkBench, and is also supplied with the Research Editions of Unix - v8, etc) Using the mouse the user can pan each page image within the window, and move to other pages.

    The program can be used in two different ways. Perhaps the most efficient way to use this program is to execute *xtroff* in the command mode (first example in the synopsis above). In the command mode a troff command string is specified that includes all the processing steps (*eqn, tbl, pic, ideal, troff*) that are needed to transform a user's document into troff output. Then whenever a change is made in the document a "rerasterize" command can be used to rerun the command string and show the new document on the screen. The "rerasterize" command is an option available on a menu that pops up when the right mouse button is pressed or in a status panel. The status panel is also enabled using the menu that pops up with the right mouse button.

    Alternatively, the output from *troff* can be used as input to this program (second example in the synopsis above.) In this case, each time the document changes it is up to the user to rerun the *troff* pipe to produce input for the *xtroff* program. This can be easily done using the "rerasterize" command.

    Fonts used by *xtroff* are rough approximations to those that will be printed in the final typesetter output. Currently only the 300 dot per inch (dpi) Imagen fonts and the 200 dpi Versatec fonts have been properly scaled for *xtroff*. All output destined for printers other than the Imagens will be shown using Versatec fonts. Although the actual bit maps used for the characters might not be correct all *xtroff* output will have the correct horizontal and vertical spacing.

    Xtroff can be controlled using a combination of mouse, menu and typed commands. Within the main text window when the middle button of the mouse is pressed the cursor is changed into the shape of a hand that grabs the text. As the mouse is moved around inside the window the displayed text (and the hand) move accordingly. When the right button is pressed a menu pops up that contains options for moving to different pages, and rerasterizing the input.

ACTIONS
    There are a number of *actions* defined in the main window. They can be invoked in a number of ways, using different *bindings*. (keys, or mouse buttons, or a combination of both). Most actions can also be invoked from the menu that pops up when the right mouse button is pressed in the main window.

    Move Around within Page
                Use the middle mouse button. When it is first pressed a

hand will appear on the page and effectively grab the text. As the mouse (and hand) move the page will move within the frame.

Another way to do this is to use the scrollbars on the right and bottom of the page.

Advance by a viewing section

A *viewing section* is the part of the page that can be displayed on the screen. Advancing to the next section will move the page so that the next section of the page is visible, or advance to the next page if at the end of a page. This command is bound by default to the SPACE bar, the mouse left button, and the cursor-down arrow key.

Previous Section This is the opposite of the previous command. It backs up to the previous section of the page, or to the previous page. It is bound to the cursor-up arrow key, and to the shifted left mouse button.

Next Page   This rasterizes and displays the next page in the document. A clock cursor is displayed while the rasterizing is done, which can take a few moments. This is bound to the cursor-right arrow, the 'N', and 'F' keys, and RETURN and LINEFEED.

Previous Page   This rasterizes and displays the previous page in the document. A clock cursor is displayed while the rasterizing is done, which can take a few moments. This is bound to the cursor-left arrow, the 'P', and 'B' keys, and DELETE and BACKSPACE.

Go To Another Page

This goes to a specific page number. Type the desired page number to the main *xtroff* window followed by the 'G' key. If you make a mistake in the page number, just hit ESC and type it again. This is not available on the menu.

Rerasterize   After changes are made to a document it is necessary to tell *xtroff* to rerasterize the file. This can be done by hitting the 'R' key, or selecting from the menu. Note that this is only really useful if you run *xtroff* using the *–command* option. If used with a file, it can still be used, provided the command to create the *troff* file is run again. If neither the file nor the command is used, and *xtroff* is reading from standard input, then rerasterize will not work, and the whole command must be run again.

Quit   This exits the program. It is bound to the 'Q' key.

EXAMPLES

To preview a file that has already been processed by troff

xtroff file-containing-troff-output

When the "rerasterize" command is issued then the indicated file will be reopened and its new contents displayed.

To typeset and preview a document use the following command

xtroff -command "eqn troff-input-file | troff -ms"

The "rerasterize" command will close any open files (or pipes) and open a new pipe. The indicated command will be run on the input side of the pipe to provide *xtroff* with its input. The command providing input to *xtroff* can contain any combination of programs as long as the final output is *troff* output. If it contains pipes 'I', or shell metacharacters, remember to enclose it within quotes.

The latter is the most common usage of *xtroff*. Typically, the user would start *xtroff* on a document, preview it, iconfiy xtroff, or put it under the other windows, and edit the document, fixing and adjusting things, and then deiconify or raise *xtroff*, and *rerasterize* to see the effect of the changes.

RESOURCES

Xtroff supports the general X Toolkit resource specifications. Here are the names and classes of the widgets used in *xtroff*.

Name,Class	Comment
xtroff,TroffPreviewer	The toplevel shell that encloses the application.
form,Form	The frame that manages the geometry of the widgets.
canvas,Window	The main *xtroff* window.
popupShell,Shell	The shell that encloses the pop-up menu.
mainMenu,Menu	The popup menu.
vscroll,Scrollbar	The vertical scrollbar
hscroll,Scrollbar	The horizontal scrollbar

In addition to the resources, *xtroff* also gets a single XDefault to determine whether the user wants the scrollbars or not. This is of the form *xtroff.scrollbar:on* or *off*. It corresponds to the command line argument *–scrollbar*.

TOOLKIT OPTIONS

xtroff also accepts the standard Toolkit command options viz. "+rv", "-background", "-bd", "-bg", "-borderwidth", "-bordercolor", "-bw", "-display", "-fg", "-fn", "-font", "-foreground", "-geometry", "-iconic", "-name", "-reverse", "-rv", "-synchronous", "-title", "-xrm". Some of the options are meaningless for *xtroff*.

FILES

/usr/local/lib/troff/*   - troff width tables /usr/local/lib/xtroff/*   - bitmap fonts for xtroff

SEE ALSO

Using and Specifiying X Resources
X(x),*x11*(x),*troff*(L)

BUGS

Searching isn't implemented because the status panel isn't implemented.

Ligatures look a little displaced.

AUTHOR

Credit for this program goes to a number of people including Brian Kernighan (Bell Labs) for first developing Device Independent Troff, University of Toronto for developing the original *vcat* program. Richard L. Hyde, Purdue University, and David Slattengren, U.C. Berkeley, wrote the original version of this program to rasterize *troff* output for the Suns. Malcolm Slaney, Schlumberger Palo Alto Research, rewrote most of the code to make it run under Sun-3 Unix and to extend the user interface. Support for X11 was added by Mark Moraes, University of Toronto.

NAME
xwatch - mailbox watch program for X11R2

SYNOPSIS
xwatch [*-toolkitoption* ...] [-option ...]

DESCRIPTION
The *xwatch* program (by default) displays a little image of a mailbox. When there is no mail, the flag on the mailbox is down. When mail arrives, the flag goes up, the mailbox beeps, and information about the new mail (author, time of arrival, and the subject of the message) is printed on the stdout. This program is nothing more than a wrapper around the Mailwatch widget not to be confused with the Mailbox widget used by *xbiff*.

When the user reads his mail or accesses his mailbox in any way, the user is in effect acknowledging that he is aware of the new mail and the flag is returned to the down position.

Xwatch looks for the left and middle mouse button events. Upon receipt of a left button event, xwatch will check for new mail immediately. If the user clicks the middle button in the icon, the icon is cleared and all new mail is considered to have been read by the user and the flag is forced down.

OPTIONS
Xwatch accepts all of the standard X Toolkit command line options along with the additional options listed below:

–help   This option indicates that a brief summary of the allowed options should be printed on the standard error.

–update *seconds*
This option specifies the frequency in seconds at which *xwatch* should update its display.

–file *filename*
This option specifies the name of the file which should be monitored. By default, it watches /usr/spool/mail/*username*, where *username* is your login name.

–down_flag *filename*

–up_flag *filename*
These options specify files which contain X11 format bitmap images to be used instead of the default images. They need not be the same size and can even be the same file. The "flag up" image is always displayed in reverse video while the "flag down" image is always displayed in normal video. If the *reverse video* option is specified, these will be reversed.

The following standard X Toolkit command line arguments are commonly used with *xwatch:*

–bg *color*
This option specifies the color to use for the background of the window. The default is "white."

–bd *color*
This option specifies the color to use for the border of the window. The default is "black."

-bw *number*
This option specifies the width in pixels of the border surrounding the window.

-fg *color*
This option specifies the color to use for the foreground of the window. The default is "black."

-rv This option indicates that reverse video should be simulated by swapping the foreground and background colors.

-geometry *geometry*
This option specifies the preferred size and position of the mailbox window; see *X(1)*.

-display *display*
This option specifies the X server to contact; see *X(1)*.

-xrm *resourcestring*
This option specifies a resource string to be used. This is especially useful for setting resources that do not have separate command line options.

X DEFAULTS

This program uses the *Mailwatch* widget whose name is "Mailwatch." Therefore, when setting resources in your resource database that are Mailwatch-widget specific, set them as in:

    *Mailwatch.down_flag: mail.icon.1
    *Mailwatch.up_flag: mail.icon.2

Xwatch understands all of the core resource names and classes as well as:

file (class **File**)
Specifies the name of the file to monitor. The default is to watch /usr/spool/mail/*username*, where *username* is your login name.

width (class **Width**)
Specifies the width of the mailbox. This defaults to the width the larger of the two icons (up and down flags) used.

height (class **Height**)
Specifies the height of the mailbox. This defaults to the height of the larger of the two icons (up and down flags) used.

update (class **Interval**)
Specifies the frequency in seconds at which the mail should be checked. The default time is 30 seconds.

foreground (class **Foreground**)
Specifies the color for the foreground. The default is "black" since the core default for background is "white."

reverseVideo (class **ReverseVideo**)
Specifies that the foreground and background should be reversed.

up_flag (class **File**)

down_flag (class **File**)
Specifies the filename to read for the up flag and the down flag icons respectively.

ENVIRONMENT

DISPLAY
>   to get the default host and display number.

XENVIRONMENT
>   to get the name of a resource file that overrides the global
>   resources stored in the RESOURCE_MANAGER property.

SEE ALSO
>   X(1), xrdb(1), stat(2)

BUGS
>   The mailbox bitmaps are ugly, but now you have an option to use better
>   looking ones if you want.
>
>   In order for *Xwatch* to display information about incoming mail, the file
>   from which the mail is scanned must be in the format which has the
>   string, "From " separating the sequential messages. If you use a mail
>   delivery program which does not store messages in this format (MMDF
>   for example), then you will get no output about new mail information and
>   *xwatch* will be virtually identical to *xbiff* except for some general bug
>   fixes.

AUTHOR
>   Dan Heller <island!argv@sun.com>

NAME
    xwd - dump an image of an X window

SYNOPSIS
    xwd [-debug] [-help] [-nobdrs] [-out *file*] [-xy] [-display *display*]

DESCRIPTION
    Xwd is an X Window System window dumping utility. *Xwd* allows X
    users to store window images in a specially formatted dump file. This file
    can then be read by various other X utilities for redisplay, printing, edit-
    ing, formatting, archiving, image processing, etc. The target window is
    selected by clicking the mouse in the desired window. The keyboard bell
    is rung once at the beginning of the dump and twice when the dump is
    completed.

OPTIONS
    -display *display*
                This argument allows you to specify the server to connect to; see
                X(1).

    -help   Print out the 'Usage:' command syntax summary.

    -nobdrs This argument specifies that the window dump should not
                include the pixels that compose the X window border. This is
                useful in situations where you may wish to include the window
                contents in a document as an illustration.

    -out *file* This argument allows the user to explicitly specify the output file
                on the command line. The default is to output to standard out.

    -xy   This option applies to color displays only. It selects 'XY' format
                dumping instead of the default 'Z' format.

    -add *value*
                This option specifies an signed value to be added to every pixel.

ENVIRONMENT
    DISPLAY
                To get default host and display number.

FILES
    XWDFile.h
                X Window Dump File format definition file.

SEE ALSO
    xwud(1), xpr(1), X(1)

COPYRIGHT
    Copyright 1988, Massachusetts Institute of Technology.
    See *X(1)* for a full statement of rights and permissions.

AUTHORS
    Tony Della Fera, Digital Equipment Corp., MIT Project Athena
    William F. Wyatt, Smithsonian Astrophysical Observatory

NAME
>   xwdtopbm - convert X11 and X10 window dump files into portable bit-
>   maps

SYNOPSIS
>   xwdtopbm [xwdfile]

DESCRIPTION
>   Reads an X11 or X10 window dump file as input. Produces a portable
>   bitmap as output.
>
>   Using this program, you can convert anything on an X workstation's
>   screen into a pbm bitmap. Just display whatever you're interested in, do
>   an xwd, run it through xwdtopbm, and then use pbmcut to select the part
>   you want.
>
>   Note that this tool only works for monochrome dump files.

3

BUGS
>   I haven't tested this tool with very many configurations, so there are prob-
>   ably bugs. Please let me know if you find any.

SEE ALSO
>   pbmtoxwd(1), pbmtox10wd(1), pbm(5)

AUTHOR
>   Copyright (C) 1988 by Jef Poskanzer.

NAME
    xwininfo - window information utility for X

SYNOPSIS
    xwininfo [-help] [-id *id*] [-root] [-name *name*] [-int] [-tree] [-stats] [-bits] [-events] [-size] [-wm] [-all] [-english] [-metric] [-display *display*]

DESCRIPTION
    Xwininfo is a utility for displaying information about windows. Various information is displayed depending on which options are selected. If no options are chosen, **-stats** is assumed.

    The user has the option of selecting the target window with the mouse (by clicking any mouse button in the desired window) or by specifying its window id on the command line with the **-id** option. Or instead of specifying the window by its id number, the **-name** option may be used to specify which window is desired by name. There is also a special **-root** option to quickly obtain information on X's root window.

OPTIONS
    -help   Print out the 'Usage:' command syntax summary.

    -id *id*   This option allows the user to specify a target window *id* on the command line rather than using the mouse to select the target window. This is very useful in debugging X applications where the target window is not mapped to the screen or where the use of the mouse might be impossible or interfere with the application.

    -name *name*
             This option allows the user to specify that the window named *name* is the target window on the command line rather than using the mouse to select the target window.

    -root   This option specifies that X's root window is the target window. This is useful in situations where the root window is completely obscured.

    -int   This option specifies that all X window ids should be displayed as integer values. The default is to display them as hexadecimal values.

    -tree   This option causes the root, parent, and children windows' ids and names of the selected window to be displayed.

    -stats   This option causes the display of various attributes pertaining to the location and appearance of the selected window. Information displayed includes the location of the window, its width and height, its depth, border width, class, colormap id if any, map state, backing-store hint, and location of the corners.

    -bits   This option causes the display of various attributes pertaining to the selected window's raw bits and how the selected window is to be stored. Displayed information includes the selected window's bit gravity, window gravity, backing-store hint, backing-planes value, backing pixel, and whether or not the window has save-under set.

    -events This option causes the selected window's event masks to be displayed. Both the event mask of events wanted by some client and the event mask of events not to propagate are displayed.

-size   This option causes the selected window's sizing hints to be displayed. Displayed information includes: for both the normal size hints and the zoom size hints, the user supplied location if any; the program supplied location if any; the user supplied size if any; the program supplied size if any; the minimum size if any; the maximum size if any; the resize increments if any; and the minimum and maximum aspect ratios if any.

-wm   This option causes the selected window's window manager hints to be displayed. Information displayed may include whether or not the application accepts input, what the window's icon window # and name is, where the window's icon should go, and what the window's initial state should be.

-metric   This option causes all individual height, width, and x and y positions to be displayed in millimeters as well as number of pixels, based on what the server thinks the resolution is. Geometry specifications that are in **+x+y** form are not changed.

-english This option causes all individual height, width, and x and y positions to be displayed in inches (and feet, yards, and miles if necessary) as well as number of pixels. **-metric** and **-english** may both be enabled at the same time.

-all   This option is a quick way to ask for all information possible.

-display *display*
              This option allows you to specify the server to connect to; see *X(1)*.

EXAMPLE
        The following is a sample summary taken with no options specified:

        xwininfo ==> Please select the window about which you
                ==> would like information by clicking the
                ==> mouse in that window.

        xwininfo ==> Window id: 0x60000f (xterm)

                ==> Upper left X: 4
                ==> Upper left Y: 19
                ==> Width: 726
                ==> Height: 966
                ==> Depth: 4
                ==> Border width: 3
                ==> Window class: InputOutput
                ==> Colormap: 0x80065
                ==> Window Bit Gravity State: NorthWestGravity
                ==> Window Window Gravity State: NorthWestGravity
                ==> Window Backing Store State: NotUseful
                ==> Window Save Under State: no
                ==> Window Map State: IsViewable
                ==> Window Override Redirect State: no
                ==> Corners: +4+19 -640+19 -640-33 +4-33

ENVIRONMENT
    DISPLAY
              To get the default host and display number.

SEE ALSO
>   X(1), xprop(1)

BUGS
>   Using **-stats -bits** shows some redundant information.

COPYRIGHT
>   Copyright 1988, Massachusetts Institute of Technology.
>   See *X(1)* for a full statement of rights and permissions.

AUTHOR
>   Mark Lillibridge, MIT Project Athena

NAME
      xwud - image displayer for X

SYNOPSIS
      xwud [-debug] [-help] [-inverse] [-in *file*] [-display *display*]

DESCRIPTION
      Xwud is an X Window System window image undumping utility. *Xwud*
      allows X users to display window images that were saved by *xwd* in a
      specially formatted dump file. The window image will appear at the
      coordinates of the original window from which the dump was taken. This
      is a crude version of a more advanced utility that has never been written.
      Monochrome dump files are displayed on a color monitor in the default
      foreground and background colors.

OPTIONS
      -help   Print out a short description of the allowable options.

      -in *file*   This option allows the user to explicitly specify the input file on
                  the command line. If no input file is given, the standard input is
                  assumed.

      -inverse Applies to monochrome window dump files only. If selected, the
                  window is undumped in reverse video. This is mainly needed
                  because the display is 'write white', whereas dump files intended
                  eventually to be written to a printer are generally 'write black'.

      -display *display*
                  This option allows you to specify the server to connect to; see
                  X(1).

ENVIRONMENT
      DISPLAY
                  To get default display.

FILES
      XWDFile.h
                  X Window Dump File format definition file.

BUGS
      Does not attempt to do color translation when the destination screen does
      not have a colormap exactly matching that of the original window.

SEE ALSO
      xwd(1), xpr(1), X(1)

COPYRIGHT
      Copyright 1988, Massachusetts Institute of Technology.
      See *X(1)* for a full statement of rights and permissions.

AUTHOR
      Tony Della Fera, Digital Equipment Corp., MIT Project Athena
      William F. Wyatt, Smithsonian Astrophysical Observatory

NAME
      xxxtopbm - convert "xxx" bitmaps into portable bitmaps

SYNOPSIS
      xxxtopbm [xxxfile]

DESCRIPTION
      Reads an "xxx" bitmap as input. Produces a portable bitmap as output.

      "xxx" bitmaps are the unknown and undocumented format found on
      ucbvax.Berkeley.Edu in the directory pub/xbackgrounds. The arrangement
      of the bits is the same as for Sun rasterfiles, but the headers are com-
      pletely different.

      Note that there is no pbmtoxxx tool.

SEE ALSO
      pbm(5)

AUTHOR
      Copyright (C) 1988 by Jef Poskanzer.

NAME
>   yorn – display a dialogue box

SYNOPSIS
>   **yorn** [**-z**] [**-standard X Toolkit options ...**] "TITLE" text to be
>   displayed

DESCRIPTION
>   *Yorn* is a utility that asks the user a question that can be answered yes or
>   no. It displays a question mark symbol, some justified text and two but-
>   tons labelled with a tick and a cross, representing yes or no respectively.
>   The question can be answered by clicking one of the boxes with the
>   mouse.
>
>   If the connection to the X server cannot be established, the title and text is
>   printed on *yorn*'s standard output and the user is requested to press *Y* or *N*
>   to answer the question.
>
>   *Yorn* can take the following option:
>
>   **-z**   No Zoom. The window will attempt to by pass the window
>   manager and appear immediately, rather than going through the
>   window manager's placement and sizing scheme.
>
>   *yorn* additionally recognizes the following standard X Toolkit command
>   line arguments:
>
>   **-bg** *colour* or **-background** *colour*
>   This option specifies the colour to use for the background of the
>   window and widgets. The default is 'white.'
>
>   **-bd** *colour* or **-bordercolor** *colour*
>   This option specifies the colour to use for the border of the main
>   window. The default is 'black.'
>
>   **-bw** *number* or **-borderwidth** *number*
>   This option specifies the width in pixels of the border surround-
>   ing the main window.
>
>   **-fg** *colour* or **-foreground** *colour*
>   This option specifies the colour to use for all text and symbols.
>   The default is 'black'.
>
>   **-fn** *font*   This option specifies the font to be used for displaying the text
>   warning message. The default is 'serif10'.
>
>   **-name** *name*
>   This option specifies the application name under which resources
>   are to be obtained, rather than the default executable file name,
>   'yorn'.
>
>   **-geometry** *geometry*
>   This option specifies the preferred size and position yorn win-
>   dow; see *X(1)*;
>
>   **-display** *display*
>   This option specifies the X server to contact; see *X(1)*.
>
>   **-xrm** *resourcestring*
>   This option specifies a resource string to be used. This is espe-
>   cially useful for setting resources that do not have separate com-
>   mand line options.

X DEFAULTS
>   *Yorn* is implemented using the Athena widgets. Each widget can indivi-
>   dually or in groups have various visual and operational aspects changed

via a '.Xdefaults' file on the client machine or the 'RESOURCE_MANAGER' property on the server. All widgets have a common set of resources (background, backgroundPixmap, etc.) and resources unique to each type of widget; a 'command button' widget, for example, also has a cursor resource. For a full list see the document *X Toolkit Widgets - C Language X Interface.*

The path names and types of all widgets used by *yorn* are as follows:

XXX.alert/yorn
> The widget that is a child of root. All the other widgets used by the yorn box are children or grand children of this widget.

XXX.alert/yorn.contents
> A form widget that manages the layout of the yorn box. Normally completely covers the 'alert/yorn' widget.

XXX.alert/yorn.contents.symbol
> A widget to display the 'query' symbol.

XXX.alert/yorn.contents.ok/yes button
> A command button widget to obtain a 'yes' answer from the user, normally displaying a 'tick' symbol.

XXX.alert/yorn.contents.no button
> A command button widget to obtain a 'no' answer from the user, normally displaying a 'cross' symbol.

XXX.alert/yorn.contents.message
> A widget to display and format the text message. The '*XXX*' may be replaced by either *yorn*'s classname, 'Xopentop', or its application name, 'yorn'.

Additionally, the following items are also fetched from the resource database:

yornsym The pathname of a bitmap file to use as an alternative to the 'question-mark-in-a-triangle' symbol displayed in the 'symbol' widget.

ticksym The pathname of a bitmap file to use as an alternative to the 'tick' symbol displayed in the 'ok/yes button' widget.

crosssym
> The pathname of a bitmap file to use as an alternative to the 'cross' symbol displayed in the 'no button' widget.

backgroundPixmap.foreground
> One of two colours (the other is the widget's background colour) required when converting a bitmap file into a pixmap for use as the widget's background pixmap.

RETURN CODES
> 0 – Termination via the tick box.
>
> 1 – Termination via the cross box.
>
> 2 – Termination due to some internal error.

ENVIRONMENT
> DISPLAY - the default host and display number of the X server.
>
> XENVIRONMENT - the name of the Xdefaults file to use (normally $HOME/.Xdefaults).

EXAMPLES

yorn "Yorn" "The file /etc/passwd exists. Are you sure you want to delete it ?"

Will open an yorn box with the title *Yorn* and containing the text *The file /etc/passwd exists. Are you* and waits for the user to click one of the buttons.

FILES

$HOME/.Xdefaults /usr/lib/X11/app-defaults/Xopentop

SEE ALSO

alert(1), gs(1)

BUGS

If the font is too large or the message too long, the text will be clipped.

The title may not be displayed if the window manager does not provide title bars around windows or the −z option is used.

AUTHOR

Gary Henderson & Mark E. Howells, Torch Computers Ltd.

3

Using and Specifying X Resources

Jim Fulton
MIT X Consortium

Copyright 1988 Massachusetts Institute of Technology

* * * *

The Xlib Resource Manager provides a set of tools for specifying and manipulating user preferences (e.g. geometry, colors, fonts). Simple programming interfaces to it are provided by the X Toolkit and by the Xlib routine XGetDefault.

Resources, also refered to as "defaults" in older versions of X, are simply <name,value> pairs that are frequently used to control the appearence or function of particular program or subsystem. They provide a convenient way to tailor whole collections of applications with a minimal amount of work.

In previous versions of X, defaults were stored in a .Xdefaults file in each user's home directory, on every machine. In addition to requiring duplicate copies of the defaults, it did not lend itself to conditional specifications (particularly if the user used both monochrome and color displays).

In X11, these problems are solved by using the window property mechanism in the X protocol to store resources in the server, where they are available to all clients. As a result, defaults may now be dynamically specified based on the particular display being used. This is particularly useful in setting up different defaults for monochrome and color displays. Furthermore, a new convention for specifying resources from the command line has been established (and is supported by all clients of the X Toolkit).

Resources are usually as "program.name.subname.etc: value", one per line in resource files, or one per -xrm argument. Names are hierarchies, usually corresponding to major structures within an application (where structures are often objects like windows, panels, menus, scrollbars, etc.). The various subnames are called components and are specified left to right from most general to least general.

If we take the "xmh" application as an example, we can see that its display is made up of sections called "panes", some of which in turn contain command buttons. The "include" button (used to retreive new mail) in the "toc" (table of contents) pane could be named as follows:

program name	pane name	object group name	subobject name
xmh	toc	buttons	include

An object's fully specified name (such as "xmh.toc.buttons.include" in the example above) is called the "instance" name for that object. In addition, each component belongs to a collection of similar components (such as the set of all panes, the set of all buttons, etc.) that can be specified using a "class" name. In the above example, if we assume that the xmh program is one of possibly several "Xmh" types of programs (just as "gnuemacs" and "microemacs" might be thought of as instances of the class of "Emacs" programs), we could build the following class name:

application type	top level area type	second level object type	third level object type
Xmh	VPane	Box	Command ...

By convention, instance name components begin with lowercase letters and class name components begin with uppercase letters. Components that are made up of more than one word have the succeeding words capitalized and concatentated without any spaces. Thus, an instance of an icon pixmap might be called "iconPixmap" whereas the class of icon pixmaps would be called "IconPixmap". The capitalization is important because resource names may contain both instance and class name components within the same specification (for example, "gnuemacs.VPaned.cursorColor: blue").

Class names allow default values to be specified for all versions of given object. Instance names allow a value for a particular version to be given that overrides the class value, and can be used to specify exceptions to the rules outlined by the class names. For example, we could specify that that all command buttons in button boxes in vertical panes should have a background color of blue, except for "include", which should be red: with

    *VPaned.Box.Command.Background: blue
    xmh.toc.buttons.include.background: red

Furthermore, resource name hierarchies do not have to be fully specified. In the preceeding example, we listed each of the individual components; however, this can be quite cumbersome. Instead of having to give a full specification for each set of objects (there might be slider bars, or edit windows, or any number of other types), we can just "wildcard", or omit, the intervening components by using the "*" separator in place of the "." separator. In general, it is a good idea to use the "*" instead of "." in case you've forgotten any intervening components or in case new levels are inserted into the middle of the hierarchy.

    Xmh*VPaned*Background: blue
    xmh*toc.buttons.include.background: red

The distiction between classes and instances is important. For example, many text applications have some notion of background, foreground, border, pointer, and cursor or marker color. Usually the background is set to one color, and all of the other attributes are set to another so that they may be seen on a monochrome display. To allow users of color displays to set any or all of them, the colors may be organized into classes as follows:

instance name	class name
background	Background
foreground	Foreground
borderColor	Foreground
pointerColor	Foreground
cursorColor	Foreground

Then, to configure the application to run in "monochrome" mode, but using two colors, you would only have to use two specifications:

    obj*Background: blue
    obj*Foreground: red

Then, if you decided that you wanted the cursor to be yellow, but the pointer and the border to remain the same as the foreground, you would only need one new resource specification:

      obj*cursorColor: yellow

Because class and instance names are distinguishable by case, both types of names may be given in a single resource specification. Section 10.11 of the Xlib manual gives the following additional examples (note, the "xmh" program may use other names, these are for example only):

xmh*background:	red
*command.font:	8x13
*command.background:	blue
*Command.Foreground:	green
xmh*toc*Command.activeForeground:	black

The resource hierarchy "xmh.toc*Command.activeForeground" specifies a particular color resource (in this case, the active foreground color) of all components of class Command that are contained within the "toc" in the xmh application. Although this is very powerful, figuring out that this can be specified at all, let alone how, is currently a problem with the documentation for many of the more complex clients of the Resource Manager. Eventually, widgets should be documented just as commands are today: there should be descriptions of the instance names, class names, and allowable values for each of the widget's resources. Application documentation would then only need to describe how widgets are combined. Until then, the best places to look for information on which resources may be specified are:

1. the manual pages for the application
2. any documentation for the widgets used by the application
3. any application resource files in /usr/lib/X11/app-defaults/
4. any XtResource tables in the the application or the widget sources

Under X11, you have a lot of flexibility as to where defaults are defined. The Resource Manager obtains resource specifications from the following places:

1. from any application-specific resource files, usually
   stored in /usr/lib/X11/app-defaults/.

2. from any application-specific resources files in the
   directory named by the environment variable XAPPLRESDIR
   (default value is $HOME) for programs written using the
   X Toolkit.

3. from the RESOURCE_MANAGER property on the root window of
   screen 0; these are stored using the xrdb program. If this
   property is not defined, then $HOME/.Xdefaults will be read
   to provide compatibility with X10 (although the resource
   specification format has changed somewhat).

4. from any user-specific defaults stored in a file whose name
   is set in the environment variable XENVIRONMENT.

5. from the -xrm command line option (for programs written with
   the X Toolkit).

Resources are usually loaded from a file into the RESOURCE_MANAGER property using the "xrdb" program from whatever script you use to start up X. Sites that use the xdm Display Manager will most likely provide for loading in user-specified resources automatically. See your system manager for details.

I have a script called "xsetup" on every machine that I use that starts up the appropriate programs for that machine (terminal emulators, a mailbox on my home machine, clocks, load average monitors, etc.). For example, I use the following on my desktop workstation to get my base environment going:

```
#!/bin/sh
xrdb -load $HOME/.Xresources
stty erase '^?'
xmodmap -p $HOME/.xmodmap
xset b 100 400 c 50 s 1800
uwm &
xclock -geometry 48x48-1+1 &
xload -geometry 48x48-1+100 &
```

The xrdb program reads my global defaults from $HOME/.Xresources. This is where I define resources that I want to have used by clients on every machine:

```
bitmap*Dashed:  off
XTerm*multiScroll:  on
XTerm*jumpScroll:  on
XTerm*reverseWrap:  on
XTerm*curses:  on
XTerm*font:  6x10
emacs*Geometry:  80x65-0-0
emacs*Background:  #5b7686
emacs*Foreground:  white
emacs*Cursor:  white
emacs*BorderColor:  white
emacs*Font:  6x10
```

I put machine-specific defaults (usually colors so that I can easily distinguish windows on various machines) in a file called ˜/.Xenv and set the XENVIRONMENT variable in my .login to point to that file. For example, I use the following defaults on my desktop workstation:

```
XTerm*Background:  black
XTerm*Foreground:  green
XTerm*BorderColor:  white
xclock*analog:  on
xclock*borderWidth:  0
xclock*padding:  2
xclock*Background:  black
xclock*Foreground:  red
xload*Background:  black
xload*Foreground:  cyan
```

For consistency, I create an xsetup script and a .Xenv file (if I want any machine specific defaults) on each of the machines that I commonly use. This allows me to just login, type "xsetup", and get right to work. Continuing the example started above, here is the xsetup file that I use on my server:

```
#!/bin/sh
xterm -geometry 80x55+0+0 &
xterm -geometry 80x65+488+1 &
xterm -geometry 80x20+0-0 &
```

```
xload =48x48-1+150 &
xbiff -rv =48x48-1+50 &
```

and the corresponding .Xenv file:

```
XTerm*Foreground: white
XTerm*Background: #c00
XTerm*BorderColor: white
tinyxterm*Font: 3x5
tinyxterm*Geometry: 80x24
bigxterm*Font: 9x15
bigxterm*Geometry: 80x55
xload*Background: black
xload*Foreground: red
xbiff*borderWidth: 0
xbiff*Background: white
xbiff*Foreground: blue
xbiff*reverseVideo: on
```

Note the use of the alternative instance names "tinyxterm" and "bigxterm". This allows me to quickly get a different "flavor" of xterm by simply invoking "xterm -name tinyxterm" or "xterm -name bigxterm".

The xrdb program uses the C preprocessor to provide conditionals based on the configuration of the server being used. This is very useful if you commonly use different types of servers (such as monochrome and color) from the same account. See the xrdb(1) manual page for more details.

Summary

X11 gives you many choices as to how to organize your screen, specify your defaults, and start up various programs. I frequently have 5 xterms, 1 clock, 2 load average monitors, 1 mailbox, an emacs, and uwm all running at once. The scheme outlined above is somewhat of a brute force approach, but works well for me.

The highlights are:

1. Use the Display Manager xdm. It is very flexible and can be tailored to provide any sort of default environment.

2. Create X startup scripts that run the appropriate programs to set up your environment (start your window manager, load defaults, etc.). I call these scripts "xsetup" on each machine.

3. Put global resources in one file that you run xrdb on from your X startup script. I call this file ~/.Xresources. In general, you should use "*" instead of "." to separate components.

4. Put machine-specific resources in another file and set the XENVINRONMENT variable to point to it. I call this file ~/.Xenv. Use "*" instead of "." to separate components.

Where to look for more information:

X(1), xrdb(1), Section 10.11 of the Xlib manual,
XGetDefault(3X), Section 4.2 of the X Toolkit manual,
application manual pages